THE CIVIL WAR POLITICAL TRADITION

A Nation Divided: Studies in the Civil War Era

ORVILLE VERNON BURTON AND
ELIZABETH R. VARON, EDITORS

The Civil War Political Tradition

Ten Portraits of Those Who Formed It

Paul D. Escott

University of Virginia Press
Charlottesville and London

University of Virginia Press
© 2023 by the Rector and Visitors of the University of Virginia
All rights reserved
Printed in the United States of America on acid-free paper

First published 2023

1 3 5 7 9 8 6 4 2

Library of Congress Cataloging-in-Publication Data
Names: Escott, Paul D., author.
Title: The Civil War political tradition : ten portraits of those who formed it / Paul D. Escott.
Description: Charlottesville : University of Virginia Press, 2023. | Series: A nation divided: Studies in the Civil War era | Includes bibliographical references and index.
Identifiers: LCCN 2022045151 (print) | LCCN 2022045152 (ebook) | ISBN 9780813949673 (hardcover) | ISBN 9780813949680 (paperback) | ISBN 9780813949697 (ebook)
Subjects: LCSH: United States—Politics and government—1849–1877. | United States—History—Civil War, 1861–1865—Biography. | Political leadership—United States—History—19th century. | Political culture—United States—History—19th century.
Classification: LCC E415.7 .E8368 2023 (print) | LCC E415.7 (ebook) | DDC 973.7092/2 [B]—dc23/eng/20221123
LC record available at https://lccn.loc.gov/2022045151
LC ebook record available at https://lccn.loc.gov/2022045152

Cover art: John C. Calhoun, by George Peter Alexander Healy, ca. 1845 (National Portrait Gallery, Smithsonian Institution [NPG.90.52]); Henry Clay, by Matthew Harris Jouett, 1818 (Transylvania University); Jefferson Davis, by Daniel Huntington, 1874 (Center of Military History, US Army); Stephen A. Douglas, from photograph by Matthew Brady, ca. 1860–65 (Library of Congress, Prints & Photographs Division); Frederick Douglass, by Southworth & Hawes, 1848 (Onondaga Historical Association); Horace Greeley, T. Lee & Co, 1872 (Library of Congress, Prints & Photographs Division [LC-DIG-pga-11424]); Abraham Lincoln (Division of Rare and Manuscript Collections, Cornell University Library); Elizabeth Cady Stanton, by Anna Elizabeth Klumpke, 1889 (National Portrait Gallery, Smithsonian Institution; transfer from the National Museum of American History; gift of the National American Woman Suffrage Association through Mrs. Harriot Stanton Blatch, 1924); Harriet Beecher Stowe, by Alanson Fisher, 1853 (National Portrait Gallery, Smithsonian Institution); Albion Tourgée, ca. 1870 (Library Company of Philadelphia, Print Department, American Celebrities Album [(I)P.9100.49f])

Para Candelas
Más gozo

CONTENTS

Acknowledgments	ix
Introduction	1
Henry Clay: Old Virtues in New Times	9
John C. Calhoun: Inveterate Ideologue	26
Harriet Beecher Stowe: The Power of Her Pen	42
Frederick Douglass: The Outsider as Resolute Prophet	58
Stephen A. Douglas: Overtaken by Polarization	77
Jefferson Davis: A Defiant Tradition and Tradition Defied	92
Abraham Lincoln: Riding the Storm to Historic Progress	111
Horace Greeley: American Enthusiast	129
Albion Tourgée: Civil War as a Sustained Clash of Cultures	148
Elizabeth Cady Stanton: Profound Radical	166
A Brief Guide to Further Reading	185
Index	193

ACKNOWLEDGMENTS

I AM very grateful to Dr. Jeffrey Crow and to the anonymous evaluators chosen by the University of Virginia Press. Their suggestions improved the manuscript and saved me from occasional errors, although the responsibility for any remaining defects is, of course, mine. I also want to thank my editor, Dr. Nadine Zimmerli, for her valuable and much-appreciated encouragement, advice, and suggestions.

THE CIVIL WAR POLITICAL TRADITION

Introduction

~

Classic works are inspirational. *The American Political Tradition and the Men Who Made It* influenced generations of readers after it appeared in 1948. With incisive prose and arresting arguments, Richard Hofstadter evaluated several presidents and other men of influence, from the Founding Fathers through Franklin Roosevelt. Thousands of college students and hundreds of future historians encountered intriguing perspectives in that book. Through his challenging, assertive essays, Hofstadter commented on the panorama of US history, its major events, and its underlying values. His portraits of major figures in US history doubled as sharp assessments of leadership and as elements of a broader, general interpretation.

Hofstadter was convinced that political history tended to overemphasize conflict in American society. His essays showed how the decisions of past leaders reflected society's "common climate of opinion," the currents of conservatism and modest reform that had shaped the past. Historically, that climate had consistently valued "self-help, free enterprise, competition, and beneficent cupidity." But Hofstadter wrote when the United States was taking on a new role in the world that contrasted with its traditional penchant for isolationism and individualism. The future, he believed, might demand unaccustomed "international responsibility, cohesion, centralization, and planning." Therefore, he offered a "critical analysis" in place of a reassuring "sentimental appreciation" of the past.

In form and in a very general sense, Hofstadter's achievement has inspired this book. It, too, consists of several essays on political or social leaders and evaluates them in the panorama of US history, especially the nineteenth century. In large measure the fundamental issues of the Civil War—the issues of slavery, race, and equality—dominated the nineteenth century, and in that sense the Civil War era extended before and after the four years of battle. The individuals who did the most to shape those issues were the makers of a Civil War political tradition. By analyzing their careers, we can discern political and social patterns in a long Civil War era.

In politics, most of the leaders profiled here contributed to a pattern of behavior, or a tradition. Theirs was a Civil War political tradition that emphasized individual ambition, short-term thinking, compromise, and a pragmatic approach to problems. Action within these norms made many careers and produced many dramatic moments, but it did not resolve the problems over slavery and race. To achieve real progress, it was necessary to challenge the established patterns, risk greater change, and adapt to consequent developments, as Lincoln did. The era's leaders of reform were more principled and systematic than the politicians, but they worked from positions of less power and achieved progress rather than complete success. Like the politicians, they learned that events could bring about greater change than individuals had been able to accomplish. Still, politicians and reformers, crises and war, were not the whole story, for the quiet but persistent power of culture imposed limits, even on monumental changes. By the end of the century, society sadly revealed the enduring strength of racism and white supremacy.

Historians' interest in the Civil War often has focused on key details of that great crisis. Many volumes scrutinize with meticulous care the growing sectional division, controversies over policy, and the battles and destruction of the Civil War. But this book, like Hofstadter's, will prioritize interpretation over detail. Like Hofstadter's, it is not based on new archival research but on a historian's perspectives. It aims to place the individuals treated, and the longer era, in a broad context of US history and the nation's economy, culture, and values. Like *The American Political Tradition*, it focuses on politics and values and deals with both change and persistent beliefs. The collective history of these ten leaders reflects the difficulties that an expansive, acquisitive, and dominant white population had in addressing the conflict between its social practices and its national ideals of liberty and equal rights.

THE INDIVIDUALS analyzed in this book shared much and differed over many things. They were enthusiastic about economic growth and geographic expansion. Racial assumptions that prioritized white people, excluding Black people and others, were so engrained that they frequently went unchallenged by men in power, even if writers and reformers tried to raise questions. Prominent among their values was a devotion to the Union. Spanning three or four generations, early leaders were united in an almost mystical reverence for the *idea* of the Union and its significance for the world. Freedom and economic opportunity achieved through the Union, they believed, made their nation a beacon for humankind. But they could interpret devotion to the Union in different ways. Although moved by the example of the Founders and their revolution for independence and liberty, they developed differing ideas of what the Union, liberty, and prosperity meant. The ideal of economic opportunity was not necessarily consistent with unity.

Their careers unfolded in a period of rapid growth and change. Not surprisingly, the political tradition of the Civil War era reflected the major forces at work in society and politics. Politics and reform bore the impress of change in the economy, in society, and in ideologies. Cultural change took place as rapidly as new developments in economic life or geographical expansion. Dozens of reform movements flourished in society along with religious awakening, even new religions. Generational change added complexity to the evolving social, economic, and political landscape. Divergent paths to economic development produced entrenched interests, stronger division, and very different views of the good society.

Certain values were almost universally shared. The hunger for wealth and a conviction that superior rights and privileges were white people's birthright ran through the majority of the population. Free-labor farmers and southern slaveholders eagerly dispossessed and cheated native peoples in order to seize lands in the West and South. Northern white people repressed free Black people, while southern planters exploited their enslaved workers to become rich in the enlarged boundaries of the country. Most men assumed that it was their right to control the lives of women. In both North and South, the desire for gain and aspirations for wealth usually proved more powerful than ideals and foreclosed or postponed social reformation. In the Civil War era's political tradition, there was recurrent conflict but also a stubborn continuity in underlying beliefs that yielded less to leaders' wisdom than to the pressure of events.

Prosperity came to both sections, but in different ways and with different results. New technologies enmeshed northerners in a transportation revolution that created a vast regional market. That newly unified market multiplied commerce and generated prosperity, but it also brought dislocations in employment and new types of competition. Swelling tides of immigrants arrived, while towns grew into cities and urban life reached new levels of concentration. Southerners lived through very different kinds of change. They expanded over the Appalachian Mountains to exploit rich soils in Kentucky, Tennessee, and especially the Gulf region. Small family farms prospered, largely outside the commercial economy, while the sweat of enslaved plantation laborers boosted production of cotton to new heights and dominance of the world's market. Greater wealth and a deeper commitment to slavery and white supremacy were the results. The liberty-loving republic became the largest and most extensive slaveholding power on the earth, while its north and northeast regions exemplified the power of a commercializing free-labor economy.

Such change steadily pushed politics toward recurrent antebellum crises. The era's political rhythm became one of conflict, evasion, and partial solutions. A veneration for the ideals of the Declaration of Independence was part of the tradition, but political "solutions" failed to preserve the nation or honor its founding values. The task of politicians, it has been said, is to construct the future. But for these generations, the future took shape rapidly, on its own, producing a temptation to ride the forces of change rather than choose a direction. They encouraged economic forces rather than questioning their direction.

Responding to these developments and adjusting the clash of interests amid the contradiction between freedom and slavery was a weighty task for any group of politicians. The nineteenth century had its full share of talented leaders. Their abundant ambition and energy led to conflicts that were both political and physical. (Henry Clay, Jefferson Davis, Horace Greeley, and even Abraham Lincoln were all involved in duels or heated confrontations, which were frequent among public figures in the prewar years.) But the politicians also sought alliances and compromises, and not all of their conflict or extremism led to wholly negative consequences. Still, their challenge was great, and there was a reluctance by many to see the future, a readiness to avoid serious problems ahead in order to manage a short-term settlement. Underlying currents of love for the Union were not enough to guide clashing interests toward a real solution. Powerful economic interests, personal ambition, and white supremacy usually were more influential in the here-and-now than righting wrong or averting catastrophe in the distant future. The leadership elite allowed and hastened a series of deeper conflicts.

In the end, it was the Civil War, rather than the plans of leaders, that produced the era's most important consequences. The enormous scale of its destruction and its changes belied the supposed achievements of previous political leaders. It demands a central place in historical memory, even though it is possible to exaggerate the significance of the war in the full scope of US history. The southern writer Shelby Foote made it fashionable to say that the Civil War "made us what we are," and there is some truth in that statement. But the Civil War was not the only large-scale, historic development that shaped the society we know today. Postwar industrialization remade the economy, while successive waves of immigration in the nineteenth, twentieth, and twenty-first centuries have changed and renewed the population. World wars and a succession of other conflicts have defined an international role exceeding anything imagined in the Civil War era.

Still, the Civil War was much more than a single large event in the distant past. Its significance today rests not in its scale or in its unprecedented costs in blood and treasure but in its consequences. The war determined the answers to two crucial issues—the legitimacy of slavery and the unity of the polity. It ended the legal enslavement of human beings and determined that the United States would be one nation. These were verdicts of the sword, but they also became amendments to the Constitution and a Supreme Court ruling (in *Texas v. White*, 1869) that secession by a state was unconstitutional. However, the Civil War changed the social order in a crucial way while leaving other core issues unresolved. It reinforced ideals of equality without removing structures and habits of inequality that slavery had nourished.

Thus, in the development of the young republic, the era's political tradition led to a fateful destination—war. That conflict brought about a social earthquake—emancipation. But the era also produced a result, in Reconstruction and after, that was much less than a reformation. The cultural preference for short-term solutions and a pragmatic approach to problems remained. Consequently, the significance of the Civil War in the long term derived partly from what it settled, but even more from what it left undone. It mandated one nation but maintained white supremacy, old patterns of thought, and two different social systems locked in a hostile embrace. Within several years the North abandoned the effort to democratize the South, and former Confederates rebuilt the racial caste system that had been central to Confederate purpose. The era saw a tectonic shift in the very foundations of society, but not one great enough to collapse the imposing edifice of racism and privilege. The values of John C. Calhoun, Jefferson Davis, Stephen Douglas, and white supremacists North and South triumphed, for generations, over the ideals of Frederick Douglass, Abraham Lincoln, Elizabeth Cady Stanton, or Albion Tourgée.

From the post–World War II decades to the present, views of the Civil War era have evolved and changed. While the United States was becoming dominant in economic power and international influence, writers viewed the period as one of great triumph. What had begun as a contest over unity became, in fact, an "abolition war" that freed millions of people and opened the path to future racial, industrial, and social progress. Ideals of freedom and equality meant that rights for African Americans and women would be on future agendas. Those were monumental steps forward. But the progress that was not achieved *then* haunts a troubled society *today*. The idea that that the United States is an exceptionally virtuous nation has been fading in the face of internal problems and international reverses. A more tempered, realistic view—one that recognizes tasks undone and wealth and treasure spent with meager results—has come slowly. A more balanced assessment incorporates the virtues and shortcomings of the leaders analyzed here.

The era's political tradition and those who made it should be seen in a human, complex light. The ideals of the Declaration of Independence and the Revolution's achievement of self-government and liberty inspired the leaders treated here. But racism, economic forces, and the great inertial power of culture also molded them and encouraged caution and short-term evasions. The influence of these forces lasted well beyond the war, and they shaped a story that is not simply one of idealism and achievement reached through conflict. It is also a story involving neglected values, conflicting goals, unreconcilable forms of acquisitiveness, and shared adherence to malign assumptions of white supremacy.

The challenge that slavery posed to leading figures in the Civil War era was enormously demanding, both socially and economically. Socially, white supremacy and racism dominated the attitudes of the electorate. Even in the North, despite zealous efforts by the abolitionists, most white people were not convinced that action must be taken to end slavery. Economically, different patterns of development had deepened and entrenched the conflict between northern and southern interests, between free labor and slavery-based social systems. Both were enjoying prosperity but were heading in different directions. Had the nation's politicians been extraordinarily wise and talented, their task still would have been forbiddingly difficult. In reality their behavior was human rather than transcendent. In a faltering, all-too-human way the leaders of the Civil War era advanced a growing, prospering nation but failed to avoid a destructive civil war. That conflict abolished slavery, but the failure of Reconstruction shackled the nation to long-lasting problems of inequality and collective injustice. From the tradition and the crises that leaders created came both new light and persistent darkness, progress and injustice. In that way the Civil War's political tradition shaped the decades leading to our present.

Henry Clay
Old Virtues in New Times

~⌣~

H<small>E WAS</small> the republic's dominant political figure for almost half a century. After election to the Kentucky legislature in 1803 and two brief stints in the US Senate, Henry Clay entered the US House of Representatives in 1811. Immediately chosen Speaker at age thirty-four, he claimed a central, often commanding, role in national politics until his death in 1852. Repeatedly winning election as a representative or senator, he promoted policies of economic development that became known as his American System. He served one term as secretary of state, was three times a leading candidate for the presidency, and founded the Whig Party. Most memorably, Clay engineered three crucial compromises over slavery and was celebrated as the Great Compromiser, the Great Pacificator, and the Prince of the Senate. His pragmatic, and sometimes evasive, approach to resolving crises became one model of statesmanship. After he died in Washington in 1852, thousands honored him as his remains traveled a thousand miles over nine days to his home to Kentucky. In Illinois Abraham Lincoln delivered a tribute, saying: "The spell—the long-enduring spell—with which the souls of men were bound to him is a miracle. Who can compass it?"

Though not handsome, Henry Clay was undeniably charismatic. According to William Seward, who was not a friend, Clay's "conversation, his gesture, his very look, was persuasive, seductive, irresistible." Affable, clever, and warm in manner, he possessed a rich baritone voice and had the ability to speak effectively for hours and without notes. Tall and thin, he was a master of the techniques used by engaging courtroom lawyers to charm the jurors. Speaking deliberately, Clay often riveted the attention of his listeners, but he also could be quick in repartee and fiery as an opponent. On many occasions the public flocked to hear him speak on issues, but his greatest skill lay in influencing others behind the scenes, laying the groundwork for legislation, for party strategy, or for agreements that cooled explosive controversies. From early prominence, his reputation grew, and he was considered part of a Great Triumvirate that was influential over four decades—Clay, John C. Calhoun, and Daniel Webster. When they first arrived in politics, all three were young men. As they aged their careers reflected the diverging paths within the country.

As a talented, dynamic westerner from across the Appalachians, Clay represented the potential of a new and growing nation. He exemplified the West's enthusiasm for economic growth and its ambivalence toward slavery's future. But he was more than a westerner—he was ever devoted to a national vision, and his life influenced generations of southern Unionists. They would remember his willingness to compromise and his devotion to national unity. Like others in the two generations that followed the Founders, Clay felt a responsibility to guard and strengthen the republic. For such men, the splendid achievement of leaders of the Revolutionary era must not be sullied or diminished. The United States, they believed, embodied for the world the example of a self-governing republic, and the ideals of the Declaration of Independence enhanced its image as a land of opportunity wedded to liberty. Preserving and carrying forward that legacy was almost a sacred duty for these political leaders. They felt an emotional, almost mystical, attachment to the idea of a United States advancing in freedom and prosperity.

The goal of national strength loomed even larger in the mind of Speaker Clay as a result of the War of 1812. Clay had been a leader of a young and angry group labeled the War Hawks who had favored military confrontation with Great Britain over its impressment of American ships and interference with US trade. But the United States barely escaped from that conflict without suffering great and long-lasting losses. Luck and the fact that the British were embroiled in a larger European conflict were on the Americans' side. The most serious blow was, perhaps, to national pride. The British invaded Washington and set fire to the Capitol, to the Presidential Mansion, and to other government buildings. President James Madison and other officials had to flee to Maryland. Destruction in Washington would have been far greater but for a torrential rainstorm that extinguished many fires within a day after the attack began. Smarting from that humiliation but proud that their young nation had confronted powerful Britain and emerged undefeated, even with enhanced prestige, Clay and other War Hawks were determined to build up the country, economically as well as militarily.

Clay and his allies swiftly made their mark. The young but powerful Speaker proposed a comprehensive economic program that revived the Federalist ideas championed by Alexander Hamilton and adopted now by President Madison. The president and others agreed that it would be necessary to maintain a relatively large standing army and improve the nation's defenses. In addition, Madison called for measures favored by Clay, policies that turned sharply away from Thomas Jefferson's idea of a limited, restrained government. Clay wanted the federal government to pursue prosperity and economic growth as the path to strength in peace or war. He called for a protective tariff behind which American industry could grow and compete successfully against cheap foreign imports. He urged the renewal and rechartering of Alexander Hamilton's Bank of the United States to bring order to the nation's money supply and credit. Finally, he advocated an ambitious program of infrastructure—known then as internal improvements—to improve the country's lamentable roads. These would become the elements of the American System that Clay advocated throughout his career.

Clay advocated forcefully for a national bank despite the fact that this reversed the position he had taken only five years before. The charge, by John Randolph of Virginia, that Clay *out-Hamiltons* Alexander Hamilton" did not embarrass him. He admitted that he was fallible and explained that the Kentucky legislature had wanted him to oppose the bank. Even more significantly, this ambitious federal program enjoyed the vitally important, enthusiastic support of John C. Calhoun and William Lowndes of South Carolina. As Speaker, Clay placed these southern allies in key positions. Calhoun became chair of a select committee that recommended the new national bank. Lowndes wrote the protective tariff bill and acted as Calhoun's lieutenant in approving the Second Bank of the United States. Together with Clay they carried the program through—improved roads, a protective tariff, and the Second Bank of the United States.

The support of prominent southerners like Calhoun, who later became a hostile foe of central power and the ideologue of state particularism, was not merely accidental. Though that support proved temporary, it reflected a shared reality in that period. For several years after 1812 there was a brief moment in which war and fluidity among parties took the edge off political conflict. It was also a time of ebullient confidence in the nation's growth, energy, and future. Everywhere citizens saw opportunity and imagined a more prosperous future. Partisan divisions lay beneath the surface, but they had subsided temporarily, and confidence in the nation's future expanded.

Significantly, however, the paths to future prosperity were not identical. Northern states had already taken decisions to gradually abolish human enslavement and were building an expanding, commercial, free-labor economy. Canals, steamboats, turnpikes, and other improvements to communication were beginning to "annihilate space," as the saying went. The future for a burgeoning internal market economy in the North was bright. In the South slavery was fueling a geographical and economic expansion untroubled by fear for the future. The wealth of slaveholders who shipped cotton abroad, like Calhoun, was soaring. Politically, southern leaders dominated the presidency and were guiding Congress and the Supreme Court. Slaveholding states still constituted close to half of the nation's population, and few glimpsed the possibility that the South would be left behind, a debilitated minority in the Congress. The demographic trends that would reduce the slave states to less than 38 percent of the population in 1860 had begun but were gradual and little noticed.

Also, and very importantly, this was a time in which the Founders' compromises on slavery briefly seemed manageable or workable for all sections. The contradiction between slavery and America's ideals of liberty was a fundamental flaw, and it had deepened since 1787 with large increases in the population of the enslaved. But North and South temporarily were not poised for conflict. New Englanders who suffered under President Jefferson's embargo had indulged in angry talk at the Hartford Convention. When the glorious news of Andrew Jackson's victory at the Battle of New Orleans arrived, an outburst of patriotic feeling left northern Federalists vulnerable to charges of disloyalty. In the South, some areas still hosted antislavery societies, and Congress, by wide margins, had prohibited the importation of more enslaved human beings in 1808. Respectable southerners could discuss slavery as undesirable or advocate colonization as a means to rid the country of human bondage. Like the Founding Fathers, many agreed that slavery was both regrettable and contrary to the nation's founding ideals. Although humanitarian currents were rising in western culture, debates over slavery had not turned acrid. Sharp differences over slavery were never far below the surface of politics, but for a moment they were less visible and far less important than achieving the War Hawks' goals.

All that changed in 1819. When Missouri sought admission as a new slaveholding state, the latent danger of sectional division suddenly became frighteningly real. Not one but two crises over Missouri threw Congress into turmoil before matters were settled in 1821. The deep and angry clashes in and out of Congress were a profound warning, what Jefferson called a "fire bell in the night." At first Henry Clay was not sensitive to the danger and was uncharacteristically supportive of slavery interests. He also was not the architect of the pieces of legislation that came to be known as his Missouri Compromise. But he became alive to the danger of disunion and repeatedly used his management of men, of time, and of parliamentary procedure to enact the necessary legislation.

When James Talmadge of New York put forward an amendment to the bill to admit Missouri, sectional hostility blazed up. Talmadge proposed, and a majority in the House agreed, that Missouri should bring no new enslaved people into its borders and should gradually emancipate the children of those already in bondage. Southerners were angrily opposed and blocked the idea in the Senate. Clay let emotions subside, and an Illinois senator advanced the idea of admitting slaveholding Missouri in tandem with Maine but restricting slavery thereafter in the Louisiana Purchase above thirty-six degrees, thirty minutes of latitude. Then, with supreme craft and knowledge of House rules, Clay broke a deadlock over the admission of Missouri and Maine, plus the restriction of slavery in western territory, by a vote on two bills, not one. This was the Compromise of 1820, which as a single bill would have gone down to defeat.

Still, the crisis was not over, for the next year Missouri presented its constitution to complete the process of admission. That constitution forbade the entry of any and all free African Americans into the state—a clear violation of the US Constitution's provision that "citizens of each state shall be entitled to all Privileges and Immunities of citizens of the several states." Since free Black people were citizens, even voters, in several northern and two southern states, the House balked. A majority demanded that Missourians change the offending clause. As a further complication, this controversy became entangled with the counting of the 1820 electoral votes for president. Clay finessed the problem by arranging for dubious language that Missouri's constitution would "never be construed" to allow a law that would restrict the rights of a US citizen. The crises over Missouri and slavery faded into the background, but they demonstrated that slavery could and would be the recurring, dangerous cause of conflict. Despite immense relief that compromise had averted a destructive collision, the compromise was provisional rather than fundamental in nature.

SLAVERY WAS an issue for Henry Clay personally, but only in a way that was and remained rooted in the past. His views were mildly progressive but racially static. Throughout his career, while criticism of slavery grew, his attitudes continued to be those of many Founding Fathers. Clay never voiced clear approval of slavery; instead, he always deprecated it in the abstract. In one of his first political acts, in 1798, he published an essay arguing for the gradual abolition of slavery. During that year and the next he published more essays and campaigned unsuccessfully for gradual emancipation in Kentucky. In 1816 he was a founder of the American Colonization Society, dedicated to "the expediency and practicability of ameliorating the condition of the Free People of Color . . . by providing a Colonial Retreat" on the west coast of Africa. Other prominent men who were founders or supporters included ex-presidents Thomas Jefferson and James Madison, President-elect James Monroe, Bushrod Washington, and Daniel Webster. The Society's first meeting took place in the chamber of the House of Representatives, with Henry Clay presiding.

In subsequent years Clay would criticize proslavery arguments and on a number of occasions helped some enslaved individuals obtain their freedom. In 1836 he became the president of the American Colonization Society and in 1839 criticized slavery in the Senate. Near the end of his life, in 1850, he declared to the Senate that "no earthly power shall ever make me vote to plant slavery where slavery does not exist." Even if a division of territory between slavery and free soil were necessary to preserve the Union, he could only "acquiesce" in such a solution. He would not vote for a law that was contrary "to my own conscience."

Yet, in the manner of many of the Founding Fathers who criticized slavery in the abstract, Clay's conscience was less than exacting. From 1799 onward he counted enslaved people as his property and depended on them financially. Their demanding labors generated the income that supported his constant activity in politics and helped him through occasional periods of indebtedness. As many as sixty human beings were his chattel property, and although visitors and neighbors testified that he was a mild slaveholder and that physical conditions on his plantation were good, some of his enslaved laborers were whipped by overseers. Within this context, he respected families, making some purchases in order to unite members of a family group, and he allowed the enslaved people at Ashland, his Kentucky estate, to visit other plantations or even to stay in

Lexington overnight. But Clay also sold the enslaved on occasion. Some rejected bondage by running away, although Clay was extremely indifferent about recovering fugitives. At one time, in 1849, when a young bondman who was traveling with him disappeared, Clay said, "in a reversal of our conditions I would have done the same thing." Rather than pursue the runaway, Clay made money available to help the young man return to Kentucky, if he wished, and he did exactly that.

Thus, Clay lived with the contradiction that he enslaved human beings and grew rich on their labors, while he disapproved of slavery. Like many others, he accepted social practices that were in his interest but contrary to his ideals. That was a moral accommodation that grew more questionable during his long career. In making some amends to his conscience, Clay freed a few of his enslaved workers while alive. Before his death he committed in his will to a scheme of gradual emancipation. The males he enslaved who were born after January 1, 1850, were to gain their freedom at age twenty-eight and females at age twenty-five. All were to receive wages in the last three years of their enslavement, in order to help them learn a trade and save money for transportation to Africa. Families were to be kept together, and if any of these individuals had to be sold before emancipation, the new owners were to be legally bound to honor Clay's plan.

Colonization of freed Black people in Africa was his lifelong solution to the racial problem, but it also was an increasingly dubious cause. The American Colonization Society sent only around ten thousand individuals to Africa before the Civil War, and when Clay became its president, interest was declining. Each year the natural increase of free Black people far exceeded the number transported. Free African Americans as well as the growing ranks of Black and white abolitionists overwhelmingly opposed the program. Despite the moral and reforming zeal of some early supporters, the American Colonization Society appeared more and more to be a means to safeguard slavery by removing a troublesome element, or as a path to a lily-white society. True, there were some in Kentucky and the Border South and others, including Abraham Lincoln, who continued to believe in the advantages of the scheme for all. But by the Civil War tenacious advocates of colonization—such as the Blair family or Wisconsin's Senator James Doolittle—clearly were devoted to white supremacy and intent on ridding the nation of unwanted Black people.

Like so many of the Founders and early leaders of the republic, Clay could not imagine a society in which African Americans lived as equals with white people. He believed that free Black people would always be a "corrupt, depraved, and abandoned class." Even though he blamed that situation on the unrelenting prejudice of society, he assumed that prejudice was permanent and unshakeable. He had little patience with abolitionists, whose agitation, in his view, only made things worse. Therefore, the only solution, in the supposed interest of free Black people, was to remove them from the country. Clay also resembled the slaveholding Founders in his blithe vagueness about when colonization or gradual emancipation might come to pass. He favored short-term personal and business interests over confronting difficult decisions. Somehow time would ameliorate difficulties and solve his and the nation's problem. Thinking of time in this way might soothe Clay's concerns and absolve his conscience of the responsibility to act. Yet as a leader of a nation dedicated to freedom, he evaded society's fundamental problem by choosing to trust vaguely in "Providence." He was not constructing the future but asking the future to heal the past.

TIME WAS not on Clay's side, and even he could see that prospects were darkening, despite the compromises he arranged. The nation's development made conflicts tied to slavery more acute and demanded solutions from politicians. With each passing decade economic change was driving the North and South in different directions, while Clay and Border States like Kentucky remained in the middle. The North's economy expanded rapidly as advances in transportation created an increasingly integrated market. That development encouraged agricultural specialization, technology, industry, and the growth of towns and cities. The rural South, buoyed by England's insatiable demand for cotton, prospered in a different way, and the enormous wealth produced by enslaved labor militated against any change of system. Slavery became ever more important, especially in the Deep South. By 1860 the value of enslaved property was far greater than all US investment in railroads and manufacturing combined. For the largest planters there was immense wealth: comprising only 3 percent of southern society, they nevertheless made up 70 percent of the richest persons in the nation.

These differences intensified the fundamental North–South conflicts related to slavery, but in fact, and in Clay's day, two additional regions were important: the West and a "middle third" of the United States along the Ohio River. The West of Clay's era consisted primarily of the former Northwest Territory and the beckoning lands on the Great Plains beyond the Mississippi River. Many thought of Clay as a westerner, and that fact plus the Missouri Compromise gave him ample prestige to contend for the presidency in 1824. He finished third, however, behind Andrew Jackson and John Quincy Adams. Clay regarded Jackson as unfit, and Adams was more likely to support the American System, so Clay threw his support to the far more puritanical Adams. When the new president named Clay his secretary of state, Jackson's supporters cried foul, and belief in a "corrupt bargain" shadowed Clay for years.

The West attracted Clay and other leaders in both North and South for its political weight and as part of a prosperous future. The rapidly growing western states had economic connections to both North and South. Internal improvements and especially railroads were opening eastern markets to states in what we now call the Midwest, pulling them into a northern market economy. Yet these states had always sent much of their production to New Orleans on the Ohio and Mississippi Rivers. Although railroads were carrying a growing share of products, steamboat traffic remained heavy into the 1850s. Each year hundreds of steamers left for New Orleans from Cincinnati, Louisville, Memphis, St. Louis, and even Pittsburgh. Leaders of the South and the North both saw the West as a prize, economically and politically, and both contended for it. By 1860 its allegiance would be to the North, if not necessarily to an antislavery Republican Party.

The "middle third," or "middle border," territory consisted of Kentucky and the southern portions of Ohio, Indiana, and Illinois. As North and South diverged, this region maintained a cultural and political distance from centrifugal tendencies either north or south. Sandwiched between regions whose economies were developing in different directions, the "middle border" shared values and outlooks of both. In a sense the culture of this region resembled that of the earlier republic, just as Henry Clay's values remained close to those of the Founders. As antislavery and abolitionist views grew in the North and proslavery theories in the South, change was slower along the middle border. White people in this middle third could discuss slavery critically in the abstract, but they did nothing practical against it and vigorously defended white supremacy. While North and South moved in contrary directions, the middle border remained behind but conflicted. By the time of the Civil War, Lincoln found that friends in Kentucky shared his and Clay's interest in gradual emancipation and colonization. Clay's Unionism also was a potent influence, even for individuals in the South, but congressmen from the middle third bitterly opposed his policy of emancipation. The moral accommodation with slavery deepened assumptions of white dominance. Such regional diversity added complexity to politics and to Clay's tasks as an architect of compromise. After only a decade his talents were needed again.

ANDREW JACKSON won the presidency in 1828, and before the end of his first term he had blocked important internal improvements, vetoed the recharter of the Bank of the United States, and shown the dictatorial or dominating tendencies that Clay feared. In the presidential contest of 1832, Clay easily emerged as Jackson's primary rival, and though Clay lost, his efforts hastened the coalescence of anti-Jackson forces into the Whig Party. For the next twenty years the Whigs would rival the Democrats, and Clay would be eminent in the party. The Whigs fought for tariffs, internal improvements, a national bank, and congressional dominance in policy-making. The opposition to "King Andrew" left the party alert against executive usurpation, and it was welcoming to many social reformers. Clay's defeat in 1832 depressed him, but before the end of the year he gathered his energies to meet another crisis.

Again it was the North–South clash that generated this next challenge. At issue was the protective tariff so essential to Clay's American System and his goals of economic development. In 1828 and 1832 Congress sharply raised tariffs on foreign goods, reaching rates as high as 50 percent. Calhoun now abandoned his nationalism, reversed his earlier advocacy for protection, and broke with President Jackson. First as vice president and then as senator, Calhoun helped South Carolina lead the South's objections, saying that protective tariffs benefited northern industry by unfairly penalizing southern consumers. The weaker section, Calhoun argued, was suffering oppression, a consolidated central government was destroying liberty, and nullification of the federal law was called for.

These economic arguments were real, but there was much more to the story. Calhoun's ambition of national leadership and power gave way to rising currents of concern in his home state. South Carolina's planters were uneasy, and social and political dangers to slavery lay at the bottom of their fears. Defying the tariff was also a way to prevent the rise of a powerful federal government that could threaten slavery and other sectional interests. Eliminating protection also could retard the growth of the northern economy and population and thus give more security to the interests of the slave South. Calhoun had reached a turning point in his career, and he threw himself into his new role as aggressive defender of slavery and the South's sectional interests.

The South Carolina legislature scheduled a state convention, and that body in 1832 declared that it had nullified the federal tariff. President Jackson was willing to reduce tariff rates, but he would not tolerate defiance of federal law. He issued a fiery proclamation and demanded from Congress a Force Bill that would enable him to send military forces to Charleston to collect federal duties. Many in Congress now looked to Senator Clay to avert a crisis that involved possible disunion and war. The challenge was complex. Clay's important tariff was at risk, and its loss might drive manufacturing areas to threaten disunion. Southern votes would be necessary for a compromise, but Clay and Calhoun had been enemies since 1824. Personal hostilities were common in the political system, and one of the few factors helping Clay was Calhoun's hostility to Jackson, which meant that Calhoun did not welcome the president's tariff-reduction plan. But a House bill proposed to end protective tariffs almost immediately.

Henry Clay drafted a different bill that would reduce tariffs but do so gradually. Not until 1840 would rates fall to 20 percent, and not until after 1842 could rates fall lower. To gain southern support, Clay made what some called a "great leap across the Potomac." He arranged to see John C. Calhoun, and through halting, difficult conversations the two made progress. Each hoped that the other's support would enable passage. In February 1833 Clay rose in the Senate and presented his plan with careful explanations over several hours. When he concluded, the presiding officer recognized Calhoun, and the Senate chamber immediately fell silent. Anxious spectators were surprised but overjoyed to hear that Calhoun firmly supported Clay's proposal, and the Senate gallery erupted in cheers. Clay became the chair of a committee to draft the final bill, and although he had to overcome a number of final complications, his legislation became law just before Congress was due to adjourn. Again, Clay emerged as the Great Compromiser whose skill saved the Union from potential disaster. His love of the Union had, in fact, been a driving force in his efforts to gain a compromise. It was a notable victory, but he could see that southern demands were becoming more adamant and that the North–South chasm was growing wider.

SLAVERY HAD loomed ominously, but not invisibly, in the background of the nullification crisis. When Henry Clay sought the presidency for the third and last time in 1844, it played a more open, salient role in wrecking his chances. The slavery issue had cast a troubling shadow over US politics since 1836, when Texans established their independence from Mexico. They promptly requested to become a state, but slaveholding Texas claimed a large territory, and its admission to the Union would sharply affect northern and southern interests. In addition, it would threaten war with Mexico.

Many leaders, like Clay, saw the dangers inherent in this situation. President Martin Van Buren blocked Texas's admission in 1836, foreseeing the divisive sectional controversy it could ignite. Still, southern proslavery interests wanted to add Texas to the Union, whereas abolitionists and many northerners feared that the admission of Texas would result in several new slave states. Texas's prospects seemed to be stalled in 1840, when the Whigs elected William Henry Harrison as president. But Harrison died after only a month in office, elevating Virginia's John Tyler from the vice presidency. Tyler had been a Democrat who joined the Whigs mainly because he feared Andrew Jackson as a danger to states' rights. As president he proved to be a conservative, proslavery southerner, and pressure for Texas's admission grew.

Clay wanted to maintain the strategy of keeping the issue out of national controversy. He was rightly confident that he would be the Whigs' candidate in 1844, and like most observers he expected Martin Van Buren to win the Democrats' nomination. To spare the nation damaging controversy and to explain his position, Clay published a public letter on Texas. He forthrightly said, "I certainly am not willing to involve this country in a foreign war for the object of acquiring Texas." With high-minded statesmanship, he went on to challenge expansionists who regarded war was "a trifling affair, on account of the weakness of Mexico." To Clay, "all wars [are] great calamities, to be avoided ... and honorable peace [is] the wisest and truest policy of this country." The United States needed "union, peace, and patience," and "good faith and justice are equally due from this country toward the weak as toward the strong." Inflicting "injustice" upon a weak nation, he said, was incompatible with American "dignity" and could entail unexpected problems and losses.

Martin Van Buren shared Clay's views, but southerners succeeded in denying the Democratic nomination to the former president. After many ballots James K. Polk, an ardent expansionist, gained the nomination, and Clay suddenly appeared to be on the wrong side of a large segment of enthusiastic public opinion. Clay then temporized and in some additional public letters backed away from his praiseworthy position, suggesting that he could support the addition of Texas to the Union. It was a shortsighted move. Opinion was evolving in the North, and the recently formed Liberty Party gained a small but significant segment of votes. In parts of New England this antislavery party polled more votes than the difference between Clay and the expansionist Polk. In New York anti-Texas voters disgusted with Clay probably abandoned him to support the Liberty Party, and Polk won that key state. For the first time concerns over slavery may well have determined the national election. The always ambitious Clay had lost his bid for the presidency, and the results signaled that slavery was becoming an ever more divisive issue.

Clay was in retirement from the Senate as the Texas issue enlarged its impact. Outgoing President Tyler engineered annexation by a joint resolution of Congress, and soon President Polk led the nation into war with Mexico. The result was a United States victory and a vast expansion of US territory to the southwest and all the way to the Pacific. Many historians have rated Polk as an effective executive because he realized his goal of expansion to the Pacific Ocean, but his success was a calamity for national unity. The future of that vast western domain—in both the original Louisiana Purchase and in the lands acquired from Mexico—now dominated the political agenda. Increasingly, conflict centered on whether slavery would expand or be limited, whether North and South shared vital interests, whether slavery and Union could remain compatible. As the minority of abolitionists slowly gained followers, a much larger number of northerners developed fears about the territorial expansion of slavery. In the South, belligerent demands for support of slave interests thrived, and states' rights opposition to national power intensified. The war with Mexico thus set the stage for deeper domestic division and for Henry Clay's last effort to craft a compromise and save the Union.

The territorial controversy was already boiling in 1849 when Clay reentered the Senate. The Gold Rush, as dramatic as it was unexpected, prompted Californians to seek rapid admission to the Union as a free state. Southerners feared that slavery would lose its veto power in the Senate and hotly objected. They argued that Congress had never organized California as a territory and that this irregular process denied slavery interests a chance to establish the institution there. Additional questions were troubling: How would all of the remaining territory won from Mexico be organized? Were lands still claimed by Texas to become additional slave states? Was the future to be tilted toward slavery, or could measures bring the government into closer conformity with its founding ideals? Southerners wanted more assistance in reclaiming escapees from slavery, whereas northerners feared that slavery would sabotage free-labor farms and destroy opportunity for settlers west of the Mississippi River.

As 1850 began, Clay assumed leadership of the effort to find a compromise, aided by the Illinois Democrat Stephen Douglas. From January into August Clay would take the floor a staggering seventy times, despite his age and growing weakness due to advancing tuberculosis. Clay was almost seventy-three, his thin form had become gaunt, and longtime colleagues concluded that he was dying. People traveled from as far away as Boston to hear him unveil his proposals in February, and an overflow crowd broke into applause when Clay rose to speak. There was a substantial pause before the sergeant-at-arms could restore order, and then Clay described his omnibus bill in a four-hour speech spread over two days. His intense labors were only beginning.

Certain parts of Clay's plan survived the legislative process with little change. These included the admission of California as a free state, a stronger fugitive slave law demanded by southerners, and prohibition of the slave trade in Washington, DC, the nation's capital. For Texas and the lands won from Mexico, Clay's original proposal had a strong antislavery bias. Mexican law had prohibited slavery in the Southwest, and he wanted to honor and assume that precedent. In addition, he proposed a new boundary for Texas that would put many slaveholders under the Mexican law and force them to move if they wanted to keep their enslaved workers. To mollify Texans over the restriction of their land claims, he proposed that the federal government would pay a large debt that the state owed on its bonds. The ideas of limiting Texas's boundary and assuming its debt would endure, but the status of slavery in the Southwest ran into controversy.

Southerners like Mississippi's Senator Jefferson Davis demanded that slavery should be allowed to go there or, as a final compromise, that the line of thirty-six degrees, thirty minutes should divide slave and free territory all the way to the Pacific Ocean. Northerners were as strongly opposed and demanded the prohibition of slavery. "Popular sovereignty" was a third position, one that would become Stephen Douglas's key principle through the 1850s. It advocated letting those who settled in a territory decide on their own whether slavery would be allowed or prohibited. What finally emerged from Congress was none of these but an evasion. As finally enacted, new territories called New Mexico and Utah would have the power to legislate on "all rightful subjects . . . consistent with the Constitution." Since northerners and southerners disagreed on what those words meant, the result might depend on the courts, and the law provided for direct appeal of a territorial legislature's action to the Supreme Court. Some later commented that Congress had enacted a lawsuit instead of a law.

Before these issues could be settled, many extensive consultations and months of labor were necessary. Finally Clay brought his omnibus bill, a package of the proposals, to a vote. He had spared no effort to persuade Congress that it was "neither southern nor northern" but "equal ... fair ... a compromise." He even held up a splinter of wood from George Washington's coffin and declared that it constituted a "warning voice, coming from the grave" that the Union must be saved. But the omnibus failed. Sick and exhausted, Clay left Washington to recuperate, but Stephen Douglas shrewdly realized that different majorities might be marshaled for each element of the omnibus. He brought the bills up separately and achieved their passage one by one. Thus, the Compromise of 1850 became law, to the immense relief of many. Ecstatic crowds in Washington rejoiced, believing that the Union had been saved from its greatest crisis. It appeared that Henry Clay had cemented the capstone to his remarkable career as the Great Compromiser.

In reality, it soon became clear that Compromise of 1850 was not a solution to the problems generated by slavery. Within a few years the fugitive slave law provoked many northerners to resist, for a number of reasons. Payments to federal magistrates under the law seemed to encourage judgments in favor of slaveholders; northern citizens could be compelled to help in apprehending enslaved people who escaped from bondage; and the spectacle of the federal government using its power to enforce slavery—in a supposedly freedom-loving nation—was repugnant to many. The territorial formula was no settlement of that key issue, either for white southerners or for antislavery northerners. Expansion into the West had a powerful allure to free-soil farmers, who saw slavery as a mortal danger to their way of life and to family-based commercial farming. Southern leaders, for their part, believed that gaining slave states in the West was essential to protect the institution of slavery and the South's power in Congress. The defeat of the bills as an omnibus package showed that true, mutual compromise had proved impossible. Henry Clay's charisma, charm, and legislative skill had done no more than delay conflict; they failed to resolve it.

AMBITION AND a talent for leadership were driving forces in Henry Clay's career. The allure of the political arena never faded for him, despite the fact that he loved Ashland, his Kentucky estate, and was devoted to his family and his wife of more than fifty years. Even after he lacked the energy to go to the Senate and suffered from a wracking cough and growing weakness, he chose to remain in Washington, DC. There he died. But Henry Clay was also a patriot. His devotion to a strong, prosperous, and united nation was the consistent goal of his politics. He strove to live up to the example of the republic's early leaders and Founders, and their values were an inspiration for his own life. His was unquestionably a constructive life in many ways.

But unlike the nation's first generation of leaders, Henry Clay lived through several decades of enormous change and development. The country whose boundaries reached the Pacific Ocean was vastly larger than the one that had fought the British in 1812. Economically and socially it had altered even more than its geography. Most critically, slavery had enriched the South while moving its values further and further away from the ideals of the Declaration of Independence. The North had developed along a very different path, one of commercial success and growing immigration, urbanization, mechanization, and industry. Slavery posed a threat to that system's growth, just as free soil and distaste for human bondage menaced the future for ambitious slaveholders. The extent of this divergence defined the challenge facing political leaders.

Clay dedicated his great energies to avoiding collisions between these forces, but his values and his vision advanced little from those of his youth. Putting his conscience to one side, he accepted the shortcomings in society that benefited him. As a political leader he sought to mitigate fundamental problems rather than resolve them, to find the short-term stopgap. He did not think realistically about the racial future, relying on time and unknown forces to solve the contradiction of a society dedicated to slavery and liberty. Meanwhile the Black population expanded greatly, and slavery extended its influence. Some of Clay's actions indicated that he recognized the potential in Black human beings, but he never questioned his society's assumption of white supremacy. The ideals and opportunities of America seemed to exist only for white people. In a long career Henry Clay achieved much, but as social and economic change increased tensions, he relied on old values to restrain opposite, diverging forces. For the nation, that proved not to be a viable strategy.

Clay was, however, very American in his deficiencies, for American society was acquisitive, ambitious, and, on the whole, fixated on short-term gains rather than long-term problems. If one regards business as the pursuit of gain, the business of America was business, even in the nineteenth century. Seeking wealth and new opportunities, both the North and the South rushed toward conflicting futures. Few citizens or political leaders were willing to consider solutions that would diminish their prosperity or deflect their paths. In these respects, Clay was essentially American, even if he was not, as his recent biographers suggested, "the essential American." His essence—the readiness to compromise irreconcilable elements—was inadequate as a solution for the country.

John C. Calhoun
Inveterate Ideologue

~

John C. Calhoun is central to public memory about the causes of the Civil War. He was the South's political warrior. A fierce, unbending advocate from South Carolina, he produced imposing arguments to defend slavery, states' rights, and southern interests. Because he always claimed to seek a solution to the Union's problems, many historians remember him as a Cassandra rather than as an insurrectionist. But he also promoted schism through the radical and aggressive nature of the theories that he promulgated. His rhetoric inspired extremism in other southern politicians who wanted to match his fame. The general image of him in historical memory as a man of constant principle is woefully incomplete. It considers only part of his career and fails to identify the essential drivers of his impact on history. To grasp Calhoun it is necessary to probe his character and understand the interaction between his personal ambition and developments in American society.

Calhoun did not begin life amid great wealth or privilege, but he was fortunate because his intellectual capacities compelled recognition. After his father died, his family sent him to Yale in 1802, although he had benefited from only a modest amount of schooling. That proved to be no handicap for the brainy youth, who graduated as valedictorian in 1804. A few years later Calhoun gained admission to the bar, and in 1811 he married Floride Colhoun, a distant cousin who was wealthy and the daughter of a United States senator from Charleston. He was on the path to power and fame, and he entered the US House of Representatives the same year as his marriage.

Immediately the twenty-nine-year-old Calhoun distinguished himself, both as a leader and as a fervent, committed nationalist. Among the young and angry War Hawks, eager to resist and end impositions by Great Britain, Calhoun stood out. He became a major ally of Henry Clay in the effort to enact an ambitious program of Hamiltonian reforms—internal improvements, the rechartering of a national bank, and the erection of protective tariffs to benefit industry. Calhoun had called for this strong, nationalist program even before Clay arrived in the capital, and his role in enacting it was central. He chaired a select committee on the currency that allowed him to shape the recommendation for a national bank. In the effort to push the entire program through Congress, Calhoun spoke often and was a vitally effective lieutenant to all of Speaker Clay's efforts.

But legislative skill was not the only distinguishing feature of Calhoun's fervent nationalism. The way that he advanced strong federal measures revealed a trait that would characterize his entire career. Calhoun saw no valid alternative to his convictions. There was nothing "more important than internal improvements," he declared. Nothing could "add more to the wealth, the strength, and the political prosperity of our country," and he rejoiced that "general concerns of the nation" predominated over "sectional feelings." "On this subject of national power," said Mr. Calhoun, "what can be more important than a perfect unity in every part, in feelings and sentiments? And what can tend more powerfully to produce it, than overcoming the effects of distance?" Dismissing the "logician" who might object that funding internal improvements was not among "the enumerated powers," he maintained that the Constitution was enacted to "provide for the common defense & general welfare." He flatly denied that such broad construction gave "a dangerous extent to the powers of Congress." In fact, "the money cannot be appropriated to a more exalted use."

The tariff was needed not merely to promote industry—it involved "the security of the country." As a southerner he was "disinterested" and was shocked that "an apathy and aversion" to the tariff had sprung up after the war with Britain. The country needed manufactures to have a strong economy. Fortunately, as well, they were "calculated to bind together more closely our widely spread republic" and demonstrate the value of internal improvements. Saying that "the liberty and the union of this country [are] inseparably united," Calhoun explained that he had studied the "causes that destroyed the liberty of other states" and concluded that tariffs would "greatly increase our mutual dependence and intercourse" and lead to "the perfection of our political institutions." Similarly, he asserted that a national bank was needed for its "important, various, and extensive" services. The bank's services would be "required" for "the national wealth" and for "the uses of commerce, agriculture, manufactures, and the arts, throughout the Union."

Calhoun's rhetoric aimed not to persuade but to overpower, to render differences of opinion illegitimate. He always preferred aggression to concession, extreme or aggressive arguments to moderate ones, and his statesmanship had the same character. He was not equivocal—to advance, he denied other possibilities; to defend, he chose to attack. The conclusion that his mind had reached always was true and unassailable, and as he grew older Calhoun became enamored of the use of cold, rigidly logical argumentation. He liked to construct an inescapable web of logic, so that to accept his premise was to surrender to his conclusion.

These were the traits of an intellectually powerful but coldly ambitious man. Calhoun was determined to become a figure of great consequence, to have a historic impact on national affairs. His ambition drove him relentlessly and never faded. He was not a man of warmth and would permit no one and nothing to stand in his way. Calhoun lacked Clay's ability to charm and secure friends but instead knew how to advance his interests amid changing circumstances. At various times he discarded allies or allied with those he had mocked, using whatever strategy would serve his purpose. Over a long career he completely reversed his position on crucial matters, always making a strong case for his point of view while adapting himself to varying conditions. Therefore, to examine his career is to gain insight into the great changes affecting the nation and especially the South and slavery.

IN THE 1810s and for much of the 1820s the political situation allowed Calhoun to pursue his ambition on the national stage as a leader for the country, but a change was coming. His prominence as a War Hawk qualified him to become secretary of war in 1817, and he remained in that post through the two terms of President James Monroe. With commendable energy Calhoun set out to right a weak, disorganized department and inject strength in the nation's defenses. He wanted steam frigates for the navy, a larger standing army, better roads to favor communication, and manufactures and reliable funding from internal taxes. He urged a wide range of reforms but did not enjoy substantial support from Congress. Nevertheless, his planning, advocacy, and actions at the cabinet level won respect from many national leaders, and his reputation in national politics continued to grow. For some time during his service as secretary of war, he enjoyed a warm friendship with Secretary of State John Quincy

Adams, with whom he frequently discussed the country's affairs. Adams called Calhoun "a man of fair and candid mind, of honorable principles, of clear and quick understanding, of cool self-possession, of enlarged philosophical views, and of ardent patriotism. He is above all sectional and factious prejudices more than any other statesman of this Union with whom I have ever acted." But this friendship with Adams, like many others, would not endure.

In 1824 Calhoun decided to seek the presidency and was recognized as one of several leading contenders. In an early sign, however, that political foundations were beginning to shift beneath his feet, the South Carolina legislature did not endorse him. Soon other supporters suggested him for second place, and his stature gave him an easy victory as vice president in the Electoral College. He served unhappily under President John Quincy Adams and began to question the American System of Henry Clay, the system that he had so fervently championed.

The change was not exclusively a personal one. Uneasiness about a strong central government was growing in South Carolina and among prominent Virginia legislators as well. Southern leaders felt their interests diverging from those of Adams's New England. Ever alert to how shifting sentiments could affect his rise, Calhoun responded accordingly. As early as 1826 he informed the popular Andrew Jackson that he had his support for president in 1828. Jackson chose the South Carolinian as his running mate, and Calhoun held onto his position near the pinnacle of national power.

Shifting perceptions of sectional power and interests would demand more change from Calhoun. A transformation in attitudes was underway among leaders in the slaveholding states. Slavery was the divisive issue always lurking below the surface of politics, and during the Missouri Crisis John Quincy Adams had realized that on slavery issues there was a chasm between his nationalism and the South Carolinian's—Calhoun loved slavery more than Union. As the decade advanced, planters developed an increased sensitivity to criticism of slavery and a deeper recognition of how vital slavery was to prosperity in a cotton South that was growing rich by feeding the ravenous textile mills of Great Britain. Slavery meant wealth from cotton, and the South's agricultural character differed more each year from a commercial North of small farms, towns, and cities. With European nations openly discussing abolition, intellectual currents in the region began to focus more closely on defense of the "peculiar institution." Given his political instincts and ambitions, Calhoun adjusted his dreams to an altered future.

Although Calhoun's fierce ambition to be great never faltered, he began to revise his goals. If he could not guide the nation to policies satisfactory to the South, he would lead the South's defense and shape its strategy. It would not be a lesser role if he could force the North to yield to his region's needs, thus serving the Union and the South. Two things spurred his full conversion to that new role: the so-called "petticoat affair" in Jackson's cabinet and the tariffs of 1828 and 1832.

The tariff controversy burst on the scene first, when Congress approved an unexpectedly steep increase in tariff duties. South Carolinians and others felt they would be exploited by protective tariffs that benefited northern industry while increasing the cost of products they purchased. More seriously, many slaveholding southerners were beginning to fear that a strong central government might have the means to interfere with slavery, causing enormous damage to the plantation economy and to a society based on human bondage and white dominance in all areas of life. Vice President Calhoun avoided, at this point, a direct confrontation with President Andrew Jackson. But he went to work behind the scenes, cooperating with his state's legislature by anonymously writing the *South Carolina Exposition and Protest*.

Calhoun now claimed that the American System that he had done so much to launch was the oppression of an "irresponsible power." The so-called Tariff of Abominations was "unconstitutional, unequal, and oppressive." It would "corrupt the public virtue and destroy the liberty of the country." Discarding the broad interpretation that he had employed to justify internal improvements, Calhoun now argued that Congress could exercise only "specific powers" that were "expressly granted." Since protective tariffs, if effective, would devastate the sale of foreign goods and curtail federal revenues, they were not a valid use of the power to lay imposts. Worse, protective tariffs would raise up "one section of the country on the ruins of another." South Carolinians, he claimed, were loath to speak of "sectional interest," but "we are the serfs of the system" that would raise the costs of producing cotton. One section would enjoy "unexampled prosperity" while the South would "languish in poverty and sink into decay."

Calhoun then enlarged states' rights theory and asserted his remedy: nullification of the federal law. The framers, he argued, had divided powers between the states and the federal government, each remaining "sovereign" over its interests. Each state retained "the right of judging . . . on contested points of authority" and reserved the power "by its veto, or right of interposition" to block an unconstitutional federal law. Thus, to "arrest" the "American System," South Carolina could "interpose" its authority and "check" the unconstitutional expansion of power by the central government. What if a state went too far in its use of interposition? Calhoun framed his answer cleverly to give the South an advantage. Congress's remedy would be to propose a constitutional amendment to validate its power. Thus, a state could nullify alone, but for the central government to prevail, two-thirds of Congress and three-fourths of *all* the states would have to support a constitutional amendment that would "terminate" the state's objection. These legalistic arguments constituted a threat, the opening salvo in South Carolina's campaign against the tariff. Action did not arrive until November 1832, when the state legislature passed an ordinance of nullification.

Meanwhile, Calhoun's position in the Jackson administration was deteriorating for social reasons. Floride Calhoun led a movement by other cabinet wives to ostracize the vivacious Peggy Eaton, wife of the secretary of war. Mrs. Eaton, in the other wives' judgment, did not meet a proper moral standard; they questioned the circumstances in which she had come to know and marry John Eaton. The attacks on John Eaton's wife enraged Andrew Jackson, who resented rumors that his own beloved wife had not been legally free to marry him. Jackson blamed her death late in 1828 on the effects of that criticism. This "petticoat affair" ended when Jackson asked for the resignation of all anti-Eaton cabinet members, but not before Calhoun suffered in Jackson's estimation. Political rivals revealed that Calhoun, as secretary of war in 1818, had wanted to censure Jackson for the general's invasion of Florida—a fact that Jackson had not known.

The larger significance of deteriorating relations between Calhoun and Jackson emerged at the Jefferson Day dinner in 1830. When the moment to offer toasts arrived, the president fixed his gaze on Calhoun and declared with steely firmness, "Our federal Union, it must be preserved." Calhoun rose and responded, "The Union, next to our liberties, the most dear." By this time Calhoun probably had concluded that his future as leader of the nation had evaporated and that he would have to seek greater prominence as the South's champion. He also saw clearly that the issue of slavery lay beneath all the sectional quarrels. He confided to a friend:

> I consider the Tariff, but as the occasion, rather than the real cause of the present unhappy state of things. The truth can no longer be

disguised, that the peculiar domestick institutions of the Southern States, and the consequent direction which that and her soil and climate have given to her industry, has placed them . . . in opposite relation to the majority of the Union; against the danger of which, if there be no protective power in the reserved rights of the states, they must in the end be forced to rebel, or submit to have . . . their domestick institutions exhausted . . . and themselves & children reduced to wretchedness.

If Calhoun had any doubts about the future of his career, they surely disappeared by 1832, the year in which he resigned his position as vice president and reentered the Senate as South Carolina officially approved an ordinance of nullification. The Palmetto State's challenge to federal law was no longer theoretical, and President Jackson reacted strongly. Vehemently rejecting the theory of nullification, he threatened military action to collect the tariff in Charleston and called on Congress for a Force Bill. Ironically, Jackson also favored a modification of the tariff, and on terms more favorable to the South than the bill offered by Senator Clay. Calhoun's hostility toward the president was so great, however, that he took the surprising step of cooperating with Henry Clay, from whom he had been alienated for several years. The Force Bill passed, Clay's phased reduction of the tariff gained approval, and the nullification crisis passed. But Calhoun's new direction was clear, both to him and to others.

For the rest of his life, Calhoun would defend slavery, raise states' rights as slavery's shield, and combat the power of the central government. Some of these themes were traditional for the Democratic Party of Jefferson and Jackson. Jefferson had sanctified the government that governed least, and Jackson, even though he took strong action to seize the lands of native Americans or to oppose nullification, had a lifelong distrust of concentrated power and privilege. Among southerners such as Virginia's John Randolph, wariness of central power had often turned into hostility. Calhoun reinforced and spread these traditions throughout the rest of his career. He did much to create a Democratic Party dedicated to these views in both the North and the South. The defense of slavery, rather than party loyalty, became his priority, but his states' rights theories sank deep roots among northern Democrats. An enduring part of Calhoun's legacy would be the Democratic Party's devotion to states' rights and southern interests, including slavery.

CALHOUN SEIZED upon the "gag rule" to stake his claim as the preeminent defender of slavery. In 1835 the abolition movement led by William Lloyd Garrison was small and unpopular—in fact despised by the great majority of "respectable" citizens. But it made itself heard, taking advantage of the steam printing press to appeal directly to citizens and to flood the country with appeals and petitions. South Carolina responded with fury, seizing antislavery materials that arrived in the mail and demanding that northern states act immediately to suppress antislavery activists and publications. Boston's mayor, surprised by South Carolina's demand, had never heard of Garrison and was even more puzzled when he investigated and caught sight of the abolitionist's modest offices. But Calhoun had no trouble hearing his state's protest and its objections to the many antislavery petitions that were arriving in Congress.

Until this point Senator Calhoun had maintained that the right of petition was "guaranteed by the Constitution" and that Congress had a "duty" to receive citizens' memorials. Without hesitation he reversed himself and led efforts in 1836 to impose on lawmakers a gag rule, a procedural order that would prohibit discussion of antislavery petitions. A South Carolina colleague succeeded in establishing such a rule in the House, and Calhoun quickly proposed one for the Senate. Mindful of appearances, other proslavery senators modified the terms of his proposal slightly, but the measure that passed and remained in effect until 1844 effectively prevented any consideration of the abolitionists' pleas. Then Calhoun went further, making striking, new proslavery declarations in February 1837.

He began in the manner that was characteristic of him. "I do not belong," Calhoun asserted, "to the school which holds that aggression is to be met by concession. Mine is the opposite creed, which teaches that encroachments must be met at the beginning, and that those who act on the opposite principle are prepared to become slaves." On the South's institution of slavery any "concession or compromise" would be "fatal." Even concession of "an inch" would lead to more compromise and defeat. "We must meet the enemy on the frontier, with a fixed determination of maintaining our position at every hazard." To "receive these insulting petitions," he said, would open the way to their consideration. More importantly, to discuss the rightness of slavery "is beyond the jurisdiction of Congress—they have no right to touch it in any shape or form, or to make it the subject of deliberation or discussion."

Calhoun then advanced from defense of slavery to ringing praise of an institution that the Founders of the early republic had regretted and described as a necessary evil. He was the first major politician to declare categorically that slavery was a "positive good." His fulsome endorsement of human bondage included warnings of disunion, pronouncements of white racial superiority, and arguments about the nature of social justice and stability in societies. Slavery was absolutely "indispensable to the peace and happiness" of both races in the South, said Calhoun:

> It cannot be subverted without drenching the country in blood, and extirpating one or the other of the races. Be it good or bad, [slavery] has grown up with our society and institutions, and is so interwoven with them that to destroy it would be to destroy us as a people. But let me not be understood as admitting, even by implication, that the existing relations between the two races in the slaveholding States is an evil;— far otherwise; I hold it to be a good, as it has thus far proved itself to be to both, and will continue to prove so if not disturbed by the fell spirit of abolition.

Calhoun then expanded on his assertion of slavery's positive good. The "black race of Central Africa," he claimed, had "never . . . from the dawn of history to the present day, attained a condition so civilized and so improved" as the one it enjoyed in the South. Few countries had a laboring class that received "so much" of benefit and had "so little extracted . . . or where there is more kind attention paid . . . in sickness or infirmities of age." The "direct, simple, and patriarchal" character of slavery in the South placed Black people in a superior condition to "the tenants of the poor houses in the more civilized portions of Europe." Taking "higher ground" than mere defense of slavery, he reiterated that "in the present state of civilization" in the South, given two physically and intellectually different races, slavery "is, instead of an evil, a good—a positive good."

Calhoun worried that abolitionism "has taken possession of the pulpit, of the schools, and to a considerable extent, of the press" in the North. It was shaping the minds of the young, convincing people that slavery was "a sin," and teaching northerners "to hate the people and institutions" of the South. "By the necessary course of events . . . we must become, finally two people" because "Abolition and the Union cannot coexist." How unnecessary and regrettable such a result would be, he then argued, for in every society "one portion of the community . . . live[d] on the labor of the other." Wealth was always "unequally divided." Not only were the South's enslaved laborers well provided for, but slavery "forms the most solid and durable foundation on which to rear free and stable political institutions."

Delivering a warning to the North, Calhoun argued that "in an advanced stage of wealth and civilization" there is always "a conflict between labor and capital." That conflict was coming to the North, he declared. But "the condition of society in the South exempts us from the disorders and dangers resulting from this conflict" and has produced a "political condition . . . so much more stable and quiet than that of the North." In this one speech Calhoun articulated or suggested almost all of the proslavery arguments that southern leaders subsequently would use to defend the institution and to claim the superiority of their society. He also had taken a position so striking, antagonistic, and unrestrained that ambitious southern politicians would strive to emulate him in the future. Calhoun asserted that the one thing white southerners needed to overcome their "imminent perils" was "concert," unity.

Later that year Calhoun solidified his position at the head of proslavery agitation. He introduced a package of resolutions that defended slavery on legal and constitutional principles. Not only did the states retain, according to these resolutions, "the exclusive and sole right over their own domestic institutions," but the central government had a duty to "give . . . increased stability and security" to them. Slavery was venerable and vitally important, and therefore any and all "open and systematic attacks" on it were unjustified, a "breach of faith," and "a violation of the most solemn obligations, moral and religious." Calhoun's resolutions also condemned any attempt to abolish slavery in the District of Columbia or to object to slavery in the territories. Sensing how important territorial issues would become, he further declared that the southern and western states must enjoy full equality in extending their population and interests into new areas.

Calhoun's attention to the territories was prescient, for territorial questions dominated controversies from that point to the Civil War. Soon he found a way to inject southern demands into issues of territorial expansion, this time relating to Texas. The nation's leaders had avoided dealing with Texas after it gained its independence from Mexico in 1836. Texans wanted to join the Union, but it was all too clear that controversy would arise over admitting that new state. Its embrace of slavery, and its claim to territory so extensive that several slave states might be formed from it, threatened serious political disruption, as well as war with Mexico. Two presidents, Democrat Martin Van Buren and Whig William Henry

Harrison kept their distance from the subject and kept Texans waiting. But after Harrison died, Vice President John Tyler, a Virginia slaveholder, took office. Turning against the Whig Party, Tyler vetoed a national bank and tariffs and resolved to add Texas to the Union.

Calhoun's chance to intervene arose from another death. Secretary of State Abel Upshur had been negotiating a treaty to admit Texas when he was killed by an explosion aboard a new naval steamship. Succeeding Upshur at the Department of State, Calhoun seized the opportunity to galvanize southern support for Texas and slavery and, in the process, inflame the situation. He put finishing touches on the proposed treaty and then wrote two provocative, unnecessary letters to the British ambassador, Richard Packenham. Britain had informed the United States of its position on Texas—it was urging Mexico to recognize Texas's independence but was not working for the abolition of slavery in Texas. It had no intention of doing anything "to disturb the internal tranquillity of the slaveholding States." Mexico and Texas were free "to make their own unfettered arrangements," even though Britain favored "the general abolition of slavery throughout the world."

Ignoring this British assurance, Calhoun announced his "deep concern" for the "safety" and "prosperity" of the United States. Britain's support for the general abolition of slavery was dangerous, because any abolition activity in Texas could spread to the slaveholding South. It would be "the most efficient means of effecting [abolition]" in the Gulf states. Calhoun suggested that Great Britain, despite its denial, *was* making "exertions" for abolition in Texas. Therefore, the United States needed a treaty with the slaveholding republic of Texas to "guar[d] against the threatened danger" and to "preserve domestic institutions" guaranteed by both nations "and deemed essential to their safety and prosperity." If abolition were to succeed in Texas, it "would involve in the greatest calamity the whole country, and especially the race which it is the avowed object of her exertions to benefit." Calhoun wedged into his letters a bold proslavery argument. He claimed that emancipation "invariably" led to "vice and pauperism" and a host of infirmities for those emancipated, and he used census data to claim that those enslaved in the South were healthier than free Black people in Maine and Massachusetts. Slavery was not just a beneficial but an "essential" institution.

Calhoun's tendentious letters sparked so much controversy that the Senate rejected his treaty with Mexico. But the two slaveholders Tyler and Calhoun devised a new path to annexation—a joint resolution of

Congress, which required only a simple majority—and Texas entered the Union. Its annexation led not only to war with Mexico but also to widespread and increasing political turmoil. Given the vast southwestern and western territories gained from the war with Mexico, the future of slavery in the territories became an inescapable, dominant issue. Calhoun had done much to put it there, and he dedicated himself to protecting slavery's interests in all the newly added lands.

When a Pennsylvania Democrat, David Wilmot, proposed that slavery should be prohibited in all the lands taken from Mexico, intense territorial battles began. Many northerners agreed with Wilmot, and before long fourteen northern legislatures had endorsed the Wilmot Proviso. The veteran Democrat Lewis Cass proposed an alternative—popular sovereignty, which would leave a future decision on slavery to those who settled in the territories. Unhesitatingly, Calhoun laid down an inflexible southern position. Because the Constitution was a compact among states, and because each state had equal rights, southerners could not be prohibited from taking those they enslaved into any territory, he argued. Thus, neither the federal government nor actual settlers in a territory could block the introduction of slavery. Only when a territory became a state could a local decision against slavery be valid.

The difference between the leadership of Calhoun and Henry Clay was clear. Calhoun did not try to evade the slavery issue or hope that it would disappear, somehow, over time. With his trenchant intellect, he focused directly on the problem and drew profound, if unsettling, conclusions. The federal government must *protect* slaveholders' rights and slavery's expansion. To preserve the Union, the North must bow to his definition of the South's rights. Calhoun established his proslavery leadership through bold, uncompromising language, and his words raised the stakes for other southerners. As the most prominent advocate for the slaveholding South, he was the inspiration for rising politicians from the region.

But Calhoun felt somewhat isolated, too solitary and exposed on the ramparts of the South's defense. The South, he believed, badly needed unity against abolitionists and the northern threat, and he had called for "concert." But too little solid support had materialized, and he feared that time was running out. To preserve the Union on acceptable terms, southerners needed to unite in their demands. For these reasons, in the last half of the 1840s Calhoun went prospecting for support among westerners and especially among his slave-state colleagues. To attract additional backing, he had to undermine one of his principled positions and soften his language. In the service of slavery's future, he did both.

Like other southern leaders, Calhoun had always hoped that the West would see its long-term interests as connected to the South's. From early days the waters of the great Mississippi Valley had tended to unite the South and the Old Northwest through river-borne commerce. Hoping to exploit those ties, Calhoun set out to build a political alliance by offering southern support for western interests. Although he had fought against internal improvements for almost two decades, Calhoun knew that westerners were eager for government help in improving their waterways and tying them to railroad construction. Therefore, in 1845 he traveled to the Southern and Western Convention in Memphis to give a keynote address. A number of southern railroad men, engineers, and editors, such as J. D. B. De Bow and B. B. Minor of the *Southern Literary Messenger*, joined him.

Calhoun spoke up for improving navigation on the Mississippi, linking the South Atlantic coast to the Mississippi Valley by "a good system of railroads," and connecting the "Valley and Lakes of the St. Lawrence by a canal." Then Calhoun broached the question of federal aid for these improvements. Claiming that the steamboat had made the Mississippi and its tributaries "an inland sea," he now supported such aid except for purely local projects that did not need federal assistance. He favored having the government grant land "to roads or canals" where that would "increase the value of the lands." He urged repeal of the duty on railroad iron and construction of levees. His speech "was heard with intense interest." But there was no immediate shift of allegiance on the part of the midwestern states.

More essential to Calhoun was increasing unity among the political leaders of the slaveholding South. To that end he worked to bring about a joint declaration of the southern men in Congress. He believed the slave states could not compel change from the North unless they stood together. But not all representatives and senators from the South were as radical as Calhoun or as wedded to his strategies. To gain their cooperation he modified his approach and toned down his language. In December 1849 he succeeded in gaining the signatures of forty-eight legislators to his "Southern Address." But although Calhoun wrote every word that appeared in the final version, it did not fully reflect his normal, slashing, aggressive style.

Drafted while debates were underway over how to treat the land taken from Mexico, much of the "Address" was a litany of supposed "acts of aggression and encroachment" against the South. Calhoun reviewed history from the Missouri Compromise forward, complaining that the North was violating sacred pledges. The "Address" complained of abolitionist activity, failure to enforce the fugitive slave law, deception about the territories, and scarce recognition of the South's sacrifices in the Mexican War. He claimed that southerners had understood that if Oregon became free territory, the Missouri Compromise line would be extended to the Pacific, allowing slavery south of that line. But now the North no longer respected that line and called for "measures of an aggressive character." These included the exclusion of slavery from new territories and voting rights for Black people in the District of Columbia. Calhoun wanted the South to insist on the right of slavery to enter every territory; the wording of his address denied that the federal government had any right "to extend or restrict slavery."

His reserved his strongest language for white southerners and slaveholders, urging them to wake up and warning of a racial catastrophe for white people. The sectional conflict, rooted in disagreements over slavery and race, was "the most important subject ever presented for your consideration." He warned that "the great body" of northerners were "united against our peculiar institution" and that "fanatics" would eventually win. The South would lose votes in the House; eventually the antislavery North would have enough power to amend the Constitution and prohibit slavery. Yet "the free and servile races at the South . . . cannot live together in peace . . . except in their present relation." The end of the peculiar institution would mean misery and desolation, such as Calhoun claimed to see in the British West Indies. "Political and social equality" would result, with voting rights for Black people, and eventually the holding of "the white race . . . in complete subjection." The "Address" ended with a clarion call for unity. White southerners must "stand up immovably in defense of rights, involving your all—your property, prosperity, equality, liberty and safety." Stakes so high justified a "resort to all means necessary."

A few months later Calhoun faced his final challenge. Debate on what would become the Compromise of 1850 was underway, and Calhoun and followers like Mississippi's Jefferson Davis feared the outcome. Calhoun now was sixty-eight years old and was dying of tuberculosis. These debates would be his last chance to lead and defend the South. He prepared a long speech but was too weak to deliver it himself. Instead, the text was read to the Senate for him by Senator James Mason of Virginia on March 4, 1850. That speech proved to be his political testament, for within a month Calhoun was dead.

The final address had a framework of restrictive logic designed to place the responsibility for unity or conflict on the North. Calhoun asked, would the South "be forced to choose between abolition and secession?" He had warned that "agitation of the subject of slavery would . . . end in disunion," but the North had permitted such destructive discussion to continue. To save the Union, southerners must feel that their section was safe, but in fact, "the equilibrium between the two sections of the government . . . has been destroyed." It was up to the North to restore that equilibrium, to give the South "adequate means of protecting itself." The way to do that was clear—to recognize the South's equal rights in the territories, to "faithfully" return enslaved people who were fugitives under the law, to end antislavery agitation, and to insert into the Constitution an amendment giving the South "the power she possessed of protecting herself before the equilibrium between the sections was destroyed by the action of this government." If northerners were unwilling to act with "justice," Calhoun then declared, "let the States we both represent agree to separate and part in peace."

Thus the final challenge that Calhoun issued included a plea for the Union. Much of his valedictory address, however, indicated that his expectations and preference were for the alternative of secession. He assailed the North with many accusations of injustice and a will to dominate. He offered no compromise in the style of Clay. He showed no concern for ideals of liberty and rights of free speech or thought in the North. He simply demanded that the South have powers that he claimed were implicit and just, and to gain them the Constitution must be changed so that his section had "the means of protecting itself, by its negative" against threatening measures. Those were words from his *Disquisition on Government*, published posthumously in 1851.

Intellectually consistent with the thrust of his *South Carolina Exposition and Protest* of 1828, the *Disquisition on Government* insisted that power and liberty must be kept in their appropriate spheres. It feared "the tendency of government to pass beyond its proper limits" and "expose liberty to danger." Any numerical majority, Calhoun warned, was capable of oppressing a propertied minority such as slaveholders. However, a "concurrent majority" was a system in which "each portion of the community" had the power of "a negative on the others"; therefore, it could protect its interests. One way to institutionalize a concurrent majority was to establish a dual executive—one president from the South and one from the North, with each possessing a veto. To Calhoun, only in such a system would peaceful cooperation, progress, and improvement be possible—although for him progress meant the perpetuation and spread of human slavery. A dual executive has never been instituted, but powerful minorities have blocked or impeded the majority's will in American democracy. During Reconstruction and after, the white South protected its interest in racial injustice by imposing limits on change.

Calhoun's speeches and writings furnished a roadmap for ambitious younger men to make demands, threaten secession, and act upon those threats. Inspiring later secessionists, he not only saw the fateful divergence between North and South, but he also guided it. Unlike pragmatic leaders who sought a short-term compromise, Calhoun focused on the distant future and the dangers threatening slaveholders' interests. In doing so he achieved the historical prominence that he always craved, but in the service of slavery, secession, and white supremacy rather than national unity, progress, and equality. His legacy favored disunion, exalted human bondage, and enshrined states' rights as a tool to protect slavery against attack or limitation.

Harriet Beecher Stowe
The Power of Her Pen

~

She belonged to a large and remarkable family. Its members played leading roles in a long list of popular reform movements: abolition, colonization, temperance, New School Presbyterianism, women's rights, public education, educational methods, even nativism. Her father and four of her brothers were ministers, and her husband was a biblical scholar and professor. One sister pioneered educational reforms, and another championed women's suffrage. Several siblings were successful authors.

Lyman Beecher, Stowe's father, held pastorates in Connecticut and Massachusetts before answering a call to win the West for Protestantism as the head of Lane Seminary, near Cincinnati. He was a noted opponent of Unitarianism, supporter of evangelism and New School Presbyterianism, and the author of widely read sermons on temperance and other topics. He led efforts for the colonization of Black people in Africa; his nativism was part of his anti-Catholicism. In 1834 the students at Lane Seminary debated colonization for eighteen nights, an event that attracted widespread newspaper coverage. When a large majority of them converted to the more radical cause of abolitionism, they left the school and moved to Oberlin Collegiate Institute, which became a hotbed of abolition and egalitarian thought. Lane Seminary did not recover from their departure, but even in this setback, Lyman Beecher made a mark.

Henry Ward Beecher, one of Harriet's brothers, became an abolitionist and the North's most prominent Protestant minister. Two other brothers who were in the ministry and the third, who was a minister and theologian, produced many publications, as did her husband, a respected biblical scholar. Catherine Beecher, an older sister, founded schools for women, published essays and textbooks, and innovated in methods of education.

She also launched a women's petition movement against the Indian Removal Bill in 1829. Isabella, a younger sister, was an activist and lecturer for women's suffrage, which Catherine stoutly opposed. The family's members attracted a great deal of attention and, frequently, controversy.

Yet she surpassed them all in impact and influence. None affected the nation as much as Harriet Beecher Stowe, who was born in 1811 and had seven children with her husband, Calvin Stowe. They lived in Cincinnati, where the couple sheltered runaways from slavery, before they moved to Maine, where Calvin taught at Bowdoin College. Before she died in 1896, Harriet Beecher Stowe authored dozens of books on a variety of topics, but none had the impact of her first major publication, *Uncle Tom's Cabin, or Life among the Lowly*. Its portrayal of slavery, as well as its comments on race, religion, and American government and law, aroused deep emotions in the North, the South, and many foreign countries. So great was its influence that Abraham Lincoln reportedly said, when he met Stowe in 1862, "So you're the little lady who wrote the book that started this great war."

Uncle Tom's Cabin did not by itself start the Civil War, but its impact *was* enormous. Stowe began publishing her novel in serial form in 1851 in an abolitionist newspaper, the *National Era*. Quickly it attracted the interest of the public and commercial publishers. In March 1852 it appeared in book form, selling three thousand copies on the first day and an unprecedented three hundred thousand copies within a year. It was enormously popular in Britain as well, where it sold more than a million and a half copies within a few years. Stowe earned no royalties from these foreign sales, but an organization in Glasgow honored and compensated her. When she lectured in England in 1853, more than a half million people signed a welcoming address to her, and huge crowds in London tried to catch a glimpse of her. In addition to sales of the book, various adaptations of *Uncle Tom's Cabin* for the stage helped spread antislavery sentiment on both sides of the Atlantic. In later years the book was reprinted, becoming the best-selling novel of the nineteenth century, second in total sales only to the Bible.

Such popularity opens a window to understanding the feelings of white northerners in the 1850s and beyond. How did Stowe manage to connect so deeply with the emotions, values, and beliefs of the citizenry? The answer lies not only in the political issues of the day but also in dominant themes of the culture. The great influence that Stowe achieved through the novel had its foundation in northerners' religious culture, their feelings about motherhood and family ties, and their attitudes about race. She was a product of intensely religiously currents of reform in the North, and her skill enabled her to tie sacred values of motherhood and family to issues of racial injustice.

THE NORTH in the 1850s had an intensively evangelized Protestant culture that had converted many. The Second Great Awakening had reached its peak in the 1820s and 1830s, with a wave of emotional revivals and camp meetings that spread from frontier states to more densely settled regions. The revival movement overturned the old Calvinist orthodoxy that only a predestined few would be saved. Instead it invited the masses—in democratic fashion—to repent of their sins, change their lives, and grasp salvation. Lyman Beecher's support for the emotional preaching and conversions of revivals had contributed significantly to the split in the Presbyterian denomination. New religious movements and denominations also appeared, many connected with social reform. Western New York experienced so much evangelization that it was called the "burned-over district," and frequent revivals occurred in a broad area running westward below the Great Lakes. As religious fervor rekindled in the 1850s, many welcomed a Third Great Awakening.

These religious experiences challenged believers to approach life with an intensity of commitment. They convinced many thousands to dedicate themselves to faith and the teachings of the Bible. Religious imperatives should apply not only to one's daily interactions with other human beings but also to an individual's relations with government and the reigning politics of society. The zeal that sparked new denominations and sects questioned established social customs as well. Were Americans living in the right way—were accepted ways of acting and thinking righteous or sinful? The Great Awakenings had laid a foundation on which Stowe could highlight the wrongs of slavery, and her novelistic skills proved equal to this important task. The heightened political tensions connected to the territorial question, the Compromise of 1850, and soon the Fugitive Slave Law expanded her access to readers' emotions and thought.

Motherhood and family also had great importance at this time for northern women, as well as for members of Harriet Beecher Stowe's immediate family. Just as male politicians of the first half of the nineteenth century worried about their duty to carry on the Founders' legacy, women confronted the challenge of republican motherhood in a rapidly changing nation. As the United States emerged from the Revolution and its founding years, the belief grew that women had a special civic obligation.

A mother's duty was to instill the civic and personal virtues on which the republic depended. Unless mothers reared their children in a way that would preserve and strengthen republican values, the American experiment would decay. A woman's role was separate from the public responsibilities dominated by men, but her obligations were so vital that they supported demands for greater educational opportunities for women. Stowe's sister Catherine was prominent in those efforts throughout her life, and in fact Catherine's school had provided a serious education and broad curriculum to her younger sister, Harriet.

The rapid expansion of the United States and the striking changes in its economy imperiled the success of republican mothers. Steamboats, canals, and railroads, along with swelling tides of immigration had brought deep change to the social environment. A hunger for wealth took hold of the land. In such a developing nation, the rearing of virtuous children faced new challenges—challenges to which women would have to adapt. Evolving ideals of affectionate, tender relations within the family and humanitarian values in the broader society also prepared Stowe's readers to respond to her messages about mothers and children.

Attitudes about race and slavery were another changing arena in which Stowe crafted her novel of far-reaching effect. By the time she wrote *Uncle Tom's Cabin*, the Atlantic world and the United States had gone through decades of growing concern over human slavery. European nations first led a battle against the international slave trade, a campaign that the United States had joined with a prohibitory law in 1808. Antislavery forces in Great Britain moved on to attack slavery itself in that nation's colonies, and France was not far behind. In the 1830s and 1840s both nations abolished human bondage in their Caribbean possessions, a momentous achievement in view of the profits extracted from slave labor. Discussion of all these questions had grown in the United States, beginning with the First Emancipation that northern states undertook around 1800 and continuing with the formation of the American Colonization Society. From the 1830s onward the new abolition movement, identified with William Lloyd Garrison's principles of immediatism and moral suasion, slowly gained ground. Territorial controversies then intensified and gave rise to war with Mexico, deeper controversy, and a political abolitionism that spawned new parties. The way was prepared for a work of fiction that could focus people's attention on slavery and matters of race.

Coming from her deeply religious, reformist, abolitionist background, and alarmed by the conflict over slavery in the territories, Stowe set out to write a novel that would engage the moral beliefs of her readers. Beyond that, she hoped to stimulate them to action and to force society to confront the critical issues posed by slavery. Clearly, she captured a very large audience. The impact of *Uncle Tom's Cabin* and its effect on Stowe's readers become clear from some of the events and themes of the novel.

ONE DRAMATIC passage in *Uncle Tom's Cabin*, more than any other, moved northerners to reflect on the depth of a mother's love and the cruelties of slavery. It was a gripping scene in the novel and the most celebrated moment of the many adaptations for the stage. Eliza was a slave on the Shelby plantation in Kentucky, where she served as maid to the owner's wife, Emily Shelby. Overhearing a conversation, Eliza learns that her indebted master has agreed to sell some of his enslaved laborers. Tom fetches a high price as a reliable, trusted worker, but a slave trader also demands Eliza's only son, a toddler named Harry. Mr. Shelby agrees, despite earlier promises that Harry would never be sold. Eliza is terrified, and Emily Shelby pleads in vain with her husband not to tear a child away from his loving mother. Desperate to hold onto her son, Eliza flees, but the slave trader who purchased little Harry sets violent agents on her trail. Cornered as she makes her way north, Eliza risks death by trying to take Harry across the icebound Ohio River on foot. In a harrowing escape she jumps from one floating patch of ice to another, a scene usually reenacted on the stage. In the novel the danger hanging over Eliza and Harry continues until pious, normally nonviolent Quakers come to their aid, even at the cost of using violence against the pursuing slave catchers.

The agony of mothers torn from their children appears often in the novel. In New Orleans, where Tom ends up after his sale, he encounters Prue, a woman utterly broken in spirit. A former enslaver had used her to breed children, all of whom she lost when they were sold away. Under a less savage master, she rejoiced in having another baby, but this child, too, died after the owner refused to pay for needed milk. After so many sorrows, Prue turned to drink, hoping to die, and was beaten to death. Later in the novel, after Tom's New Orleans master dies, he is sold again, and at auction he meets another mother sold away from her daughter as well as a woman separated from her husband and four children. Simon Legree buys those two women, planning to force one to be his concubine and to give the other to a cruel Black driver for sexual exploitation. On Legree's plantation all three encounter Cassy, a light-skinned quadroon who has lost her daughter and been forced to submit to Legree's advances for years. To be replaced by the younger concubine is a blessing for Cassy, but nothing can remove the pain of losing her daughter.

Readers understood the torment endured by Eliza and these enslaved women, for family ties were vital to pious white Christians. Stowe indicated that on the Shelby plantation Black families previously had been fortunate to stay together, sharing life's joys and sorrows in love. But for Eliza and the other enslaved women encountered in the novel, the destruction of families was the deepest pain imaginable, one that sometimes could not be borne. Through her sympathetic portrayal of Eliza and the sad plight of other mothers, Stowe humanized Black people in bondage to her white readers. Demonstrating that the victims of slavery felt love, joy, sorrow, and pain made them real to northern white people in a new way. Most northerners had no contact with African Americans, for almost 99 percent of the residents of the free states were white, and the culture had taught them to dismiss all Black people as disgusting, subhuman, and unworthy of concern. In *Uncle Tom's Cabin* many readers discovered that the enslaved were human—sentient beings like themselves who suffered enormous wrongs.

That discovery was Stowe's greatest achievement, but she had additional goals. To enlighten northerners about the depth of slavery's corrupting power, she linked the theme of motherhood and family ties to questions of American politics and law. After Eliza crossed the Ohio River—cold, hungry, and still hunted by slave catchers—she sought refuge at the home of a white couple, Senator and Mrs. Bird. Mr. Bird has just returned from the state legislature, where he had voted for a stronger law to capture "fugitives" escaping from slavery. The senator explains to his wife that he has a duty to combat "reckless Abolitionists" and support his "brethren" slaveholders across the river in Kentucky. His wife, Mary, on the other hand, worries about the "poor colored folks" who are fleeing from bondage; to refuse to give them shelter and food would be "downright cruel and unchristian." She demands to know if her husband "think[s] such a law is right and Christian?" Senator Bird explains that he has constitutional obligations to the South: "There are great public interests involved." Given the dangerous "agitation rising" over slavery, Americans must "put aside . . . private feelings." Legislation against fugitives fleeing from bondage is "necessary." Senator Bird even says that it is "Christian and kind" for Ohio to support southern slaveholders.

Mrs. Bird's response is unequivocal. Religious faith guides *her* action and should correct the path of lawmakers. "I don't know anything about politics," she says, "but I can read my Bible; and there I see that I must feed the hungry, clothe the naked, and comfort the desolate; and that Bible I mean to follow." That faith nourishes her "gentle and sympathetic nature," one that cannot tolerate cruelty. Her husband has approved "a shameful, wicked, abominable law," and she vows, "I'll break it . . . the first time I get a chance." Senator Bird's reply pinpoints the conflict between Christian faith and America's constitution and laws. Encouraging runaways from slavery would "involve a great public evil," he says. "Obeying God," answers Mary, "never brings on public evils. I know it can't." It is vital "to *do as He bids us.*"

Mrs. Bird knows that her husband is a decent man and could not support such a law "when it comes to practice." At that moment Eliza, her "garments torn and frozen" and one foot bleeding, arrives with little Harry, seeking shelter. It turns out that the Birds had recently lost a beloved child who was Harry's age. The senator suggests that his dead son's clothes could warm Harry, and soon the senator is breaking the law in order to help Black human beings escape from bondage. Thus, in an effective chapter of the novel, Stowe informed her readers that God's law condemned American law and contradicted the Constitution's support for slavery. The nation's statute books called on citizens to do what their hearts told them was wrong.

In the husband-and-wife conversations of the Shelbys and the Birds, Stowe also expanded on the cultural assumption that women were more moral and virtuous than men. The virtue that equipped the American mother to raise children with upright, republican values was needed more widely. In 1851, as the slavery controversy heightened, Stowe called on American mothers to exercise moral leadership, to defend Christian values against slavery. Decades of abolitionist agitation had not redeemed the nation, and therefore women needed to call the men and lawmakers to account. The teachings of the Bible, her characters showed, were paramount, for human bondage contradicted both religion and the Declaration of Independence.

Eliza's husband, George, who also was running away to freedom, strongly reinforced that message. "What laws are there for us?" he asked of a sympathetic white man who once had hired his labor. "What country have *I*?" demanded George. When enslaved, Black Americans "don't consent" to the laws, and "all they do for us is to crush us, and keep us down." George knew that America's laws contradicted the nation's core principle of freedom. White people's "Fourth-of-July speeches . . . tell us all, once a year, that governments derive their just power from the consent of the governed. Can't a fellow *think*, that hears such things? . . . Sir, I haven't any country. . . . I'll fight for my liberty to the last breath I breathe. You say your fathers did it; if it was right for them, it is right for me!" George also justified himself "to God Almighty;—I'm willing to go with the case to Him, and ask Him if I do wrong to seek my freedom."

Religion and fidelity to God's laws were absolutely central to Stowe's novel, so much so that one scholar characterized *Uncle Tom's Cabin* as an altar call to the nation—an invitation to America to repent of the sin of slavery. Despite the piety of Mrs. Bird and others, the preeminent religious figure in the novel was Uncle Tom. Before he was sold, Tom presided over heartfelt services of worship and prayer on the Shelby plantation. He was "a sort of patriarch in religious matters, in the neighborhood" and "was looked up to with great respect . . . the simple, hearty, sincere style of his exhortation might have edified even better educated persons. But it was in prayer that he especially excelled." Tom knew a great deal of Scripture and constantly exerted himself to be close to Christ. The commandment to love one another and the duty to serve others shaped his entire life in the novel. Tom sacrificed himself through sale to the slave trader so that other enslaved people could remain together on the home plantation.

In the decades after publication of Stowe's novel, the words "uncle Tom" came to mean a servile Black person who ingratiated himself to white people in betrayal of his race. Stowe's Uncle Tom, however, did not pander to white people or cower before their power. He was, in fact, a man of extraordinary courage and Christian faith. So great was his religious commitment that he was truly otherworldly, in a religious sense that Stowe held up to praise. He did not war on slavery because his eyes were fixed on God and on the reward of heaven for those who followed God. Tom always sought to follow Christ's example. Striving to make his own actions honest and upright, he constantly encouraged others to follow a religious path. Although he was aware of evil in this world, his priority was always the world to come.

Tom's concern for others appeared first in his willingness to be sold in order to protect from sale all the other enslaved people on the Shelby plantation. Then, in transit to New Orleans on a steamer, he unhesitatingly risked his life to save Eva, a little girl who had fallen overboard. Purchased by Eva's father, Augustine St. Clare, Tom prayed for and counseled others in the household, showing special concern for the soul of his intelligent but world-weary master. With sincere warmth, Tom tried to aid and show love for everyone with whom he came in contact. The ultimate test of his religious character came, however, after St. Clare died and Tom fell into the hands of the brutal Louisiana planter Simon Legree.

In the slave warehouse Tom had comforted others and especially the two women, Emmeline and Lucy, who also were sold to Legree and sent to his isolated plantation. In the women's despair Tom read the Bible to them and cooked cornbread for them when he was "almost faint for want of food." When Lucy could not pick cotton quickly enough, Tom helped to fill her basket, and for that Tom was ordered to give her a flogging. In response, he said, "I'm willin' to work, night and day . . . but this yer thing I can't feel it right to do;—and, Mas'r, I *never* shall do it,—*never!*" Facing Legree's rage, Tom declared "in a mild voice" that "the poor critter's sick and feeble." Whipping her would be "cruel . . . it's what I never will do. . . . Mas'r, if you mean to kill me, kill me; but, as to my raising my hand agin any one here, I never shall,—I'll die first!" He made it clear to Legree that "my soul an't yours, Mas'r! . . . ye can't buy it!" for it already belonged to God.

For that defiance Tom received a brutal whipping from which it took many days to recover. But before long Legree challenged him again and demanded that Tom reveal what plans Cassy and Emmeline were making to gain their freedom. Tom was unbending, explaining to his owner that he would believe in God "to the last!" A religious vision restored Tom's cheerfulness and peace despite renewed beatings. Finally, Legree declared, "I've made up my mind to KILL YOU . . . unless you'll tell me what you know about these yer gals!" "With a slow, firm, deliberate utterance" Tom refused, and—as the depraved owner carried out his threat—pleaded for Legree's soul. "I'd *give* ye my heart's blood . . . as the Lord gave his for me," said Tom. "O, Mas'r! don't bring this great sin on your soul! . . . my troubles'll be over soon; but if ye don't repent, yours won't *never* end!" Stowe described Tom's murder in a chapter titled "The Martyr," and it was clear that she presented Tom as a Christ-like figure.

Little Eva also exemplified the sacrificial Christian faith and simple goodness that slavery and racism negated. She loved the family's Black servants and after a separation from Mammy "flew across the room; and, throwing herself into her arms, she kissed her repeatedly." Like Tom, she was eager to take care of others, and she "put herself on an equality with every creature that comes near her." The reason Eva loved having many enslaved people around her was not to command them, as her selfish mother did, but because it meant there were "so many more round you to love, you know." She lavished love on a troublesome enslaved house servant and confided to Tom that "I would be glad to die, if my dying could stop all this misery."

Eva and Tom formed a close bond immediately, and the little girl began reading the Bible with him and teaching him his letters. Her affection for others knew no boundaries of color, and her concern was encompassing. "The child's whole heart and soul seemed absorbed in works of love and kindness." She wanted all the victims of bondage to learn to read so that they could "read the Bible" and "learn God's will." Before her death from tuberculosis, Eva told her mother that it would be best to sell all the mother's jewels "and buy a place in the free states, and take all our people there, and hire teachers, to teach them to read and write" so that they could "read their own Bible" and be able to write and receive letters. She told her father, "I wish, papa, they were all *free*," and she gained from him a promise to free Tom. Eva then implored all in the household to accept Christ. Because she knew that religion was more important than society's laws, Eva was another exemplary figure in the novel.

STOWE SOUGHT to undermine northern racism as well as southern slavery. For Miss Ophelia, Augustine St. Clare's cousin from Vermont, practicing Christianity despite racial difference was an enormous challenge. This character embodied New England's habits of order, discipline, puritanical rectitude, and narrowness, and her role in the novel gave Stowe a means to comment on the North's racial failings. Miss Ophelia condemned slavery and insisted that slaves were "immortal creatures." But she could not imagine kissing Black people, nor did she want to touch them. Seeing her discomfort when Eva sat on Tom's lap, St. Clare tells his cousin that "personal prejudice" was stronger among northerners than among southerners. "You loathe them as you would a snake or a toad, yet you are indignant at their wrongs." Rather than have anything to do with Black slaves, "You would send them to Africa, out of your sight and smell, and then send a missionary or two." Ophelia admits that "I've always had a prejudice against negroes," and shrank from any physical contact with them.

St. Clare is brutally candid about the racism of Americans in both sections. Southerners have twisted "Scripture doctrine" to justify enslavement, but "all the world over, it's the same story,—the lower class used up, body, soul and spirit, for the good of the upper." White people hold Black people as slaves, he says, "because my brother Quashy is ignorant and weak, and I am intelligent and strong . . . therefore, I may steal all he has. . . . Because I don't like work, Quashy shall work." St. Clare believes that "human virtue" is weak and "a mere matter, for the most part, of latitude and longitude, and geographical position, acting with natural temperament." His father and Miss Ophelia's father, two brothers, were much alike, until one went south and the other stayed in Vermont. The veneer of northern virtue about slavery was very thin. If emancipation were to occur, St. Clare asks his sister, what would northerners do to help the freed people? Southerners were "too lazy and unpractical" to "educate these millions," but "is there enough Christian philanthropy, among your northern states, to bear the process of their education and elevation?" Spending thousands on foreign missions was one thing. Doubting that you could "endure to have the heathen sent into your towns and villages," St. Clare observed that "the unchristian prejudice of the north is an oppressor almost equally severe."

Stowe's basic agreement with this judgment is clear, in part, from the action of the novel. Miss Ophelia has the New England Puritan's sense of religious duty, so she steels herself to help Topsy, a young, enslaved girl who is unreliable, untruthful, and theft-prone. Ophelia had not been able to bear "hav[ing] that child touch me," though she hoped Topsy did not know it. After Eva died, Ophelia resolves to help Topsy. "*I* can love you," she declares, "though I am not like that dear little child [Eva]. I hope I've learnt something of the love of Christ from her. I can love you; I do, and I'll try to help you grow up a good Christian girl." Readers learn that Ophelia took Topsy back to Vermont, educated her, and helped her reform. But it was a difficult trial for Ophelia, and Topsy ultimately does not become part of New England society but instead departs for missionary work in Africa.

In "Concluding Remarks," Stowe insisted that she had based the elements of her novel on actual events, and she appealed to citizens of both sections to see "what slavery is." Using flattery she appealed to northerners by speaking of hardworking New England "farmers . . . strong-hearted, generous sailors and shipowners of Maine . . . brave and generous men of New York, farmers of rich and joyous Ohio." Then she asked if they could continue to "countenance and encourage" slavery. The free states were guilty. They had "defended, encouraged, and participated" in the nation's system of human bondage "and are more guilty of it, before God, than the South, in that they have not the apology of education or custom." Northern Christians owed the "African race some effort at reparation," she argued, for the wrongs the nation had imposed. It was not enough to say "We don't want them here; let them go to Africa." The church had a responsibility, she declared, to educate Black people to "moral and intellectual maturity, and then assist them in their passage to those shores." Stowe's sense of moral duty was strong, but it ended with colonization abroad, rather than fair treatment and equal rights in the United States. That preference for the outworn and impractical concept of colonization flowed from long-standing, engrained societal assumptions of racial difference.

Given that Harriet Beecher Stowe was so religious, her view of Black people as an inferior race is complicated. Hers was a kind of romantic or religious racism. Her words suggested that Black people were superior in some respects and inferior in others, but unquestionably she saw them as different, in both moral and intellectual capacity from white people. Stowe credited Black people with superiority in important religious virtues. No other race has "received the Gospel with such eager docility as the African." She praised "their gentleness, . . . their aptitude to repose on a superior mind and rest on a higher power, their childlike simplicity of affection, and facility of forgiveness." One day, she predicted, the lowly Black people would emerge victorious. Their African continent would awake "with a gorgeousness and splendor of which our cold western tribes faintly have conceived." More importantly, the Black race "will exhibit the highest form of the peculiarly *Christian life*." Perhaps it was God's design to "chasteneth whom he loveth," Stowe said, and to make "poor Africa . . . the highest and noblest in that kingdom which he will set up, when every other kingdom has been tried, and failed; for the first shall be last, and the last first." Black Africans would "reign with Christ when his kingdom shall come on earth."

White people, by contrast, belonged to hypocritical, "cold western tribes." Northerners praised the "sublime heroism" of distant Hungarian youths seeking freedom but showed scant sympathy for "despairing African fugitives" on their doorsteps. Their religion, observed Augustine St. Clare, did not thrive but declined in "the dead sea of your respectable churches," where believers bent their faith to "fit every crooked phase of selfish, worldly society." Yet Stowe affirms that the cold white tribes held power. George Harris, the most intellectually impressive Black person in the novel, was half white, and Stowe has him describe the Anglo-Saxon's destiny. Even if "the African race . . . may prove to be, morally, of an even higher type," says Harris, "to the Anglo-Saxon race has been intrusted the destinies of the world, during its pioneer period of struggle and conflict. To that mission its stern, inflexible, energetic traits were well adapted." Other characters in the novel assert that "The Anglo Saxon is the dominant race of the world, and *is to be so*."

What place was there, then, in Stowe's imagination, for Black people in the United States' future? Despite her praise for Black people's religiosity, she saw them as an exotic race, stolen from a "far-off mystic land of gold, and gems, and spices, and waving palms, and wondrous flowers, and miraculous fertility" and endowed with "a sort of tropic warmth and fervor." They seemed not to belong to the white, European, American experiment. Although the reader can admire and respect several of the Black characters in the novel, Stowe envisions their future, under freedom, outside the United States. In the closing pages of her novel, Stowe has George Harris make a lengthy case for colonization of African Americans in Liberia. Thus, like many northerners, Stowe assumed that Black people did not belong in the United States. She shared attitudes that George Washington Cable summarized in 1885: "the idea that [the Black person] is of necessity an alien. He was brought to our shores a naked, brutish, unclean, captive, pagan savage.... As a social factor he was intended to be as purely zero as the brute at the other end of his plow-line.... Generations of American nativity made no difference... still he remained, to us, an alien."

Stowe's George Harris declares: "The desire and yearning of my soul is for an African *nationality*. I want a people that shall have a tangible, separate existence of its own." To that goal he decides to dedicate his life. He describes Liberia favorably, as "a republic formed of picked men, who, by energy and self-educating force, have... raised themselves above a condition of slavery.... There it is my wish to go, and find myself a people." Colonization, he believes, is part of God's plan. Through that movement "*Our nation* shall roll the tide of civilization and Christianity along [Africa's] shores, and plant there mighty republics." The "development of Africa is to be essentially a Christian one." In that "*field of work*" the mission of American Black people would be "to spread over the continent of Africa" the "sublime doctrine of love and forgiveness." This idea—of slaves, educated in the United States, returning to Africa to Christianize the continent—appealed to Stowe's religious nature. But, ironically, it also was a facile rationalization for bondage voiced by southern ministers and apologists for slavery. In addition, it was a destiny that few African Americans approved or embraced.

Through George Harris's declarations, Stowe acknowledges that the colonization movement in the United States had been used "as a means of retarding our emancipation." But Harris argues that transporting freed slaves to Africa would not amount to desertion of the millions left in slavery. By building a free Black nation, the colonists supposedly would generate respect for the race and fortify the case for freedom in the United States. What the status of freed Black people might be in that indefinite future remains unsaid. But Harris had little faith that Black people would otherwise be able to battle racism and achieve freedom and respect in the United States. Answering all critics, he insisted, "I want a country, a nation, of my own." The achievement of his dream would remove a problem for white Americans.

Harriet Beecher Stowe's primary goal was to touch people's hearts about slavery. In this endeavor she tried not to be sectional. She wanted to encourage her fellow citizens, North and South, to address the problem together. *Uncle Tom's Cabin* was not popular in the South—frequently white southerners reacted with anger and denials. Yet Stowe had been careful to avoid any blistering attack on southern slaveholders or their wives, who knew of the sexual exploitation of enslaved women. The Shelbys of Kentucky appeared as basically kind and attractive people, although they accepted the benefits of slavery and did not live up to their principles. Mr. Shelby put maintaining his comfortable lifestyle above his promise to respect enslaved families, but his wife and son did all they could to redeem that betrayed promise. Augustine St. Clare in New Orleans analyzed the wrongs of slavery and the hypocrisies of all Americans in an unsparing, incisive way. Unfortunately, as an individual who had lost his purpose in life, he lacked the energy and wholeness to act on his insight. Even in the case of his wife, Marie, Stowe indicated how the slave system had twisted an ordinary individual toward appalling self-absorption and selfishness. Marie had been corrupted, but she was not inherently evil. Vermont's Ophelia also was far from perfect, and in addition, the most depraved and brutal character in the novel, Simon Legree, was a northerner who had moved to the South. Stowe's message was that the problem of slavery was a national problem and that human character manifested the same strengths and weaknesses in both sections.

Ophelia's decision to reform herself, to take Topsy to New England, and to love and educate Topsy there spoke to the North's responsibility toward racial justice. But Topsy goes to Africa to evangelize the continent, just as George Harris hopes to build a Black nation in Africa. The decisions of Topsy and George may well have reinforced the feeling among many northerners that slavery and race were not their problems. Instead, they were a defect of the South, and their solution would not affect northern society or its way of life. Northerners could look disapprovingly at the

South without feeling a necessity to reform their own social patterns, and for many generations they did so. George's belief that building a Black nation abroad would ultimately help African Americans, in some indefinite future time, also was as vague as the Founders' hope that slavery would someday disappear. Thus, the novel's success in depicting the *wrong* of slavery was not matched by a sense of urgency toward the solution.

Harriet Beecher Stowe stands out due to her immense influence on the North's encounter with the slavery issue. Her lecture tour of England in 1853 also advanced antislavery activities there. She was the agent of significant change in the feelings of many individuals, a reformer who mattered. Although she spoke out in 1869 for greater legal rights for married women, *Uncle Tom's Cabin* was her greatest achievement. Despite carrying racist attitudes whose grip on American society should not be underestimated, Stowe aroused potent antislavery emotions among formerly indifferent citizens. Through her work northerners grew more concerned about slavery's impact on the nation and listened more attentively to Free Soil or Republican parties. That was a vital contribution to change, for politicians generally were responding to citizens' concerns rather than initiating action on their own.

To reach her audience, Stowe drew on her own maternal instincts, on her religious convictions, and on the heritage of the Great Awakenings, and she invented a narrative that could prod society toward reform. Her novel brought the hopes and dreams, the suffering and pain, of slaves to life. It humanized millions of Black people for white readers who had considered the enslaved—when they thought of them at all—only abstractly as strange and inferior beings involved in a distant and different system. To be sure, northerners also had economic and political reasons to be alarmed over slavery's demands, and those could prove more important than morality. But it is difficult to explain the growth of antislavery attitudes in the North of the 1850s without the awakening of the religious and humanitarian concerns that Stowe shared and stimulated.

Stowe's immersion in the culture allowed her to touch readers' emotions and advance reform, but it also exposed her to other long-established cultural assumptions. Among those were the ideas, practices, and norms of white supremacy. African Americans needed both emancipation and equality. Such immense changes—in the Western Hemisphere's largest slaveholding economy and in the free states where very few Black people could vote—required both emotional and ideological changes. What Harriet Beecher Stowe did, to her great credit, was to change people's hearts. She showed them how to empathize with the suffering of the enslaved. But it was a more difficult task to change people's minds, to convince them that Black people deserved political and social membership in American society. Many northerners refused to recognize the small free Black population as part of their society, and they assumed that victims of slavery in the South were an ignorant, degraded, un-American population. Changing hearts, Stowe convinced many that the enslaved were *human beings*, but changing minds—to argue that these Black Americans should be part of the polity—was far more challenging. Harriet Beecher Stowe was not fully equal to that challenge. Like the great majority of white people, she saw Black people as different, not American, exotic. They seemed not to be part of the republic's mission.

It would be unjust to condemn Stowe too harshly, for in comparison with prominent men like Henry Clay, Stephen Douglas, or others, she faced the problem of slavery, calculated its evil effects, and stimulated vitally important forces of change. She transcended her society's acceptance of slavery, but she could not transcend deeper assumptions of white supremacy. Attitudes of racism and white supremacy had given shape to society and had solidified their influence through more than two hundred years. Tragically, those attitudes had regained force by the time of her death in 1896. For all Stowe's sensitivity and commitment to religious and family values, she did not see African Americans as, simply, Americans. In her heart they were God's creatures. But in her mind, they remained outsiders, different and apart. That was, regrettably, how most white people of the nineteenth century saw Black people as well as Native Americans. The limits of Stowe's vision testify to the strength of white supremacist attitudes.

Frederick Douglass
The Outsider as Resolute Prophet

~

Few abolitionists began life more differently than Frederick Douglass and Harriet Beecher Stowe. She was born into a prominent, influential, and well-educated family; he was born into slavery, never knew his father, and quickly lost most contact with his mother. Stowe never knew financial insecurity; Douglass began with nothing and often worked to the point of exhaustion to make ends meet and support a large family. Yet both made an indelible mark in the campaign against slavery, and both achieved notoriety, fame, and influence. Each became a well-known author, and Douglass in addition became a famous lecturer whose image was one of the best known in the nineteenth century.

Frederick Douglass's rise and achievements were remarkable. He was an independent person who showed, throughout his life, both enormous resourcefulness and personal courage. After learning to read largely on his own, he continued a thorough self-education and developed such a mastery of language that his three autobiographies attracted a wide readership. His skill as an orator impressed many thousands in the United States and in the British Isles. Yet America's racist white majority never embraced a Black man demanding the inclusion of his people. Douglass often faced physical violence and racist hate, and at various times he withstood scathing attacks even from fellow abolitionists and Black leaders. As one of the two or three most famous, most effective figures in the abolitionist cause, he played a role in the coming of the Civil War, and during the conflict he fought successfully to influence Abraham Lincoln and federal policy.

The independence that Douglass demonstrated throughout his life was perhaps his most remarkable trait. It bolstered him through innumerable confrontations with white racism and gave him an honest, authentic voice. To chart a lonely course for oneself, to go against the grain of society, to challenge even one's allies and supporters is uncommon because it is enormously difficult. Human beings need acceptance and a substantial degree of affirmation from their fellows, and for that reason true independence is psychologically demanding and rare. Frederick Douglass repeatedly assailed established views, challenged consensus, and stood alone. He never wavered in his fight for emancipation and equal rights, guided by religious faith and a determination to help the oppressed men and women of his race. From the Bible he drew the strength and inspiration to be a prophet, lashing out at his country over the wrongs it inflicted on African Americans. In the Constitution and Declaration of Independence, as well as his own experience, he found the goals of freedom and equal rights for which he fought unceasingly.

Through years of progress or defeat, Douglass was outspoken, delivering harsh judgments where they were needed. He consistently raised his prophetic voice against slavery, racism, and white supremacy. His success was different from Harriet Beecher Stowe's, and it was as vitally important as it was incomplete. Where she touched hearts, he challenged minds, urging them to reform laws and government. A change of heart could end with reflection in one's living room chair, but changing laws involved confrontation with powerful interests. Whenever it was possible, Douglass moved the minds of policy-makers, and he persisted when it was not. Unlike Stowe, he remained for most Americans an outsider, a Black man who excoriated racism and demanded that the nation live up to its core values. A Black patriot, he demanded justice and regeneration from a white-dominated nation that was in a hurry to expand and grow rich.

BORN INTO bondage on the Eastern Shore of Maryland around 1818, Douglass—then named Bailey—never knew his father, who was probably a white man, and was raised until age six by his grandmother. Sent to a different plantation owned by the Auld family, the young boy was fortunate to receive from white people some tutoring and exposure to religion. A Black lay preacher deepened his faith and sharpened his desire to be literate and to study the Bible. While only a teenager Douglass began to teach and preach to other enslaved people, until neighboring slaveholders violently broke up his meetings. When he was sixteen he physically fought a white farmer determined to dominate him, a battle that he described twelve years later in his first autobiography. Showing his talent with words, Douglass wrote that the whippings he had suffered transformed him "into a brute." But due to new courage and confidence from the successful fistfight, he explained to his readers that they had "seen how a man was made a slave; you shall see how a slave was made a man."

By age nineteen Frederick Bailey was working as a hired-out enslaved laborer in Baltimore's shipyards. In that city he met Anna Murray, a free Black woman who was five years older and hailed from the same area of Maryland's Eastern Shore. She helped him plan his escape to the North through Delaware to New York City. There Anna joined him, and they married before moving on to Massachusetts, where he chose a new surname. As a fugitive from bondage working as a day laborer, Frederick Douglass still was in danger. But he continued to read and study, seized the opportunity (rare in the North) to vote, became active in a Black church, and was licensed to preach in 1839. After subscribing to the *Liberator*, Douglass was inspired by William Lloyd Garrison's demand for immediate action against the sin of slavery. He attended antislavery meetings and within a year had been noticed by some of Garrison's followers. At age twenty-three, he accepted their invitation to become an antislavery lecturer. Douglass's long public career had begun.

As a speaker the young Douglass created a sensation before interested audiences. Northerners saw an enslaved man who was handsome, intelligent, and articulate—a living condemnation of the institution. Eager to help his people, Douglass signed on for a marathon of lectures between 1842 and 1845, first in Massachusetts, then through New York State, into Rhode Island, and finally as part of a tour of five states from Vermont to Indiana. Often, he spoke every day, except when traveling, and he developed techniques of sarcasm and skillful arguments against religious defenses of slavery. He became a major asset to the band of Garrisonian lecturers.

Douglass's reception before religious, reform-minded audiences was enthusiastic, but the large majority of Americans were hostile to abolitionism. He and other Garrisonians often met with threats and violence. Angry roughnecks blocked church meetings and forced the abolitionists to speak outdoors. On many occasions they threw bricks, rocks, or rotten eggs at Douglass, ejected him from railroad cars, or shouted racist epithets and vulgarities. In Indiana a mob knocked him unconscious and broke his hand. Douglass spoke again the very next day, although his hand never fully healed. It was an education for the young man, an education both in the depth of northern racism and in the beliefs and priorities of Garrison's brand of abolitionism. It also was a test of his stamina and his readiness to sacrifice for the cause, spending long periods away from his family for modest financial compensation. Douglass faithfully defended almost all of Garrison's ideas, but his independence appeared as early as 1844, when he refused to make the Liberty Party a special target of criticism.

In a four-month break from these speaking tours, the ambitious Douglass found time to write his autobiography, *Narrative of the Life of Frederick Douglass, an American Slave*. It captured the cruelties of slavery, the resentment of injustice, and the longing for freedom that motivated Frederick Bailey. The book was quickly a success, selling five thousand copies in the first four months and thirty thousand by 1860—impressive totals even if not on the unmatched scale of *Uncle Tom's Cabin*. The *Narrative* furthered the abolitionist cause and made Douglass more prominent, but his notoriety was not an unmixed blessing. As a fugitive from slavery's oppression in a nation whose laws enforced the capture of men and women like him, he was always at risk. To escape from danger and to gather financial support for abolitionism, Douglas sailed to the British Isles on what turned out to be another lecture tour of more than two years.

In Ireland he arranged for a local edition of his book and gave numerous lectures, sharing stories of his enslavement and refuting religious defenses of slavery. He thrilled many audiences but did not hesitate to argue that bondage in the US South was something worse than the "slavery" and poverty suffered by the Irish. In Scotland and England he deepened the Garrisonian movement's ties to many well-educated and active British abolitionists. They in turn praised him, supported him financially, and arranged for sales of the *Narrative*. Douglass was often homesick and sometimes insecure and temperamental. He was learning much about continental conditions and reforms while perfecting his jeremiads against slavery and America's hypocrisy. Ultimately British sympathizers raised funds and bought his freedom from Hugh Auld. Douglass was very grateful but also took advantage of the opportunity to condemn the idea of human property and to emphasize the need to free "millions" more. He vowed, "I shall neither be made to forget, nor cease to feel the wrongs of my fellow countrymen, who are yet in chains."

Returning from abroad, he declared in New York City that on British shores he had everywhere seen "a recognition of my manhood, and an absence, a perfect absence of everything like that disgusting hate with which we are pursued in this country." That contrast prompted him to add: "I cannot agree with my friend Mr. Garrison in relation to my love and attachment to his land. I have no love for America, as such; I have no patriotism . . . no country" because the United States was "supporting and perpetuating this monstrous system of injustice and blood." Foreign experiences had watered the seeds of independence from Garrison. Douglass resented the movement's surveillance of him in Great Britain as well as its slight support for his family. He returned with money from British sympathizers that would help him launch the *North Star*, a newspaper of his own.

After enduring racist and false newspaper attacks that he had been intimate with one of the abolitionist Mott sisters, Douglass embarked on a western speaking tour with Garrison. They faced violent mobs, rotten eggs, bricks, and denials of service. Both men became ill, and when they were separated by their travel schedules, Garrison grew distrustful. He decided that Douglass had shown no concern for his mentor, although in fact Douglass had tried in vain to obtain news about the abolitionist patriarch. When Douglass decided to move forward with the launch of his own newspaper, the *North Star*, a breach between the two men opened.

The disagreement with Garrison involved more than journalistic ambition; it also was ideological. Garrison was a purist who insisted on severing all connections with sin. He kept separate from political parties and from churches that would not combat slavery and emphasized an exclusively moral campaign against slavery. One of his priorities was ending the nation's support of human bondage. Disunion, he maintained, would purify the government and, supposedly, weaken the South's oppressive institution. As a young lecturer Douglass had supported the movement's arguments, but he was growing impatient for practical progress, for action that actually benefited the enslaved people of the South. Political activity did not seem wrong to him.

Garrison charged Douglass with disloyalty and unsound views at the 1851 meeting of the American Anti-Slavery Society. The convention voted to strip the *North Star* from its list of recommended publications. Douglass defended himself, believing that the organization should focus on emancipation rather than on rigid orthodoxy, on progress rather than on theoretical consistency. At the next year's meeting many leading Garrisonians assailed Douglass, treating him as an enemy. Only thirty-four years old, he withstood the bitter hostility of his closest allies and replied, "I CONTEND THAT I HAVE A RIGHT TO CO-OPERATE WITH ANYBODY, WITH EVERYBODY, FOR THE OVERTHROW OF SLAVERY IN THIS COUNTRY."

In an address given a few years later, Douglass fully explained his thinking. Garrison's "doctrine of *no union with slaveholders*' . . . leaves the slaves and their masters to fight their own battles," he pointed out. In reality, it "leave[s] the slave to free himself." Garrison's disunion principle treated American slavery as if it existed in some foreign country. That was an abandonment of the original purpose of the American Anti-Slavery Society—"to free the slave." Douglass admired the efforts in Congress against slavery by the wealthy New Yorker Gerrit Smith, who was giving steady support to the *North Star*, and Douglass gave early praise to the Liberty Party for asserting "the power and duty of the Federal Government to abolish slavery in every State of the Union." He likewise criticized the Free Soil Party for opposing only the extension of slavery and leaving "the slave in his fetters." But Douglass saw the value of a broadly based attack on slavery. Harriet Beecher Stowe's novel, he pointed out, had sparked discussion everywhere. Poets and intellectual leaders were joining the antislavery ranks, and more northerners were becoming convinced "that slavery must be abolished at the South, or it will demoralize and destroy liberty at the North."

DOUGLASS'S WORK as a Black editor helped him develop his own views and put them into practice. He called on those of his own race to pursue education and self-betterment, while he also denounced in strident terms the "black laws" that kept African Americans from voting or enjoying citizens' rights throughout almost all of the North. By reporting on the 1848 election and the intensifying controversies over slavery, he expressed his growing interest in political action that could have practical consequences. That year the *North Star* took the important step of supporting the Free Soil Party and its nominee for president, the former chief executive, Martin Van Buren. Douglass even attended that party's convention, and he also participated in the Seneca Falls convention for women's rights. He would always maintain that women deserved equal rights with men, although in the Reconstruction period Douglass would give first priority to Black people's interests. Douglass also followed the 1848 revolutions in Europe and gave a public address in which he said that in revolutions "some lives may indeed be lost." The editor, orator, and activist was becoming steadily more independent of Garrisonian precepts.

Douglass's paper could not have survived but for the labors of Martin Delany, who favored both abolition and emigration, and Julia Griffiths, an older, well-educated, committed British abolitionist who became the paper's business manager and a frequent contributor. Nothing was easy about the *North Star*'s operations, and the problems went far beyond weekly deadlines. Douglass felt that Delany was not finding enough subscribers or raising enough money in his travels for the paper. Griffiths lived for months in the Douglass household, despite the awkwardness this created internally and the scurrilous rumors about interracial sex that it generated externally. The wealthy Gerrit Smith did much to sustain the paper's determined editor and its finances. Still, Douglass broke down for a while under these pressures. But as slavery issues heated up in the 1850s, he continued to support the Free Soil Party. Then he pressed forward ideologically, rejecting Garrison's view of the US Constitution.

The Constitution was a proslavery document according to Garrison, who outraged many northerners in 1854 when he burned a copy and called it "a covenant with death, and an agreement with hell." Douglass had been studying the document and the writings of Lysander Spooner, Gerrit Smith, and others. In 1845 Spooner had published *The Unconstitutionality of Slavery*, whose arguments the Garrisonians almost universally rejected. Douglass, however, chose to advance the opposite point of view from 1851 onward. Breaking with Garrison and impatient for practical steps against bondage, he concluded that the Constitution could be "wielded on behalf of emancipation." What impressed Douglass most were the sweeping purposes in the Preamble, the Constitution's expectation of ending the slave trade in 1808, and its avoidance of the word "slave" (a point that would be important to Lincoln and Republicans as well). In a famous speech on July 4, 1852, he praised Spooner, Smith, and others who had "vindicated the Constitution from any design to support slavery for an hour.... The Constitution is a GLORIOUS LIBERTY DOCUMENT," Douglass declared. He saw no purpose of slavery in the Constitution and praised the "great principles" of the Declaration of Independence. Whatever one's views about the Constitution's text, Douglass chose the wiser strategy of using, for freedom, a document sacred to the majority of citizens.

He argued that both "the constitution and the Bible ... are disregarded and trampled upon" by the nation's support of slavery. Identifying himself "with the American bondman, making his wrongs mine," Douglass declared that "the character and conduct of this nation never looked blacker" than it did on 1852's Fourth of July. The Compromise of 1850 had deepened "the great sin and shame of America." The fugitive slave law had turned New York into slave-state Virginia. Agreeing with Ralph Waldo Emerson, Douglass lamented that "the power to hold, hunt, and sell men, women, and children as slaves" was now national. Hunting down the enslaved stood "superior to the right of marriage, and to all rights in this republic, the rights of God included!" He went on to condemn the churches as "not only indifferent" to slavery but on the side of "the oppressors." Using the language of Isaiah, Douglass told the nation's "eloquent Divines" that "YOUR HANDS ARE FULL OF BLOOD." To ordinary citizens he declared that slavery "brands your republicanism as a sham, your humanity as a base pretence, and your Christianity as a lie."

The 1850s were discouraging years for abolitionists. After passage of the Compromise of 1850 and its fugitive slave law, the Kansas-Nebraska Act opened vast territory for slavery's expansion where it had been prohibited by the Missouri Compromise of 1820. Then the *Dred Scott* Supreme Court decision denied that Black people were part of the polity or had any rights that white people must respect. It seemed that the government was becoming thoroughly proslavery. Believing in God, the Declaration of Independence, and the progressive "tendencies of the age," Douglass had declared that "the doom of slavery is certain." But he could share the discouragement felt by many. Briefly in 1860 and 1861 he even spoke favorably about ideas of emigration championed by other Black leaders. That was the one exception to what was otherwise his lifelong insistence that Black men and women were American citizens, entitled to all the rights of the nation and determined to stay in the United States.

Douglass continued to fight against slavery, supporting men and women fleeing from bondage and opposing slave catchers, even asserting that violence against kidnappers and slaveholders was justified. He quoted Isaiah that "There is no peace, said my God, to the wicked." On another occasion he declared, "Every slaveholder who meets a bloody death . . . is an argument in favor of the manhood of our race." He continued to lecture widely on sometimes exhausting tours and to write, bringing out the second version of his autobiography. Although he had supported the Free Soil Party in 1852, by 1856 the Republican Party gained more votes, with its platform against slavery's extension, than the Liberty or Free Soil parties ever had. Douglass scored the weaknesses of its platform, calling its focus only on the territories "lame, halt, and blind" since it admitted the right of slavery to exist in the South. "Freedom in Kansas," he wrote, was hopelessly inadequate to battle the nation's sin of slavery. Still, he endorsed Republican John C. Frémont for president, reasoning that such a ballot was the "deadliest blow upon slavery that can be given at that particular time." Then he returned to denouncing the Slave Power and demanding more of Republicans. If his rhetoric revealed the inadequacy of the Republican program, it also allowed that party to seem more moderate to a racially prejudiced electorate.

In 1859 John Brown sought to recruit Frederick Douglass for his assault on slavery at Harpers Ferry. The two men had met on various occasions over a period of twelve years, and Douglass admired Brown's fervent antislavery zeal. He put Brown up at his home in Rochester, New York, in 1858 and helped him correspond and meet with other antislavery figures. Brown's appeal for Douglass's participation was touching and eloquent, but Douglass refused to give him any further aid. Brown's plan was seriously flawed. As a person formerly enslaved, Douglass knew that attacking the US armory at Harpers Ferry would provoke a swift reaction and would work against any large movement of those in bondage to Brown's side. The military power of state and federal forces would crush the raid, and that was precisely what happened. Hearing that he was to be arrested as a conspirator, Douglass fled to Canada and then to England. He returned in April 1860 and stayed off the lecture circuit for four months, until it seemed clear that any legal action against him had been abandoned.

In that year's presidential election Douglass was conflicted but insightful in his analysis. He accurately understood that the Republican Party was a coalition of diverse elements, some of which were anti-Black, and that the party's platform was "only negatively antislavery. It is opposed to the political power of slavery, rather than to slavery itself." But his impression of Lincoln was rather positive. He saw the "untried" Illinois lawyer as "honest" and possessing "great firmness of will." He judged Lincoln to be "fully committed to the doctrine of the irrepressible conflict" and wrote in his paper that "antislavery sentiment" was the "vital element" of the party. On election day Douglass voted for a tiny radical party. But in the preceding months he worked for Lincoln's election, trusting Lincoln's firmness and hoping Republicans would eventually decide that the federal government could abolish slavery.

WHEN SECESSION occurred, Douglass opposed compromise, and when war began, he was ready. Immediately he became the tribune of emancipation, the strongest voice arguing that the war to preserve the Union must become an abolition war. His voice was not a solitary one, for many Black abolitionists argued energetically for emancipation and Black rights during the war. Douglass's example helped energize a chorus of northern Black leaders—including such men as J. W. C. Pennington, James McCune Smith, Charles Lenox Remond, Henry McNeal Turner, John

Rock, John Mercer Langston, Henry Highland Garnet, and others. They continued to work in abolitionist assemblies and in the Black convention movement to advance the cause of emancipation. Southern Black people also seized opportunities to speak out in many cities and towns by 1865. Demonstrating their knowledge of congressional leaders and the democratic process, these southerners added their petitions, demands, and impressive arguments to the efforts of northern Black leaders. But among this swelling Black chorus, Douglass was the best-known figure, and his colleagues often chose him as a spokesperson or chairman at their meetings.

A few days after the first shots were fired, Douglass argued that "slavery has done it all" and that "any attempt now to separate the freedom of the slave from the victory of the Government . . . will be labor lost." In many previous jeremiads against American racism, Douglass had emulated the Old Testament prophets, but now he was truly and accurately prophetic: "The American people may refuse to recognize it for a time; but the 'inexorable logic of events' will force it upon them in the end; that the war now being waged in this land is a war for and against slavery; and that it can never be effectually put down till one or the other of these vital forces is completely destroyed."

In May 1861 he reemphasized his insight that "there is but one . . . effectual way to suppress and put down the desolating war which the slaveholders and their rebel minions are now waging against the American Government. . . . War for the destruction of liberty must be met with war for the destruction of slavery. *The simple way, then, to put an end to the savage and desolating war now waged by the slaveholders, is to strike down slavery itself*, the primal cause of that war."

However, Douglass was right that the Republican Party would be slow to oppose slavery itself. The Republican platform of 1860 had promised to respect slavery where it already existed, and Lincoln had reaffirmed the platform's pledge in his Inaugural Address. He had even given his support to a proposed constitutional amendment that would have prohibited any federal interference with the domestic institutions of the states. With the war underway and the North suffering defeat at Bull Run, Lincoln did not rush to act against slavery. Instead he worried about retaining the support of the loyal but slaveholding Border States. He also needed the support of legions of Democratic voters in the North who were determined to hold him to his pledge to respect slaveholders' rights. Therefore, Lincoln took no action against slavery in 1861 or early 1862 and overruled two generals who proclaimed emancipation in their theaters of war.

Douglass therefore intensified his arguments. Slavery was "a tower of strength" to Confederates, he declared. Their newspapers declared it to be such, and it was a fact. "Why? Oh! why," asked Douglass, "in the name of all that is national, does our Government allow its enemies this powerful advantage?" The North must realize that "the Negro is the key of the situation—the pivot upon which the whole rebellion turns." Slavery was more than just the cause of the war; it also held the key to military victory. Confederates used enslaved labor to bolster their rebellion, both by raising food for the rebel armies and by doing heavy fatigue work at forts and with military supplies. Thousands of enslaved men and women, however, were escaping into Union lines, volunteering to fight the rebels and providing intelligence to Union generals. Making use of the "Negro pivot" would strengthen the North and simultaneously weaken the South. The flood of pro-Union slaves escaping into the army's lines was a powerful, practical argument for emancipation.

Douglass had hoped that Bull Run would have taught the government "to distinguish between its friends and its foes at the South." But when it did not, he attacked Lincoln's policy, and in his characteristic style, he did not mince his words. Douglass forcefully denounced Lincoln's policies for shielding slavery and censured the president for overruling "his most earnest and reliable" antislavery generals. The president's policy was to reconstruct the Union while allowing slavery to "retain all the power that it ever had." Therefore, Lincoln was "no more fit" to lead than James Buchanan had been. Only by destroying slavery could the president preserve the Union.

When Congress decided in the spring of 1862 to prohibit the return of runaways who came into Union lines, Douglass rejoiced, saying, "I trust I am not dreaming." But he knew he had to maintain the pressure for emancipation. In August Lincoln told a group of Black leaders from Washington, DC, that they should take the lead in colonization because "it is better" for the races "to be separated." An angry Douglass denounced the president for furnishing "a weapon to all the ignorant and base" men who commit outrages on Black people and for showing "his pride of race and blood, his contempt for negroes." Other Black abolitionists and journals expressed outrage and demanded a change in policy.

The rising criticism and discouraging lack of military progress forced Lincoln's hand. The president decided that he must change his policy in order to defeat the rebellion. On September 22 he issued his Preliminary Emancipation Proclamation, declaring that on January 1 he would free the enslaved people of rebel states that did not return to the Union. In response *Douglass' Monthly* proclaimed, "We shout for joy that we live to record this righteous decree." Still, he knew that "the necessities of the war" as much as "the dictation of justice and humanity" had brought the change and that he must push the revolution forward.

Douglass also knew that emancipation was no cure for the pervasive racism in American society. Ending slavery might, in fact, increase racist hatred. The problem was not simply a long history of racist attitudes and practices. Almost half the northern electorate favored the Democratic Party, and during the Civil War Democrats churned out an unending stream of racist propaganda. They charged from the beginning that Lincoln was a radical abolitionist who threatened the rights of white people, and they denied the humanity of Black people through inflammatory arguments and degrading images. For any advance that the government made toward freedom, there were equal attacks on Black people from the Democrats. White northerners of whatever political loyalty heard a steady barrage of vicious racist commentary throughout the war.

Therefore, Douglass redoubled his demands that Black men be allowed to fight for the Union and to gain their full rights as citizens, including suffrage. As early as August 1861 he had pointed out that governors and generals were frantically calling for "Men! men! send us men!" "The national edifice is on fire," reasoned Douglass. "Every man who can carry a bucket of water ... is wanted.... This is no time to fight with one hand, when both are needed ... no time to fight only with your white hand, and allow your black hand to remain tied." It was vital that the Union gain the strength of Black soldiers, but even more important was the fact that Black soldiers would gain the right to claim full citizenship. "Once let the black man get an eagle on his button," said Douglass, "and a musket on his shoulder and bullets in his pocket, and there is no power on earth which can deny that he has earned the right of citizenship in the United States."

Through the rest of the war Douglass would fight for Black rights—with determination, with hope, but also with his eyes open to the enduring power of white supremacy. He threw himself into recruiting Black soldiers, publicized their courage, and took advantage of a nascent friendship with Abraham Lincoln to urge freedom and equality. His respect for Lincoln grew, but access to the White House did not turn his head—in the 1864 presidential race he supported John C. Frémont's candidacy, which promised "equal rights," until Frémont withdrew. Douglass never hesitated to criticize various shortcomings in the government's policy. He assailed the treatment of the formerly enslaved in occupied Louisiana and demanded equal pay for Black soldiers and protection of Black prisoners of war. Looking to the future, he knew that progress depended heavily upon the right to vote.

In the North free Black men were allowed to vote only in five New England states and, with enough property, in New York. These voters comprised a tiny portion of the Black population of the free states. Douglass knew that it was essential to take advantage of and sustain the revolutionary momentum generated by the war. At the end of 1863 he told the American Anti-Slavery Society, "our work will not be done until the colored man is admitted as a full member in good and regular standing in the American body politic." Objections that Black people were uneducated were inadmissible, and not only because many white men and immigrant voters lacked education as well: "If [the colored man] knows enough to take up arms . . . and bare his breast to the storm of rebel artillery, he knows enough to vote. (Great applause)." Any rule on qualifications for voting, Douglass insisted, must apply equally to all races.

When Lincoln, in the war-weary summer of 1864, wavered in his insistence on freedom as a war aim, Douglass spoke boldly. As author of the "Address to the American People" of the National Convention of Colored Men, Douglass denounced the "evident" fact that Lincoln's administration had shown that it "is not only ready to make peace with the Rebels, but to make peace with slavery also." He then went on, declaring, "We want the elective franchise in all the States" in both present and future. Discrimination must be erased from the statute books in favor of "one law for the white and colored people alike." Prejudice would exist "in social and domestic relations," but "in the matter of government, the object of which is the protection and security of human rights, prejudice should be allowed no voice whatever." The excuse that "colored men" initially were not called to military duty had been "entirely swept away" by the courageous service of "two hundred thousand colored men" fighting for the Union, and suffrage entailed the right to testify in court, to buy and sell property, "and all other rights."

One month later Douglass demanded that Maryland "wipe out all those black laws that disgrace your statutes. You must give us the right to vote, to hold office, testify in courts and sit in jury boxes." He then went on to address the white people's fear of social equality: "What we want is perfect civil, religious, and political equality. We do not ask for social equality. . . . That will settle and regulate itself." Douglass challenged white people who seemed to be afraid of competition with his race. "Is our degradation necessary to your elevating? Must our hands be tied in order that you may thrive? I cannot believe it.... Away with your conditions to freedom. All we ask is a fair and equal chance, and we are willing to abide the results."

Throughout the war years, Douglass's example had encouraged thousands of prominent and little-known Black people in both sections to demand their rights. With the war ending, Douglass stood by his strong, independent positions. To the dismay of many, William Lloyd Garrison proposed to disband the American Anti-Slavery Society because its work supposedly was over once slavery was abolished. Douglass, with Charles Lenox Remond, George T. Downing, Wendell Phillips, and others, argued passionately against that idea, because the work of elevating Black people to full freedom was far from over. "Slavery," Douglass insisted, "is not abolished until the Black man has the ballot." The "'immediate, unconditional, and universal' enfranchisement of the black man, in every State" was essential, and especially because the "malignant spirit" of southern traitors would oppose freed people and the national government. "The strength to counterbalance this spirit" had to be found "in the Negroes of the South." Garrison lost his motion and retired, and Douglass prepared to fight on, opposing all racist attitudes and practices. "This war shall not cease until every freedman at the South has the right to vote," he insisted. He wanted "simply justice," and to those who asked, "What shall we do with the Negro?" he had a brief answer: "Do nothing with us! ... Let [the Negro] alone! Untie his hands, and give him a chance."

THE YEARS of Reconstruction and after brought exciting progress and then discouraging national regression. The changes were not entirely surprising to Frederick Douglass, who lived until 1895. He had seen the depths of white racism and the peak of emergency-induced change. Douglass continued to lecture frequently, travel widely, revise his autobiography, argue eloquently for equality, face criticism from Black rivals, and weather scurrilous charges about his private life. He remained influential, but in the last twenty years of his life society was unreceptive to his message. The industrializing, post-Reconstruction United States had little energy for reform in what was called the Gilded Age. The North was occupied with economic growth and the hunger for wealth, and the white South had regained positions from which it could resist equality. Douglass continued arguing for Black rights and human rights, though the scars of lost battles accumulated.

As a well-paid lecturer soon after the Civil War, Douglass energetically defended freedmen's rights and decried anti-Black violence in the South. In 1866 he led a group that demanded to meet with President Andrew Johnson. At that meeting Douglass insisted on Black rights and "equality before law." Johnson grew irritated, predicted that Black suffrage would start a race war, and urged colonization abroad. After arguing fruitlessly with the president, Douglass authored the group's public statement of protest. Soon he declared that Johnson was not the Moses of the formerly enslaved (as the president was fond of saying) but their oppressive pharaoh. Progress would have to come through the congressional Republicans.

As Reconstruction advanced, Douglass wrote in national magazines and defended the Radical Republicans' approach to Reconstruction. At the beginning of 1867, for example, he argued in the *Atlantic* that Black suffrage was needed "to break the force of a blow already descending with violence" in the South. In addition to all the claims that his people had on the nation for justice, Douglass declared that the nation needed the "moral and mental energies" of millions of Black people recognized as enfranchised, "country-loving citizens." On the Fourteenth Amendment his views proved controversial: not because he criticized the amendment's failure to *require* Black suffrage but because he prioritized the needs of the freedmen over women's suffrage and angered women's rights leaders. By 1869 that clash became worse as Congress passed the Fifteenth Amendment, which could benefit the voting rights of the formerly enslaved but ignored the rights of women.

In 1870 Douglass started another newspaper, the *New National Era*. He worked to combat the Lost Cause ideology and remind Americans that the Civil War had been over the wrong of slavery. He foresaw that the way the war was remembered would affect the future. The nation must not admire "those who struck at the nation's life" but should honor and remember instead "those who fought for liberty and justice." His nationalism was leading to a wider interest in international affairs, and he extended many of his views on human rights. In 1869 he spoke in Boston about the numerous races within the republic, a fact which is "itself a strong argument in favor of composite nationality." Douglass defended the interests of despised Chinese immigrants, for whom he favored naturalization and "all the rights of American citizenship." He argued that national policy should be governed by "wisdom" instead of "by race pride. . . . There are such things in the world as human rights." The only tarnish on his advanced views of racial tolerance and understanding concerned

American Indians, a people whom most white Americans seemed to want to eliminate. Whatever Douglass's private thoughts might have been, he expressed no sympathy for the Indians' efforts to save their western lands from white aggression, and he criticized them for spurning modernity. He did not defend their culture or feel that their rights should impede the progress of white-dominated civilization. That view fit with the ideas of a dominant, conquering Anglo-Saxon civilization that Harriet Beecher Stowe and many others shared.

Douglass loyally supported President Grant and the Republican Party against the counteroffensive of southern white people. He gave campaign speeches for Grant and supported Grant's desire to annex Santo Domingo. After Senator Charles Sumner blocked a proposed treaty in the Senate, Douglass agreed to assist a commission sent to consider the purchase of the Samaná region of the island. He defended imperialistic designs on the Caribbean as an opportunity for the United States to assist the nonwhite people there and asked why expansion was unpopular only in regard to Black nations. The United States could become a "perfect illustration of the unity and dignity of the human family." He claimed that annexing Santo Domingo and bringing progress to the island would "discourage slavery and promote the freedom of mankind." A decade later he served for two years as minister and consul general to Haiti.

Although Douglass became a Republican stalwart, he remained independent enough to speak uncomfortable truths bluntly and directly. In 1876, at the unveiling of the Freedmen's Monument in Washington, DC, he honestly assessed President Lincoln and the power of white racism in American society. Lincoln was "preeminently the white man's President," said Douglass, and "entirely devoted to the welfare of white men." In the first year of his presidency he proved willing to "sacrifice the rights of humanity in the colored people to promote the welfare" of white people. Lincoln told Black Americans "to leave the land in which we were born ... refused to retaliate our murder and torture as colored prisoners ... [and] told us he would save the Union if he could with slavery." All these facts reflected the dominance of white supremacy in society and in Lincoln's personality as "a white man."

But Douglass also was fair-minded and grateful. He credited the martyred president with using shared racial prejudices to gain the "sympathy and the powerful cooperation of his loyal fellow-countrymen" and then leading them to end "the great crime of slavery." As a white American, Lincoln often put white people first, but as a person who "loathed and hated slavery" he gave Black people a chance to belong. If Lincoln seemed "tardy, cold, dull, and indifferent" when "viewed from genuine abolition ground," he was "zealous" and "radical" when measured "by the sentiment of his country, a sentiment he was bound as a statesman to consult." Still, African Americans remained outsiders, "at best only his step-children." In the next two decades that observation applied to the nation's posture, as Congress and the Supreme Court moved away from equal rights and elemental fairness.

Douglass campaigned loyally for the Republican Party. He gave speeches for its presidential candidates and defended its record, even as patronage and office-seeking replaced reform and progressive policies during the Gilded Age. The atmosphere of the time affected Douglass himself, to some extent, as he praised capitalism and lectured frequently on "Self-Made Men." Still, he sometimes demanded more of his party, and in 1876 he warned that former Confederates could not be trusted and would only take advantage of the conciliatory positions of President-elect Rutherford B. Hayes. In 1878 he qualified President's Grant's original call for intersectional peace. "Yes, let us have peace," Douglass said, "but let us have liberty, law, and justice first." The three Reconstruction-era amendments should be "faithfully executed and cheerfully obeyed in the fullness of their spirit and the completeness of their letter." For his political loyalty Douglass received in 1877 the position of marshal, an administrative post in the judicial system of the District of Columbia. Even that appointment was controversial, as white supremacists and some Black leaders objected.

Just as he demanded more of his party, Douglass also inveighed against intellectual and cultural currents that were reinforcing racism in the postwar decades. In 1881, for example, he published an article titled "The Color Line" in the *North American Review*. Although he recognized that "prejudice of race has at some time in their history afflicted all nations," Douglass fiercely denied that racism was "natural, instinctive, and invincible." In thorough fashion he showed that the racism that had caused African Americans to suffer "most" did not exist always or everywhere. His own experience in England was one proof of that fact. Racial prejudice was neither "instinctive" nor "an ineradicable part of human nature." It was a "prejudice against condition" and not part of "the nature of the Caucasian race." The institution of slavery had generated "contempt and scorn" for Black people and spawned justifying "arguments in favor of oppression." But "the higher the colored man rises" above slavery's degradation, "the less prejudice does he meet."

The postwar years were often difficult for Frederick Douglass personally, as well as politically. In 1872 his home in Rochester, New York, burned, probably as a result of arson. He was supporting a large family whose members sometimes struggled with unemployment, illness and death, or painful disagreements. In 1874, when a severe financial recession was threatening many businesses and banks, Douglass was asked to become president of the vulnerable, overextended Freedmen's Bank. His prestige could not save the institution, and a few months later he had the humiliation of presiding over its bankruptcy and the resulting damage to thousands of Black depositors. His newspaper failed that same year. Rumors about his ties to other women—especially to a German admirer, Ottilie Assing—had never disappeared. Assing, who translated some of Douglass's works into German and evidently loved him, had lived for months at times in the family home, to the irritation of his wife, Anna, who loyally managed the household but was not an intellectual companion for her husband.

Anna died in 1882 from a stroke. Douglass mourned her as "the main pillar of my house," perhaps feeling some guilt over the many years he had been away and had placed heavy responsibilities on her, perhaps too because they had not been intellectual companions. During the next year younger Black leaders challenged Douglass's preeminence and loyalty to the Republican Party, often in bitter, personal exchanges. Shortly after Douglass criticized his party for its inaction over voter suppression, the Supreme Court struck down the Civil Rights Act of 1875. He joined in protests but must have been discouraged. By 1884 he was surely in need of personal comfort, even if it led to more attacks on him as an individual and as a Black man.

In January 1884 Douglass married Helen Pitts, a well-educated, reform-minded woman forty-six years old who had taught contrabands in Virginia. For more than two years she had been working as a copyist in the Recorder of Deed's Office in Washington, DC, which Frederick Douglass ran after being appointed by President James Garfield. She was well-suited to Douglass in intellect, values, and progressive sentiments. However, she was white. White racism immediately surfaced in denunciations of her as "low" or "common" and of Douglass for taking a white wife. Black newspapers and critics joined in the assaults, saying the "Negro Idol has fallen" or that he no longer could be a leader of his people. The marriage caused ugly tensions in his own family, and Helen's father and uncle broke permanently with her. Relying yet again on his courageous independence,

Douglass answered that "God Almighty made but one race." Believing that "in time the varieties of races will be blended into one," Douglass observed that "what the American people object to is not the mixture of the races, but honorable marriage between them." All evidence indicates that the couple's eleven years together, ending with Douglass's death in 1895, were happy, brightened by extensive foreign travel.

After the triumph of emancipation in the Civil War and Black suffrage in Radical Reconstruction, Frederick Douglass lived through more than twenty years of national retreat from equality. No longer did he have an opportunity to push the nation forward with his words of American idealism and biblical prophecy. Those years were a disappointing coda for a life of high achievement, but social forces and the spirit of the times worked against him. His idealism and protests did not shine as brightly during those decades as they had before, but he did not abandon his call to the nation to act justly and live up to its ideals. His hope that the United States would live out its creed survived, as did his conviction that African Americans would never surrender their fight for equality. His was a resolute, prophetic voice. He fulfilled the role of a prophet—to prod the nation toward justice, even when the prophet's challenge is not heard by all.

Stephen A. Douglas
Overtaken by Polarization

AT MIDCENTURY, Stephen A. Douglas was the nation's most representative leader. On a broad range of issues, he embodied the popular sentiments of the country. An enthusiastic westerner, he rose to prominence in an exciting period of "Manifest Destiny" and western expansion. In years of energy and optimism he promoted economic growth and new realms for commerce and development. He was a bumptious leader of the "Young America" movement in which proud US citizens applauded the efforts of European revolutionaries to overthrow monarchies. His support for slavery and his hostility toward abolitionists coincided with key southern interests, and his racism and belief in white supremacy affirmed the prejudices of most northerners. In an era of technological advances, he praised steam power, American invention, railroads, the telegraph, and the Atlantic cable, and became a regent of the Smithsonian Institution. Repeatedly and zealously Stephen A. Douglas advocated measures, such as a Pacific Railroad and free homesteads, that later were adopted and enacted by political rivals. He displayed energy, intelligence, and a strong personality that won him many devoted followers.

Twice considered for president, triumphant over Abraham Lincoln in the Illinois Senate race of 1858, he achieved his ambition in 1860 and won nomination for president. But that coveted nomination came from the northern wing of the Democratic Party only, and in the ensuing campaign Douglas realized that he could not win. Instead of ruing his fate, he decided to campaign vigorously, in person, to save the Union. That devotion to the Union was another value supposedly shared by all, or by most. Thus, on one important issue after another, Douglas's stands and beliefs probably had represented the sentiments of the majority of Americans.

But he also had contributed to the polarizing conflicts over slavery that trapped and debilitated him. His career revealed some continuities but many changes that were taking place in American society and culture. Ultimately the politics of slavery brought Stephen Douglas's defeat and the Union's fracture.

BORN IN Vermont and educated in New York, Stephen A. Douglas moved to Illinois, where it was easier to enter the bar, in 1833. Only twenty years old, he quickly spied the bright future that awaited him. "I have become a Western man," he wrote, and "have imbibed Western feelings, principles, and interests." He said that he felt "an enthusiasm, which seemed to others wild and romantic, in regard to the growth, expansion, and destiny of this republic." To him it was clear that the United States should expand to the Pacific and that his mission was to further that destiny. "The spirit of the age" and "the genius of progress" were making his country a "young giant" and "the favored nation of the world." Ordinary citizens shared his enthusiasm and confidence about the westward march of American democracy.

Like many, Douglas gloried in America's representative government and praised Andrew Jackson's strong leadership and equalitarian rhetoric. He attached himself to the Illinois Democratic Party and in 1836 won election to the state House of Representatives. Soon he was appointed to some relatively minor state posts before he became Illinois's secretary of state, and then in 1841 he won election to the state Supreme Court. Resigning that position in 1843, he ran for a seat in the United States House of Representatives and won. When Douglas arrived in Washington, he carried with him a robust enthusiasm for the annexation of Texas. Resolutions that he introduced eventually "formed the basis for the joint resolutions" that annexed Texas in 1844. Two years later Douglas voted for the war with Mexico, and he subsequently proclaimed that Texas was acquired "upon broad national grounds" supported by "the patriotism and pride of every American." As a bright young expansionist, he began to attract some attention. Short, but with a barrel chest and powerful-looking build, Douglas also had a large head and forceful way of speaking. Respect for his oratory helped him gain a popular title, "the Little Giant."

Douglas was tempted to join the army and fight in Mexico, but Democratic President James K. Polk urged him to stay in Congress to defend the administration. Eager to expand the nation westward, Douglas stood for party unity against the divisive forces of the slavery controversy. Northern Democrats were growing irritated with the pro-South tilt of Polk's policies and appointments, and many of their constituents did not want to see slavery expand. Pennsylvania's David Wilmot, a Democrat, offered a proposal that slavery should not be allowed in any lands won from Mexico. Southern interests fought back tenaciously. Although the Wilmot Proviso never passed both houses of Congress, it generated great controversy and won the endorsement of fourteen northern state legislatures. Douglas was one of only four northern Democrats to oppose the Proviso. Showing greater sensitivity to southern, slaveholding interests, he argued instead that extension of the Missouri Compromise line was the right policy. That 1820 compromise had divided lands in the Louisiana Purchase between slave territory and free territory at thirty-six degrees, thirty minutes, and Douglas favored allowing slavery and free soil to share the new territories.

After he had won a second term in the House, the Illinois legislature sent Stephen Douglas to the US Senate in 1847. By 1848 he had adopted the formula for establishing new territories that he would champion through the rest of his career—popular sovereignty. Lewis Cass, the Democratic Party's nominee for president in 1848, made popular sovereignty well known and advanced it as a solution to the growing controversy over slavery in the lands taken from Mexico. Cass pointed out that eventually Congress would need to make arrangements to admit new states from the West, but "in the meantime" he argued that Congress should leave to the settlers themselves any decisions about establishing or prohibiting slavery. That formula had the advantage of avoiding explosive battles in Congress over lands that for some years were likely to have few white settlers and even fewer enslaved Black people.

Popular sovereignty had a more fundamental importance for Stephen Douglas. The genius of the American system of government, he believed, was its federal principle that allowed geographical expansion and local variation along with the preservation of liberties. Popular sovereignty in the territories was a functional analogue to states' rights and local self-government, which were core beliefs of the Democratic Party. Douglas believed that western settlers had the inherent right of local self-government. Popular sovereignty allowed them, he said, "to govern themselves in respect to their own internal policy and domestic affairs." It would facilitate the westward expansion of the republic that he believed was so important.

As a westerner, Douglas held that the Mississippi Valley had been the core of the "Great West" and "the heart of the Republic." Its fertile lands and river commerce had united the country. With railroads and technological advances, the addition of new western lands would benefit the Mississippi Valley and further strengthen the nation. He knew that settlement on the Great Plains would stimulate the economy of Illinois by encouraging the production of goods sent to Chicago. Nothing should restrain "the onward march of civilization, Christianity, and free government," he declared. Native Americans would have to give way, because western lands could not remain "a howling wilderness . . . roamed over by hostile savages." Sometimes Douglas spoke of "steady growth and gradual expansion" as a "law of our national existence. It is the decree of Providence."

In the House Douglas had chaired the committee on the territories, and he gained the corresponding assignment when he entered the Senate. For eleven years, from 1847 until the end of 1858, Douglas dominated the committee on the territories and brought to that role an unrelenting focus on promoting territorial governments and growth in the West. Repeatedly he argued for transcontinental railroads and policies to award land, free of charge, to actual settlers. He even favored "national industrial universities" to aid farmers and mechanics. Many in both North and South had great interest in the possibility of seeking new opportunities in the West.

But it was an unexpected crisis, rather than constructive proposals for western lands, that gave Douglas, at age thirty-seven, a national reputation. The "meantime" that Lewis Cass had hoped would postpone confrontation over the territories lasted little more than a year. The discovery of gold suddenly lured many thousands to California, and in 1849 settlers requested admission to the Union as a free state, even before California could be organized as a territory. Proslavery southerners now feared that they would lose their equal power in the Senate and become a minority, whereas Free Soil forces wanted to apply the Wilmot Proviso to the lands won from Mexico. Deep sectional division suddenly threatened national unity as well as the country's future ability to benefit from its vast domain.

At this point Douglas stepped forward as a skillful legislator. He made himself the hardworking and ingenious assistant to the Great Compromiser, Henry Clay. A package of bills designed to satisfy North and South included an ambiguous version of popular sovereignty for the western territories. After months of intense debate, when Clay's "omnibus bill" came to a vote, it failed. Clay, elderly and sick, left Washington, but

Douglas found a solution. He split the legislation up into five separate bills and cobbled together different majorities for each one. Southerners were sure to favor some measures; northerners favored certain others. By identifying and relying on a small group of compromise-oriented lawmakers, Douglas found a way to pass all five. Many anxious observers in Washington and throughout the country were immensely relieved. They had feared that the Union would break apart and end America's greatness, but thanks to Douglas, the danger had passed.

Stephen Douglas could take pride in the Compromise of 1850, for which he deserved much credit. His efforts as a public servant had satisfied a large majority of the nation's citizens. His own devotion to the Union and his desire to foster a brilliant future for the West had won affirmation. Douglas benefited personally because his prominence was growing; the Little Giant now cast a much larger shadow. But he also knew that his apparent success in legislative management hid some serious divisions. Many southern and northern lawmakers did not agree on *when* settlers in a territory could decide to institute or prohibit slavery. Northerners argued that the decision could come at any time, but southern leaders followed Calhoun in demanding that settlers could prohibit slavery only when their territory became a state. The compromise measures had evaded this disagreement with ambiguous wording—territorial governments could pass laws on "all rightful subjects . . . consistent with the Constitution." The divisive demon of the slavery controversy was not contained. Soon it would reappear to challenge the North, the South, the unity of the republic, and Douglas's career.

By 1854 violent confrontations were developing over the Compromise's fugitive slave law, but a proposal from Stephen Douglas soon aroused anger that dwarfed them. He introduced a bill to organize the Kansas and Nebraska territories on the Great Plains, promoting the kind of westward expansion that attracted Americans. Territorial governments would encourage settlement, railroad construction, and the economic development that Douglas championed. His Kansas-Nebraska bill incorporated the idea of popular sovereignty, following the example set by the Compromise of 1850. Although Americans generally were enthusiastic about westward expansion, Douglas quickly discovered how difficult it was to satisfy both proslavery forces and those opposed to slavery's expansion.

His first moves pleased southerners and solidified his high standing with them. But their leaders quickly drew his attention to a problem—Kansas and Nebraska lay north of the Missouri Compromise line that prohibited slavery in that part of the Louisiana Purchase. How could settlers exercise popular sovereignty and decide whether to allow slavery, if its entrance was legally prohibited? One afternoon during a carriage ride in the nation's capital, Senator Archibald Dixon of Kentucky pressed Douglas on this point and demanded repeal of the Missouri Compromise. Dixon's insistence was a reminder of the deep division that had arisen over the Wilmot Proviso and the Compromise of 1850. At length, Douglas relented, saying: "By God, Sir, you are right. I will incorporate it in my bill, though I know it will raise a hell of a storm." Foreseeing such opposition, Douglas requested help from the secretary of war, Mississippi's Jefferson Davis. Together they convinced President Franklin Pierce to pressure all Democrats to support the bill as an administration measure, and the bill became law.

The storm was far greater than Douglas had imagined. Antislavery senators Salmon Chase and Charles Sumner, along with representatives such as Joshua Giddings and Gerrit Smith, published in newspapers a scathing attack called "The Appeal of the Independent Democrats." "The Appeal" showed that many northerners rejected the kind of expansion that southerners desired. Douglas's bill was, they said, "a gross violation of a sacred pledge," a menace to freedom, and a threat to the Union. It amounted to "an atrocious plot to exclude" worthy settlers from Europe and the North from a vast domain that had been set aside for freedom. It would convert an "immense region" on the Great Plains "into a dreary region of despotism, inhabited by masters and slaves."

Their "Appeal" set off a political earthquake in the North. Meetings of protest multiplied across the region, expressing so much anger that a new party formed—the Republican Party, that dedicated itself to opposing the extension of slavery. Douglas himself quipped that on a trip back to Illinois he could have relied on burning effigies of himself to light his way. "Never before," declared a Washington, DC, newspaper, "has a public figure been so hunted and hounded."

Douglas defended himself in a powerful speech in the Senate. Accusing his foes of hypocrisy, he first pointed out that the Northwest Ordinance of 1787 had not revealed a determination by the Founders to exclude slavery from all territories; after all, "slavery was permitted" in territories south of the Ohio River. Then he confronted the central complaint of "The Appeal"—the repeal of the Missouri Compromise line. Who had failed to honor that line, he asked? Not Stephen Douglas, for in 1848 he had proposed its extension to the Pacific Ocean through all the land taken from Mexico. Free-soil forces in the House, "northern votes," were the legislators who had defeated Douglas's proposal after it passed in the Senate. "Every man" opposing the Kansas-Nebraska bill, he said, "was opposed to the Missouri compromise in 1848." According to Douglas, the defeat of the Compromise line in 1848 "created the necessity for making a new compromise in 1850." At that point Congress adopted the principle of "congressional non-intervention as to slavery in the Territories." Popular sovereignty, allowing settlers "to do as they pleased upon the subject of slavery," became the new and accepted rule. "The great principle of self-government" replaced a division of the territories.

Douglas made other notable points. Facts on the ground showed that federal laws had never been a complete bar to slavery in the territories. Some slavery had existed in Illinois territory, despite it being within the Northwest Ordinance. Some settlers in Nebraska who claimed to favor free soil had brought Negroes with them, as domestic servants or "help" for their wives. He also claimed that the Founders had aimed at "a natural or geographical line" that would "correspond, as near as might be, to the laws of climate, production," and other factors. That natural line would identify where slavery was "desirable or undesirable" to actual settlers. These laws of climate and production—nature's realities—would ultimately decide the question, and Douglas asserted: "it is worse than folly to think of [Nebraska] being a slaveholding country. I do not believe there is a man in Congress who thinks it could be permanently a slaveholding country."

The speech was logical and pointed. At its end he arraigned his opponents as evil "abolitionists," a word that still connoted dangerous irresponsibility to many. What Douglas elided, however, was the fact that free-soil advocates had always wanted more than the prohibition of slavery above some line. They, like David Wilmot, wanted to exclude slavery completely from *all* the lands taken from Mexico. Douglas—as an experienced politician—should have known that free-soil forces were not ready to abandon their ideals of freedom or renounce the Missouri Compromise. But, like other national leaders of the Democratic Party, he assumed that most northerners accepted slavery and slaveholders' rights. Determined to move forward, he focused on the immediate gains for western development, Illinois's commerce, and his own prominence in the Democratic Party. He probably assumed that the depth of white racism would carry him past short-term difficulties.

Quickly Douglas learned that his support for slaveholders' expansive ambitions endangered his popularity in the North. His bill spawned meetings, protests, and speeches for months. In one of those protests an

Illinois acquaintance, a lawyer and one-time congressman, renewed his political career. Abraham Lincoln spoke at Peoria and developed a variety of arguments against the Kansas-Nebraska Act. He probed the various discomforts that proud, freedom-loving Americans felt about slavery, but he also appealed directly and effectively to the white supremacists, who were very numerous among Douglas's supporters. "We want them [the territories]," Lincoln said, "for the homes for free white people. This they cannot be, to any considerable extent, if slavery be planted within them." Poor people, said Lincoln, go to free territories to better their condition. They had to flee from slave states, however, in order to find opportunity. Douglas's bill was popular with slave states but was damaging him in free states. The first half of a vise began to close around him, and the slavery controversy promised more pressure.

The problem for Douglas became finding a bridge between adamantly opposed groups, for if free-soil forces were outraged, southern leaders were even more determined and insistent. The question of slavery was forcing more voters each year toward new and uncompromising positions. It was overshadowing issues that had been popular in all sections. How one felt about human bondage was becoming the identifying feature of a politician. What, then, did Douglas feel about the question of slavery?

ALTHOUGH MOST northern voters were not aware of it, Stephen Douglas had a significant connection to the institution of slavery. In 1847 he married Martha Martin, who was the daughter of a wealthy planter from North Carolina whose wealth derived from many enslaved laborers. As a wedding gift, Martha's father proposed to give the couple a plantation that he owned on the Pearl River in Mississippi. Douglas turned down that gift. He pointed out that he had no knowledge of plantation management, and he no doubt was aware that his enslaving people would not be a political advantage for him in the North. The next year, however, Martha's father died and willed the plantation to his daughter and her heirs. The Douglases had become parents of two young boys when Martha died in 1853. Stephen Douglas thus became responsible for overseeing the plantation and its human "property" in the interests of his sons.

Through much of the 1850s he was significantly involved in the affairs of the plantation. He received detailed reports about the work and the land's productivity, and he oversaw the sale in New Orleans's market of the cotton produced. Financially, the proceeds from enslaved labor were valuable for his sons and for his family's position. By 1857 Douglas decided that a change was desirable, since the land was subject to flooding and productivity had declined. In that year he entered into a partnership with a man who furnished new land in Washington County, Mississippi. Douglas's contribution to the venture was 142 enslaved human beings plus some mules and wagons. According to historian Robert Johannsen, the new plantation remained very successful financially until just before the fall of Vicksburg in 1863.

These facts, although little noted, were not a secret in the North. On a few occasions Douglas's connection with slavery was attacked and criticized by opponents. In response, he usually had little to say. Douglas did not advocate for slavery, but like other Democrats he staunchly defended the right of southern white people to enslave Black men and women. He seems not to have been disturbed by the moral issues of slavery. Rather, he approached the issue as a pragmatic politician, holding that slavery was a local institution with which the federal government should not interfere, except to discharge its duties under the Constitution. He saw his duty as representing the people he served, and as a Democrat with national ambitions he was not going to attack slavery. To him and to most Democrats, slaveholders' rights were more important than human freedom, and white supremacy was the nation's guideline.

In a private conversation in 1854 Douglas described the peculiar institution as a "curse beyond computation," but he was referring to its pernicious effect on national politics and sectional unity. In 1858 Abraham Lincoln would charge that Douglas did not care about the morality and the effects of slavery, and Lincoln probably was right. That attitude of "don't care," said Lincoln on various occasions, ignored that slavery was a wrong; it was "blowing out the moral lights around us" and "eradicating the light of reason and the love of liberty." Douglas's political positions had coherence and consistency but lacked a vital moral dimension. He was, as Lincoln charged, "indifferent" to Black slavery and convinced of the validity of white supremacy. His America fit the image of an expansive, dominating Anglo-Saxon nation described by one of Harriet Beecher Stowe's characters. In regard to the future and the opportunities for his northern constituents, Douglas did not expect slavery to expand. He believed that popular sovereignty would yield free territories and free states while permitting the local self-government that he praised. If most voters shared the attitude that Lincoln denounced as "don't care," Douglas's fortunes could flourish and carry him to the presidency. But the political terrain was becoming more disjointed and hazardous.

PASSAGE OF the Kansas-Nebraska Act was a legislative achievement for Douglas; in his time as chair of the Committee on the Territories he had advocated without success for several other territorial governments. But rather quickly Kansas became a severe test and problem for him. Popular sovereignty did not provide a route to peaceful settlement but quite the opposite. Proslavery and antislavery forces mobilized to seize Kansas and control its politics, by any means necessary. Proslavery "Border Ruffians" from Missouri, led by sitting United States Senator David Atchison, rode across the border on election day to stuff ballot boxes for slavery. New Englanders encouraged free-soil settlers to head west, and some antislavery groups sent boxes of the new, breech-loading Sharps rifles. After Henry Ward Beecher declared that the Sharps rifles had moral authority, they were nicknamed "Beecher's Bibles," and put to use against armed opponents. Pro- and antislavery settlers clashed at almost every election, scores of people died, and the abolitionist zealot John Brown invaded Kansas to murder several proslavery settlers. The escalating violence over slavery intensified bitter disputes over land claims.

Violence and electoral chaos became the rule in the territory, and soon "Bleeding Kansas" had rival proslavery and antislavery governments, each one claiming to represent the true wishes of the territory's settlers. Democratic President James Buchanan made the lamentable situation worse. Buchanan had pledged publicly that the settlers in Kansas would be able to decide whether or not to have slavery. Then, after it become increasingly clear that the proslavery territorial government was greatly in the minority, he urged Congress to accept its proposal for statehood, embodied in the Lecompton Constitution. That constitution itself was a fraud, since it provided that settlers could decide to admit or bar enslaved people in the future, yet by law bondage would continue for the enslaved already in the territory and for their descendants.

Stephen Douglas faced aroused, insistent southern Democrats who demanded approval of the Lecompton Constitution. But he also faced political danger on his northern flank. Northern voters feared that slavery interests, aided by a biased federal government, would monopolize future western lands. Popular sovereignty was in danger of becoming irrelevant as a guiding principle. Douglas could not turn his back on northern voters and accept the bankruptcy of popular sovereignty. At a painful political crossroads in 1857, he broke with his party's president, spoke out against the Lecompton Constitution, and demanded that the will of territorial settlers be respected. His stand, though effective, was costly to his presidential ambitions, because it turned many influential southern leaders against him. Although he continued to be popular with many Democratic voters in the South, he had become unacceptable to much of that region's leadership. To represent his northern electorate, however, Douglas probably had little choice, and for a time his respect rose in the North. Some influential leaders of the new Republican Party even looked with favor on the possibility of his reelection to the Senate against Abraham Lincoln.

Judicial rulings presented further difficulties. At the beginning of 1857 the Supreme Court had handed down the *Dred Scott* decision, a ruling that had enormous consequences for Douglas as well as for the Republicans. The Court held that African Americans could not be citizens and that Dred Scott had not become free by living in free territory. Inaccurately, the Court asserted that Negroes had never been citizens and claimed that the Founders believed that Black people had "no rights which the white man was bound to respect." This racist decision greatly reassured southern leaders and resonated with racist northerners, including many northern Democrats. But the Court also ruled that Congress had lacked the power to prohibit slavery in any territory, and its reasoning strongly suggested that territorial legislatures lacked such power as well. For Douglas and northern Democrats, popular sovereignty seemed to be invalidated, while Republicans faced a decree that their core principle—no extension of slavery—was unconstitutional. For the Republicans, however, the Supreme Court's decision was so shocking and alarming that their party gained strength. Stephen Douglas, on the other hand, confronted the challenge of defending popular sovereignty without further alienating proslavery southerners.

The Lincoln–Douglas debates in 1858 focused attention on these issues. Douglas had a ready tool to reassure northern supporters and solidify Democratic support: racism. He exploited racism and white supremacy to attack Lincoln and the Republicans, charging that they were dangerous abolitionists who imperiled the superior status of white men. Repeatedly he called them "Black Republicans" and identified them with Black leaders. "Lincoln's ally," said Douglas, was "FRED DOUGLASS, THE NEGRO, PREACHING ABOLITION DOCTRINES." Lincoln's supporters, he claimed, tried to put Frederick Douglass on the stand at a Democratic meeting, and "they had the same negro hunting me down" while another Black abolitionist was "traversing the northern counties ... speaking in behalf of Lincoln." Stoking white men's sexual fears, Douglas charged that at one of the debates Frederick Douglass arrived "in a carriage driven by the white owner, the negro sitting inside with the white lady and her daughter. ('Shame'—heard from the crowd.)" Ought "the negro," he asked, "to be on a social equality with your wives and daughters, and ride in a carriage with your wife, whilst you drive the team?"

Stephen Douglas identified himself completely with the beliefs of white supremacy. "I say that this Government was established on the white basis," he declared. "It was made by white men, for the benefit of white men and their posterity forever, and never should be administered by any except white men. I declare that a negro ought not to be a citizen" whatever his place of birth, due to "the fact that he is a negro, belonging to a race incapable of self-government, and for that reason ought not to be on an equality with white men. (Immense applause.)" African Americans, Douglas asserted, were a "barbarous race," one of the "inferior and degraded" races of the world. By contrast, he claimed that Lincoln wanted to make them equal according to words in the Declaration of Independence. But the Founding Fathers, said Douglas, had established a government for white men of European background. He invited voters "who believe that the negro is your equal and ought to be on an equality with you socially, politically, and legally" to "vote for Mr. Lincoln. ('Down with the negro,' no, no, &c.)" Douglas knew that racism was potent among Democrats and among many Republicans as well.

To defend popular sovereignty as a tool that could deliver the territories to white northern settlers, Douglas took issue with the Supreme Court's decision, arguing that it had not limited a territorial legislature. But in addition, during his debates with Lincoln, he made the case for simple nonaction. "It matters not what way the Supreme Court may hereafter decide as to the abstract question," said Douglas. "The people of a territory can, by lawful means, exclude slavery from their limits prior to the formation of a State Constitution . . . for the reason that slavery cannot exist a day or an hour anywhere, unless it is supported by local police regulations. (Right, right.) Those police regulations can only be established by the local legislature." Thus, "by unfriendly legislation" or a simple refusal to give support to slavery, settlers could "effectually prevent the introduction of it into their midst."

The applause that greeted these assertions showed that Douglas had reassured northern Democrats who wanted the territories to offer opportunity for free settlers only. But leading southerners were alert to his apostasy and denounced Douglas as unreliable. To them he was betraying the constitutional rights of slaveholders, rights affirmed by the highest court in the land. White southerners had an undeniable right to take slaves into the territories, thundered Mississippi's Senator Albert Gallatin Brown: "The Supreme Court awards it. We demand it; we mean to have it." Douglas never recovered from this critical loss of support within the national Democratic Party. In the summer of 1859 he published a long, scholarly, legalistic article in *Harper's Magazine* defending his interpretation of popular sovereignty. The article convinced a few, such as Reverdy Johnson, a respected lawyer and former senator from Maryland, but it changed no minds among the most aggressive and influential leaders from the South. They now were resolutely determined to deny Douglas the party's nomination for president.

When the Democratic National Convention assembled in Charleston, South Carolina, in 1860, Douglas had only a few southern supporters, even though he was more popular among the rank-and-file than among the section's elected leaders. Northern delegates were more numerous, however, and Douglas decided that he would stand firm in his positions and make no concessions. Although his supporters offered some conciliatory measures for the party platform, southerners were adamant on the right to take enslaved people into any territory in the future. Eight southern states walked out of the convention at Charleston, and a reassembled convention in Baltimore some weeks later was no more unified. The Democratic Party split, with Stephen Douglas as the nominee of the northern branch and Kentucky's John Breckinridge the nominee of southern Democrats. Douglas probably had "the support of a majority of Democrats in the nation," as judged by historian Robert Johannsen, but an undivided Democratic Party behind his candidacy was impossible. No longer was there a national party contending for the presidency, and that fact weakened any prospect that the nation could remain united.

THE SLAVERY issue had shredded many institutions and beliefs that formerly had unified the country. Belief in the importance of the Union was one of the few values that remained widely held, though it was losing ground among southerners. A Constitutional Union Party hurriedly formed in the hope of somehow holding the nation together. Douglas resolved that "We must make the war boldly against the *Northern abolitionists* and the Southern *Disunionists*, and give no quarter to either." His southern supporters urged him to visit the region and campaign, and he decided to defy tradition and campaign in person. In the late summer he visited six cities in the Border States of Virginia, North Carolina, and Maryland and spoke to enthusiastic crowds. There he defended popular sovereignty and denounced both Republicans and Breckinridge Democrats for sectional perspectives that threatened the Union. By the fall, however, he concluded that "Mr. Lincoln is the next President. We must try to save the Union. I will go South."

In October Douglas went to Memphis, Huntsville, Nashville, Chattanooga, Atlanta, Macon, Columbus, and Montgomery, where he often faced hostile crowds. At one point he was pelted with eggs, but he continued on to Selma and Mobile, Alabama, in the days just before the election. Once he knew that Lincoln had won, he made one more appeal for unity in New Orleans. He argued that "the mere election of any man to the Presidency . . . does not" furnish a valid reason "for dissolving the Federal Union." He called on southerners to recognize that "four years will soon pass away" and predicted that Lincoln would lack the power to "do wrong," even if he wanted to do so. Perhaps a few southerners were converted, like the planter in Montgomery who mused, "Well, if Lincoln is elected, *perhaps* we can stand it for four more years." But Douglas's best rhetoric was no match for the tide of secession feeling.

Still, Douglas's strength as a national political figure, as well as the fact that the country had become geographically polarized, emerged in the electoral results. Abraham Lincoln carried the free states and the Electoral College with just under 40 percent of the popular vote. Douglas finished second, winning 29.5 percent of the popular vote, well ahead of Breckinridge and Bell. But he finished last in electoral votes, despite the fact that he was the only candidate to win electoral votes in a slave state, Missouri, and in a free state, New Jersey. Breckinridge ran ahead of Douglas in most of the South, and John Bell, the nominee of the Constitutional Union Party, showed notable strength only in the Border States. Douglas's appeal to many voters in free states and in slave states had ceased to be an advantage.

In what turned out to be the last months of his life, Douglas returned to the Senate and tried to find solutions that would avert secession and the breakup of the Union. He was appointed to the Senate's special Committee of Thirteen, charged with trying to find a solution to the Union's crisis. After working closely with Kentucky's Senator John Crittenden, Douglas announced his readiness to accept the Crittenden Compromise, which proposed to divide current and future US territories into free-soil or slaveholding areas along the Missouri Compromise line. Douglas reported that southern leaders on the committee, Jefferson Davis and Robert Toombs, also would support Crittenden's measures *if* the Republicans on the Committee of Thirteen did so. But Lincoln instructed his colleagues not to agree, since that contradicted the Republicans' core principle and might encourage efforts to spread slavery to the Caribbean, Mexico, or Central America.

After secession occurred, Douglas remained firm in his defense of the Union. He praised Lincoln's Inaugural Address as more conciliatory than confrontational. Once war began, however, he urged the new president to call for more troops than Lincoln initially sought. To friends he expressed confidence in Lincoln as a man and leader and declared that he would stand by him. Stephen Douglas had always been an expansive nationalist and Unionist. He had not changed his views on the issues that had been most important throughout his career, but the political environment moved away from the centrist, racist leadership he offered. By the time Douglas died of typhoid fever in May 1861, the most important issue that remained for him was defense of the Union. In his final actions he helped rally the North to the goal of preserving the Union through war. And it was through war, rather than through the statesmanship of politicians, that slavery came to an end and the Union endured.

Jefferson Davis

A Defiant Tradition and Tradition Defied

The South's planter-politician is a stereotype in the collective memory of the antebellum and Civil War eras. For many people that stereotype derives mainly from the history of Virginia, South Carolina, or the Eastern Seaboard states. It connotes rigid states' rights advocates from old families and established wealth, aristocrats with a classical education, patriarchal values, and a genteel country lifestyle based on enslaved labor. The First Families of Virginia—a few dozen families that had inordinate influence during colonial days—helped to establish the stereotype, which fit presidents Jefferson, Madison, and Monroe. Later, defenders of the Confederacy adopted it by deifying J. E. B. Stuart as a gallant cavalier and Robert E. Lee as a model aristocratic gentleman. Literary apologists for the South and for Virginia especially, such as John Esten Cooke, George William Bagby, and Thomas Nelson Page, did much to burnish those images and lodge them in the public mind.

How does Jefferson Davis of Mississippi fit into this picture? As the would-be nation's chosen president, we would expect him to enhance the myth. He was wealthy, and he was an ideologue who argued for states' rights and southern interests throughout the sectional crisis. (Like other ambitious southerners, he strove to emulate Calhoun in bold defiance and renown.) But other similarities to the myth are few. In fact, much about Jefferson Davis does not conform to the popular and mythologized version. Many aspects of his life contradict the popular stereotype and provoke a collision of myth with reality. Davis's personal history and his record as Confederate president reveal important facts about the South and the Confederacy—facts that champions of the Lost Cause and Confederate memory prefer to ignore.

By background and personal history Jefferson Davis was a different and more accurate representative of the rich planter-politicians who did much to start the war. Davis was not from an old or established family, and his education was technical and military rather than classical. His prewar career may have seemed predictable, but as president of the Confederacy he proved to be a shockingly unconventional southern leader. His decisions diverged so significantly from what the political elite expected that some prominent editors questioned his sanity. After the war he was as much ignored as remembered, because only parts of his legacy proved useful to the myth of the Lost Cause. Not only did Davis contradict parts of the myth, but he also challenged fundamental beliefs of the Confederacy he led.

JEFFERSON DAVIS was born in Kentucky in 1808, the year before Abraham Lincoln's birth in the same state. His father, like Lincoln's, was a farmer who moved west in search of opportunity and prosperity. Davis was the last of ten children (a fact explaining his middle name, Finis); his oldest brother, Joseph Emory Davis, had been born in 1784. In 1811 that older brother moved with the family to Mississippi. There Joseph Davis practiced law, became locally prominent, and began acquiring a huge tract of remarkably fertile alluvial land near the Mississippi River. He took advantage of the many opportunities open to an ambitious and intelligent man in a new and almost unsettled state. He became one of the richest planters, the enslaver of hundreds, and a figure of recognized influence due to his material success.

The fact that Joseph Davis fathered and acknowledged three illegitimate daughters posed no social problem for him in those early years of white settlement. Gaining wealth was the key to power and standing—past family history or impeccable morality were unimportant. Joseph Davis did not decide to marry until he was forty-three, when he wed a sixteen-year-old girl and thereafter concentrated on the affairs of his plantation. To Jefferson Davis's great good fortune, his oldest brother chose to act almost as a second father, taking the young boy under his wing. After sending him to local schools and for one year to Transylvania University in Kentucky, Joseph helped him gain an appointment to West Point. Joseph Davis had in one generation become a wealthy man of influence, a new southern aristocrat. His support was crucial to giving Jefferson Davis entry, within that same generation, into the rising, ambitious aristocracy of the Gulf South.

Jefferson Davis resigned his army commission in 1835. Farming the fertile soil acquired by his brother and taking advantage of the booming demand for cotton, he quickly became a wealthy man. He used a loan from Joseph to buy 16 enslaved workers in 1835 or 1836; by 1840 his enslaved workforce numbered 39 and by 1860, 113. Jefferson Davis recognized the talents of a few of these enslaved people and gave them substantial responsibilities, but most labored under the supervision of white overseers, at least one of whom Davis discharged for "mean and vicious . . . conduct." The value of the Briarfield plantation that he ran tripled in the 1850s to $75,000, a princely sum in a period when the average income of a free person in Mississippi was only $124. Davis's enslaved laborers alone were worth, in today's value, around $2.5 million. With little debt, he could enjoy great wealth and concentrate on politics. Davis was a planter—defined as a person who enslaved more than twenty people. Such individuals possessed more than half of all enslaved human "property," and although they made up only 3 percent of southern society, they constituted 70 percent of the richest individuals in the nation. Their slaveholdings alone had a value in 1860 greater than all US investments in railroads and manufacturing combined.

The Davis family was a good example of the new wealth in areas like Mississippi that was changing the South and its elite. Many prominent men from these newer states were newly minted aristocrats. They could claim great and growing riches, but they did not have or care about an old, distinguished lineage. This was one of several important ways in which the trans-Appalachian region, and especially the Gulf states, were different from Virginia and the original Atlantic Seaboard states. The soil was much richer, and the society was more flexible, more open to ambition, and less bound by old conventions. White manhood suffrage prevailed. The area's settlers were new and very much on the make, eager for expansion, status, and wealth.

It is true that some eastern planters purchased lands farther west, but they usually chose to keep their homes in Virginia or the Carolinas and hired overseers to manage their new property. The Gulf region became the rising economic powerhouse of the slave South due to its fertile soil. It was the region where constantly increasing crops of cotton fueled most of the exports to British textile mills, and many fortunes were made. Ambitious new planters prospered and sunk their profits into more land and more slaves. Aggressive southern politicians, eager to make their mark and rise in power, came from these Gulf states. In the 1850s the tide of migration had reached Louisiana and Texas, but many areas still were very thinly populated.

These newer, more western slave states from which Jefferson Davis came rapidly gained influence within the South. In 1820 settlement beyond the Appalachian Mountains was substantial only in Kentucky and Tennessee. In that year only 11 percent of the population in all the states that the Confederacy would claim lived in the Gulf region, which stretched west from Alabama to Texas, or in Arkansas, Missouri, and sparsely settled Florida. But by 1860 this newer South contributed over 42 percent of the population and was approaching parity in numbers with Virginia, the Carolinas, Georgia, Kentucky, and Tennessee. Its percentage of the Black population similarly had risen from 21 percent to 42 percent. In wealth the Gulf states had surpassed the Atlantic Seaboard, and its politicians were expecting to wield even greater influence. This younger South was also more tightly connected to slavery as the key to a prosperous future.

Leaders from the Gulf and western slave region tended to follow older political models, despite the fact that their origins were different. By the time the region was rising in importance, Calhoun and others had established the defense of slavery and states' rights as orthodoxy. Belligerent assertion had priority over calm persuasion in politics, perhaps even more so than in the Seaboard states. A man made his mark by claiming a prominent role for himself and defending that claim through violence, if necessary. Public figures were quick to resist criticism as calumny. Rigid conceptions of personal honor in society added tension to many social or political interactions. Fighting a duel, or battling a rival with a cudgel, fists, or a knife, frequently was part of a political career. Such confrontations conferred respect rather than eliciting social disapproval. Whether a man was large or small, strong or weak, manly assertion included violence in words or deeds.

Jefferson Davis followed the norm in a number of these characteristics. In personality he could be warm to intimates, but more often he was touchy and proud, quick to take offense, sure that he was right, and insistent on his rectitude. An exaggerated sense of dignity was far more important to him than popularity. On two occasions he quarreled very publicly with his senatorial colleague Henry S. Foote, and one physical confrontation between them almost ended in a duel. Davis's wife, Varina Howell Davis, referring to the ability to compromise and be sociable, said that he "did not know the arts of the politician, and would not practice them if understood." She also described him as "abnormally sensitive to disapprobation; even a child's disapproval discomposed him. He felt how much he was misunderstood, and the sense of mortification and injustice gave him a repellent manner."

One of the Confederacy's attorneys general, Thomas Bragg, liked Davis but admitted that he was "somewhat irritable when opposed." To James Seddon, who served as secretary of war during most of the Confederacy's life, the president was "the most difficult man to get along with he had ever seen." As president, Davis tried to keep his office open in order to receive delegations from different states or members of the Confederate Congress. But he often spoiled this gesture by turning snappish and lecturing or criticizing his visitors. When the War Department's J. B. Jones saw the president conversing "with several members of Congress, standing in the street," he was surprised. The chief executive did not often "descend from his office to this mode of conference." Official correspondence with state leaders or with military officers not infrequently ended on an angry note.

Ironically, Jefferson Davis made a special effort during the war years to discipline himself and avoid giving offense. In the prewar years he had lashed out often at political opponents and as US secretary of war had carried on long, unsightly controversies with military officers. There was an interminable, spiteful quarrel with General Winfield Scott over certain expenses for which Scott sought reimbursement. Secretary Davis also clashed with General John Wool over such matters as a testimonial sword. In 1862 Davis told his wife that he wanted to "learn just to let people alone who snap at me." She saw that he was trying to respond to unsolicited advice "in softly modulated, dulcet accents." But Davis's self-control and self-knowledge were limited. He pictured himself as rising above "those who engage in strife for personal or party aggrandizement," but the *Richmond Examiner* declared that Davis was "capable of employing the great powers of Government for the unworthy gratification of animosity." Recurrent malaria and a very painful eye condition surely aggravated his irritability.

Like other southern politicians, Davis was hungry for military glory. After graduating from West Point, he had cut his officer's career short to marry Sarah Taylor, a daughter of Colonel Zachary Taylor, only to see her quickly die of malaria. A second chance for military fame came with the Mexican War, and Davis promptly left his seat in Congress to serve as colonel of the First Mississippi Regiment. He and his troops fought in the

Battle of Monterrey and then won fame by defeating a far superior force at the Battle of Buena Vista. Davis suffered a painful wound in the foot that ended his active service but enhanced his reputation. Long after the war was over, he devoted many hours and much turgid correspondence to defending the record of that battle against any criticism or slight. At one point he nearly fought a duel over the issue. Mississippi's legislators rewarded their war hero with election to the US Senate.

The same war that won Davis glory plunged the nation into a serious crisis over the future of all the lands won from Mexico. That crisis gave him an opportunity to cement his reputation as a fervent defender of slavery and the South's rights. Davis always defended slavery, praising it as "a moral, a social, and a political blessing." John C. Calhoun was aging and nearing the end of his career, and the younger Mississippian was eager to become the recognized successor to the South Carolinian. In an era of expansion, Senator Davis took the unbending position that slavery must have an "experiment," must be allowed to expand into *all* of the new but arid southwestern lands. He regarded this as a basic constitutional right of the South, and he speculated that there could be great opportunities for slave labor in mining and irrigated agriculture. The expansive proslavery optimism of Davis and other southern leaders extended even to gaining future possessions in the Caribbean, Mexico, or Central America. Any attempt to exclude slavery from the lands won from Mexico, Davis insisted, was an unconstitutional violation of slaveholders' rights.

In 1850, as conflict intensified in Congress, Davis urged the South to unite and take a firm stand. He regarded opposition to the South's claims as "Abolitionism," while others called for a compromise that would protect the sacred Union. Davis declared that the most he would accept—as an extreme concession to benefit the Union—was a division of territory along the Missouri Compromise line reaching all the way to the Pacific. But nothing beyond that should be considered, and if the North refused to agree, he believed the South must resist. He encouraged the Nashville Convention, where delegates from nine slaveholding states argued for extension of the Missouri Compromise line. Like Calhoun, Davis denied that he sought disunion but warned that it could be caused by the North's "sectional aggrandizement" or by abolitionists' love for "the African race."

Davis rejected the Compromise of 1850 as unsatisfactory, and he resolved to continue the battle against what he saw as northern aggression. Democrats in Mississippi split over how much resistance was appropriate, with some organizing a pro-Union party. Support for the Compromise gained ground in the state. But Davis, adhering to his strong stand, demanded respect for what he claimed were the rights of the South. He told nonslaveholders that slavery was vital to them, because it established equality among white people. All previous civilizations, he said, had drawn "a line . . . between the rich and the poor," but in the South nonslaveholders "*stand upon the broad level of equality with the rich man.*"

Then Governor John Quitman, who had supported an expedition to seize Cuba, resigned in order to defend himself against a charge of violating federal neutrality laws. Mississippi Democrats called on Davis to replace Quitman, and he resigned his seat in the Senate to fight an uphill battle for the governorship. He denied that he wanted to dissolve the Union, but that reassurance was not sufficient. Davis's loss was painful and disappointing to him, but he soon accepted appointment as secretary of war in President Franklin Pierce's Democratic administration. That cabinet position gave him further opportunity to advance slaveholding interests.

To this point Davis fully reflected Calhoun's example. He was among the most extreme advocates for the South, yet he asserted a love for the Union. From 1852 until the end of the decade he maintained both positions, but northerners saw that his actions leaned heavily toward southern interests. As secretary of war, Davis worked to strengthen the army and to defend slavery. The admission of California gave him an opportunity, from a military perspective, to call for a transcontinental railroad. Because defending California would be difficult without a railroad connection, Davis ordered surveys of possible routes. Not surprisingly, he found that a southern route was most advantageous, and he promoted the Gadsden Purchase, which would make a southern line more attractive.

There was more to please proslavery expansionists. Davis championed President Pierce's desire to purchase the slaveholding island of Cuba from Spain. When that idea failed to interest the Spanish, Davis defended the Ostend Manifesto, written by three proslavery US ambassadors. The Manifesto declared in bellicose terms that should Spain refuse a fair price for Cuba, "we shall be justified in wresting it from Spain." Cuba should not be allowed, the Manifesto declared, "to be Africanized and become a second St. Domingo, with all its attendant horrors to the white race." In addition, Davis spoke in favor of filibustering expeditions to conquer territory in the Caribbean or Central America, and the Pierce administration recognized the short-lived government of William Walker, who had defeated Nicaragua's army and taken power there.

Davis's most notable proslavery act as secretary of war concerned the territories, not the military. He gave a crucial boost to the Kansas-Nebraska bill proposed by Illinois's Stephen Douglas. After Douglas bowed to southern demands and agreed to repeal the Missouri Compromise line in his bill, Davis provided vital support at a crucial moment. Knowing that the repeal of the Missouri Compromise line would anger northerners, Douglas needed President Pierce to support his bill and pressure Democrats to back it. Davis, who was on good terms with the president, agreed to take Douglas to see Pierce on a Sunday, when the president normally refused to transact any business. The meeting succeeded, Pierce made the bill a priority of the administration, and Congress opened the Great Plains to settlement by slaveholders.

In all these controversies Jefferson Davis energetically promoted slavery's expansion. His influence in the cabinet was important, and he had longstanding ties to Missouri senator David Atchison, who was determined to help "our people" go into Kansas "and take their '*niggers*' with them." Atchison boasted that he was ready "to shoot, burn & hang" if necessary, and he joined gangs of Border Ruffians who, with blatant illegality, rode across the border to vote for slavery in Kansas elections. Proslavery activists like Atchison did their full part to incite violence in Kansas. As secretary of war, Davis ordered US officers to act responsibly as they made futile efforts to maintain peace, but his support for slavery's interests was clear.

Conflict in Kansas dominated the end to Pierce's administration and soon plunged James Buchanan's presidency into turmoil. Davis again was representing Mississippi in the US Senate as Buchanan took office and the Supreme Court handed down the *Dred Scott* decision. That decision stiffened slave-state radicalism. Davis and his southern colleagues rejoiced that the ruling declared the Missouri Compromise unconstitutional and affirmed slavery's right to expand. Consequently, they redoubled their efforts to establish slavery in Kansas. For southern Democrats, this was an opportunity to add a slave state to the Union, and Davis called Kansas "the pivot of this sectional conflict." Despite the fact that a large majority of settlers in that territory were opposed to slavery, Buchanan and Davis backed the proslavery Lecompton Constitution. Stephen Douglas denounced the Lecompton Constitution as a mockery of popular sovereignty, and many northerners saw it as another aggression by the Slave Power. Ultimately, Kansas did not gain admission under the Lecompton Constitution, and southerners had to disguise their defeat and renew their demands.

At this point Davis's posture changed. He remained a radical exponent of southern rights, but from the summer of 1858 onward he put more emphasis on the love for the Union that he and Calhoun had claimed to feel. Working with allies within the Democratic Party, he sought ways to avoid disunion while defending the South. By the time of the secession crisis, this modification of his positions had made him a dignified, rather than irresponsible, champion of the South and a leader more acceptable to older states like Virginia.

During the battles over Kansas, Davis had endured months of extremely painful eye problems. To recover his health and escape the summer heat in 1858, he traveled to New England. There he met with support from quite a number of northern Democrats, for much of the party's northern wing was devoted to white supremacy and staunchly defended slaveholders against Republicans. His speeches won applause at the Maine State Fair and in Boston's Faneuil Hall. New Englanders like Massachusetts's Caleb Cushing, who had been attorney general in Pierce's cabinet, showed Davis that they could be trusted. His hopes grew that the Union could be preserved, with the backing of northern Democrats for southern interests.

On the Fourth of July he predicted that "this great country will continue united," and a few days later he asked, "Has patriotism ceased to be a virtue, and is narrow sectionalism no longer to be counted a crime?" In Maine he declared, "The whole confederacy is my country, and to the innermost fibers of my heart I love it all, and every part." In Boston he recounted with pleasure that "I have learned . . . in New England the vast mass of true States Rights Democrats to be found within its limits," and he expressed confidence that they would help southerners "whip the Black Republicans." To Franklin Pierce he wrote, "The difference is less than I had supposed." Perhaps most important in a substantive sense, he denied that slaveholders wanted to "forc[e] slavery upon any community." In practical terms, Stephen Douglas's Freeport Doctrine was correct, for without "police regulations [to give security] to slave property . . . the owner would be practically debarred . . . from taking slave property into a territory" whose inhabitants were opposed to it.

In Mississippi much opinion now was becoming more radical, and Davis used fiery rhetoric to defend his image while discouraging ideas such as reopening the international slave trade. Back in Washington sectional conflict increased with John Brown's raid on Harpers Ferry and as the next presidential election approached. Davis feared the Republican Party, convinced that it was a revolutionary threat. He counseled others that "the vital element" of the party was hostility to slavery, even if its official positions were more constrained. Among his fellow Democrats he emphatically joined those who had concluded that Stephen Douglas was an unreliable ally and must be blocked from gaining the presidential nomination. Davis introduced into the Senate a series of "Resolutions on the Relations of States." These insisted on slavery's inviolability from government interference and repeated Calhoun's theories that "neither Congress, nor a Territorial Legislature, whether by direct legislation or legislation of an indirect and unfriendly nature, possess the power to annul or impair the constitutional right of any citizen ... to take his slave property into the common Territories." This language was a direct attack on Douglas. Its purpose was to ensure that southerners in the party would deny him the Democratic nomination. Davis stopped short of demanding laws to establish a territorial slave code, however, for he merely asserted that Congress had a duty to act *if* rights were denied in the future.

The opposition of Davis and many others to Douglas seemed likely to prevail, but Davis hoped the party could somehow remain united. He consulted with Franklin Pierce and others to seek some solution. Davis urged nominating a "man who will be accepted by both sections without a platform." However, those efforts failed, delegates from eight southern states walked out of the convention at Charleston, and a second meeting in Baltimore also failed to achieve unity. The Upper South was far less eager than the Deep South to provoke a confrontation that might lead to war. The Democratic Party split, and the victory of Abraham Lincoln appeared ever more likely. Davis's last effort to unite the Democrats came when he approached the three other candidates: Stephen Douglas; John Breckinridge, the nominee of southern Democrats; and Tennessee's John Bell, nominated by a new Constitutional Union Party that opposed disunion. Davis suggested that all three withdraw in favor of some conservative candidate, but Douglas refused, saying that he was the only candidate capable of winning in the North. The election produced the expected result—a victory for Abraham Lincoln.

Proslavery southerners then divided into those favoring immediate secession and others who wanted to wait, to cooperate with other states, and to seek a solution. Davis was firmly in the cooperationist camp. He recommended, in vain, that South Carolina postpone its secession, and he was among a minority of Mississippi's congressional delegation in advising the governor to avoid separate state action. By January 1861 it was becoming clear that Mississippi would secede, but Davis hung back. He warned the Senate that a war would be terribly destructive. On the Committee of Thirteen he agreed to support the Crittenden Compromise (which revived the idea of the Missouri Compromise line for any and all future territories) if Republicans on the committee would do the same. After Abraham Lincoln instructed his colleagues to say "no," Davis sadly delivered his farewell address to the Senate and returned to Mississippi.

Jefferson Davis's Confederate career was about to begin—a career that would depart radically from venerable southern traditions and separate him from most of the Confederacy's political elite. Both his leadership and the Confederate states' experience departed widely from its long-influential depiction in the Lost Cause myth. Davis challenged both the political elite's expectations and some central values of the slaveholding South. The stress of warfare revealed that southerners were not united, like the proverbial band of brothers, in defense of constitutional liberty instead of slavery. Four slaveholding states in the Border South, of course, did not secede. But in addition, within the Confederate States both class and regional differences produced deep fissures in what the Lost Cause later presented as a unified, harmonious society.

Jefferson Davis had his hopes set on military glory as war loomed. He hoped "to be a general in the army" of the Confederacy, but the Montgomery Convention named him president of the Provisional Government, and a year later he was elected without opposition as president of the "permanent" government. Davis's relative moderation at the end of the decade had put him more in tune with the Upper South, and his reputation was that of a determined but dignified southern advocate. In a sober, realistic mood, he took up his duties. Although many who should have known better were celebrating secession and predicting an easy victory in war, Davis feared that the conflict would be "long and bloody." In fact, the new Confederacy was deficient in a long list of material and human resources, and the strains of war would fracture its unity.

Davis hoped that a homogeneous white southern population, one dedicated to slavery and free of abolitionists, would show its strength. He began his presidency building loyalty to the new government and working to convince any who had doubts about the wisdom of secession. The Confederacy had not destroyed the American Union, he argued. Instead, it had vindicated the true principles of the Union and preserved the Founders' legacy, a legacy that the North had betrayed. "The Constitution framed by our fathers is that of these Confederate States," said Davis. The new nation was, supposedly, the embodiment of true American ideas of government. Southerners were "the last best hope of liberty," whereas Lincoln's government "tramples on all the principles of constitutional liberty." Northerners were a danger to American liberty and had to be left behind.

From his first days in office Davis committed himself to Confederate nationalism and to independence. Having discarded one nationality, he declared his absolute devotion to the new one. As soon as he first arrived in Montgomery, Alabama, he declared that "the time for compromise" had "passed." Southerners must "make all who oppose us smell Southern powder and feel Southern steel. . . . Our separation from the old Union is complete. NO COMPROMISE; NO RECONSTRUCTION CAN NOW BE ENTERTAINED." For Davis, Confederate independence was the absolute priority—a goal to be pursued even if unexpected, unwelcome measures proved necessary. His inflexible determination would endure to the end of the war, despite setbacks, fierce internal criticism, and fading commitment on the part of others.

Davis proceeded to build from nothing a strong government—in fact, one so strong that it shocked and dismayed a growing host of critics. The new Confederate constitution gave Davis and the central government great powers, because it was much like the US Constitution. It declared that Confederate laws were supreme over state legislation, and it contained a "necessary and proper" clause that gave scope to legislation. Davis recognized that he needed to use all its powers. The shocking, very unsouthern aspects of his leadership were just beginning, for he was ready to embrace unexpected measures to gain independence.

The Confederate Congress was far less realistic and was "incredulous of a long war," especially at first. It failed to establish adequate taxation or require long terms from volunteers for military service. In the heady first days of the war the Confederacy had a superabundance of enthusiastic volunteers, but most were allowed to commit to only twelve months in the ranks. By the spring of 1862 the bulk of the Confederacy's army was about to disappear. Davis then called for and obtained the first conscription law in American history. The states' rights Confederacy became the first American government to compel men to serve in the army.

Some governors and politicians protested fiercely; Georgia's chief executive, Joseph E. Brown, charged that conscription was "at war with all the principles" for which "Georgia entered into this revolution." Conscription, he claimed, "strikes down" his state's "sovereignty at a single blow" and was worse than anything the United States government had ever done. The *Charleston Mercury* denounced conscription as "the very embodiment of Lincolnism" because it was a power "to coerce sovereign States." Some drafted citizens went to court to try to overturn the law, but Davis prevailed. Quickly he showed that conscription was only the first of many controversial measures.

Before long the Confederate Congress saw, too late, that it had to agree to higher taxes. These were objectionable to many, even though the failure to tax adequately subjected southern society to rampant, runaway inflation exceeding 7,000 percent. That level of inflation alone caused severe suffering among the population. Even tougher measures proved necessary to feed the armies. In the spring of 1863 the government started to collect a tax-in-kind, taking one-tenth of the nonperishable foodstuffs from every southern farm. Thousands of agents fanned out over the countryside to publish regulations and designate warehouses to which farmers had to bring their crops. Despite the introduction of the tax-in-kind, the army always relied more heavily on impressment—the simple seizure of food, horses, wagons, or any other useful and needed material from southern farmers. Such seizures often were far heavier than the tax-in-kind, and they were unequal in their impact, since impressments burdened only areas in which the army happened to be operating. Even government officials admitted that impressments were "harsh, unequal, . . . odious" and "productive of such discontent" that their only justification was "absolute necessity." But the necessity was constant.

Inflation and shortages convinced Davis that greater control over the economy was needed to obtain the uniforms, arms, ammunition, medicine and other supplies that were required. Therefore, the government used the conscription laws to marshal the Confederacy's manpower and allocate it where needed. With conscription covering an ever-larger range of ages and eventually claiming males from ages seventeen to fifty, the Confederacy used exemptions or details to put workers into essential factories or occupations. Control of the workforce included requisitions for enslaved labor, so that enslaved Black people could build fortifications and perform much of the army's skilled or fatigue labor—a measure resented by many planters. In addition, the Confederacy established subsidies and guaranteed profits in order to encourage key businesses. Before the war was over the Confederacy passed laws to regulate shipping and ensure that ships carried material that was important to the war effort. Significant control also extended over the South's inadequate system of railroads.

Davis demanded and three times received authority to suspend the writ of habeas corpus, a striking restriction of individual liberties. He used that power to act against sedition and opposition that increasingly appeared. Military authorities arrested and imprisoned more than four thousand people, many of whom languished in jail. Facing challenges to his authority, or to conscription and other laws, President Davis went into the state courts and won on the strength of the Confederate constitution's provisions. The dimensions of Confederate control over society steadily expanded. In Richmond a passport system developed informally because the city was both militarily important and thronged with strangers. Soon that system extended its reach more widely, and by 1863 it had become nearly ubiquitous. A British visitor traveling through the Gulf states found that soldiers demanded his papers "continually, and on the railroad every person's passport was rigidly examined." Armed guards supervised railroad cars, and sentries patrolled many public highways. Members of the Confederate Congress complained that they had to go "to the Provost Marshal's office and ge[t] a pass like a free [N]egro."

The central government militarized Confederate society to an extent never before seen. Davis used his powers to enforce unity when it faltered in certain regions and among hard-pressed citizens. Officials of the Conscription Bureau rounded up draft evaders or soldiers overseeing their leaves. Detachments from the army repeatedly raided areas where deserters had congregated and arrested thousands. Thousands of other Confederate officials descended on farms to demand the tax-in-kind or to supervise impressments. Army officers burned stores of cotton to prevent its falling into Union hands. The business of government and of the Congress was almost entirely war related, as the Confederacy struggled to mount an effective opposition to the US forces. In a surprisingly short time, a government that began with no employees or procedures grew into a bureaucracy bigger, in relation to population, than that of the United States.

Jefferson Davis's approach to Confederate policy was, in the main, intelligent, realistic, and utterly committed. But it was far from what many leaders and citizens had expected. All this was shocking to political leaders schooled in states' rights ideology, and it was jarring to rural farmers and nonslaveholders who previously had felt the hand of the central government very little if at all. The decades of prewar rhetoric about the dangers of central power lived on in beliefs of states' rights and resistance to domination. As a result, Davis and his government had to struggle against fierce internal opposition as well as northern armies. The opposition from politicians was loud and insistent, and governors often fought to defend their constituents from demands of the central government. Widespread resistance from ordinary citizens proved injurious to the overall war effort and gave the lie to later claims of southern unity against northern aggressors.

A senator from Texas expressed the feelings of many members of the elite when he declared that a war "for the vindication of the sovereignty of the states [and] the liberties of the people" had instead conferred "absolute despotic power . . . upon the executive and the military." The "original object of the war," he claimed, was "lost sight of," and the changes shocked "the habits of the people." The central government lost the "moral support" of the citizenry because it became "as perfect a military despotism as ever existed upon the face of the earth." A measure of this man's alienation was that he condemned martial law as "clearly unconstitutional," even though suspension of the writ of habeas corpus was one of the constitution's enumerated powers.

Other members of Congress were equally outraged and critical when strong measures failed to produce victory. South Carolina's Representative W. W. Boyce decided early in the war that "Davis has no military genius" and was taking the Confederacy to "the brink of ruin." As problems deepened, he accused Davis of doing "everything that a centralized military despotism could do. Indeed, if you were appointed military dictator," he asked in anger, "what greater powers could you exercise than you do now?" Newspapers joined in, blaming the president for "every military misfortune of this country." Davis's disillusioned vice president, Alexander Stephens, tried to organize opposition that would circumvent the president's authority. A number of leaders felt, even if they labored on, that the revolution was a failure and that the heart of the people was not in it.

The common people of the Confederacy suffered in massive numbers. Most white families lived on small farms with no enslaved labor, and therefore the absence of men in the armies meant a critical labor shortage on the farm. Impressment, inflation, the tax-in-kind, crop failures, and the destruction of war made suffering worse. Many families went hungry and depended on the desperate, inadequate efforts of local governments to provide aid. As a result, despairing letters called on soldiers to return home, and many declared that a man's first duty was to provide for his family. Desertions increased, and local opposition became violent. When men came home, the government's efforts to round them up drove them into opposition. Armed bands of deserters fought authorities, took control of local areas, and stole from the rich to support their loved ones. By 1863 the assistant secretary of war reported that "the condition of things in the mountain districts of North Carolina, South Carolina, Georgia, and Alabama menaces the existence of the Confederacy as fatally as either of the armies of the United States." Within a year, military commanders worried that soldiers from Texas or Louisiana would refuse to obey any orders that might require them to leave their homes and cross the Mississippi River.

By the fall of 1864 Jefferson Davis faced grim realities and began a bold challenge to the core institution of southern society: slavery. He admitted that "two-thirds of our men are absent" and that the army needed new recruits. These could only be obtained from the enslaved population, and Davis argued that enslaved Black southerners, who were persons as well as property, needed a motivation to serve. Freedom as the reward for service, coupled with the promise of future residence in the Confederacy, would supply that motive. In his November address to the Confederate Congress, Davis presented this idea gingerly, calling at first for the purchase of forty thousand enslaved men to be used as laborers. But after indicating that Black soldiers might be necessary, he declared, "should the alternative ever be presented of subjugation or of the employment of the slave as a soldier, there seems to be no doubt what should then be our decision." For Davis, who was totally committed to independence, that decision was clear. But his determination challenged what most regarded as the very purpose of the Confederacy.

The Confederate president and his allies worked with determination to gain support for arming and freeing slaves. His government reassured state leaders and others that white supremacy was not in question. Freed soldiers would remain "an inferior race ... unfitted for social or political equality." States could pass laws that would give their families "ultimate emancipation after an intermediate stage of serfage or peonage." Davis made General Robert E. Lee, whom many saw as the nation's only possible military savior, his spokesman, and Lee affirmed his support, saying that slaves were needed and would make good soldiers. Lee called for action "without delay" and proposed "immediate freedom to all who enlist, and freedom at the end of the war to the families of those who discharge their duties faithfully (whether they survive or not), together with the privilege of residing at the South." The governor of Virginia, some military commanders and units, and a few others supported the plan.

But most politicians and editors were enraged and apoplectic, for "if a negro is fit to be a soldier he is not fit to be a slave." Davis's idea contradicted Confederate society's central value and abandoned "the object for which we undertook the war." The president's "extraordinary suggestion" not only was "insane," it was "inconsistent, unsound, and suicidal," cried the *Charleston Mercury*. One Richmond paper declared that freeing slaves would be "an act of cruelty. . . . If the slave must fight, he should fight for the blessings he enjoys as a slave." Another insisted that "the [N]egro is in his proper situation," for slavery is "a state superior and better for him than that of freedom." The president, inexplicably, had adopted "the whole theory of the abolitionist." Confederate legislators denounced the administration's "insane proposals," called them "wild schemes and confessions of despair," and asked, if slaves became free in the country, "Who would consent to live in it?"

Furious over Davis's "insane proposals" and anxious over the dire military situation, some began to call for the president's removal. The *Daily Richmond Examiner* blamed "every military misfortune of this country" on Davis personally, and the *Daily Richmond Enquirer* hoped the government would make Lee "*generalissimo* of all the armies." A well-informed clerk in the War Department recorded in his diary that "a large number" of people "openly declare in favor of Lee as Dictator." Although this could be done only "by revolution and the overthrow of the Constitution," some in Congress and in the executive branch favored the idea. The *Charleston Mercury* demanded Davis's impeachment, and Richmond's *Examiner* called for a convention of states to change the government. Senator Louis Wigfall of Texas tried to interest three states' governors in a plan to strip Davis of his military powers. Wigfall, surprisingly, wanted to make a less successful general, Joseph Johnston, "dictator." Plans for dictatorship came to nothing, but in February 1865 the Confederate Congress established the office of general in chief, and Davis appointed Lee to the post.

Even then, fierce resistance to arming the Confederacy's slaves continued. After months of bitter invective, while military defeat became ever more certain, the Confederate Congress finally acted on March 13, 1865. By a margin of one vote in the Senate, the government gained the authority to enlist slaves as soldiers, but "nothing in this act shall be construed to authorize a change in the relation which the said slave shall bear toward their owners." The Confederate Congress obviously agreed that the enslaved man "should fight for the blessings he enjoys as a slave." Thus, the debate made two things undeniably clear: Jefferson Davis was dedicated to independence over the preservation of slavery, but the new nation's lawmakers disagreed and stood emphatically behind slavery. Human bondage was, beyond question, the Confederacy's reason for being, "the object for which we undertook the war."

JEFFERSON DAVIS had been unpopular during most of his years as Confederate president—at times even extremely unpopular. Before his death in 1889 his reputation had begun to revive, but not because white southerners belatedly recognized the value of his centralizing leadership or policies. Rather, the disappointment and humiliation of defeat caused a proud and once boastful population to contest the North's interpretation of its victory and insist on the virtue and superiority of southern culture. The Lost Cause myth had many powerful exponents among army veterans and influential elite women, and that myth served a variety of purposes. It was valuable psychologically, socially, and politically. It helped the South fight changes brought by Reconstruction, and it bolstered the power of the elite while reinforcing white supremacy. A political elite that had quarreled frequently during the war found unity in Reconstruction and after as it fought to deny Black rights and maintain an unyielding white supremacy.

Jefferson Davis was part of that postwar consensus. He never enjoyed the praise and reverence that advocates of the Lost Cause bestowed on Robert E. Lee, but his image became that of a southern leader who was loyal and had suffered unjustly. This change began right after the war, when the United States government imprisoned Davis for two years at Fortress Monroe in Virginia. His health, never stable and good, suffered during part of that imprisonment, and newspapers treated his illnesses as a form of persecution. Eventually Davis gained his release, as federal authorities could not decide whether it was wise to try him as a traitor. In the years of Reconstruction and after, his relatively few public statements always supported white southern resentments. For example, he held that the South had been "cheated not conquered," and he deplored what he called an oppressive "Yankee and Negro" rule. Reconstruction had been a "night of despotism," and freedom and efforts at equal rights for Black people had merely made them "more idle and ungovernable than before." As an object of memory, Davis's betrayal of the proslavery gospel faded, and the public tended to remember him as yet another southern leader cruelly mistreated.

But Jefferson Davis's impact on the postwar United States was substantial, because during the war he had done much to inflame sectional hatreds and make them enduring. The dynamics of war always encourage the contestants to demonize each other; the enemy becomes not merely a foe but something that is inherently evil, a vile threat to the good. As president of the Confederacy, Davis had done all he could to stir up such feelings and to embed such images in southerners' minds. Painting the northern enemy as unrelentingly savage had been his tool to enhance southern resistance. The necessity of resisting an evil North was central to his ideological appeals, which aimed to strengthen the resolve of Confederates.

As early as 1862 Davis accused the United States of inhumane warfare, of practices violating "the usages of civilization and the dictates of humanity." "Hyenas," he said, were preferable to Yankees. He reacted to the Emancipation Proclamation by charging that it was an effort to "incite servile insurrection." According to him, Lincoln's purpose was to arouse slaves to "a general assassination of their masters." Emancipation thus would be remembered as "the most execrable measure recorded in the history of guilty man." At other times Davis accused the Union army of "every crime conceivable," of the burning of "defenceless towns" and the "pillag[ing]" of people's homes by a "brutal soldiery." Defeat, he told Confederates, would mean "subjugation, slavery, and . . . utter ruin." Denouncing the "wickedness of the North," he asked Mississippians if they were willing to "be the slaves of the most depraved and intolerant and tyrannical and hated people upon earth." Northerners' "malignant rage" would result in "nothing less than the extermination of yourselves, your wives, and children." All this nourished the myth of a noble and badly mistreated region.

Jefferson Davis's time as president of the Confederacy proved to be brief. But no one, perhaps, did more to encourage the sectional enmity and divisive stereotypes that have lasted to our present day. His commitment to Confederate independence reinforced the distinct southern identity nourished by the Lost Cause. His dedication to white supremacy, which he had insisted would continue through Black serfdom or peonage, enlarged the United States' enduring problem with white racism and systemic inequality. Davis's wartime actions revealed much that was false about the postwar image of the Confederacy. But his words left a legacy that aided the Lost Cause myth and did much to poison American politics and culture. Southern leaders would resist every reform of Reconstruction, work to reenslave Black people, and nourish hostility toward the North for generations to come.

Abraham Lincoln
Riding the Storm to Historic Progress

~~~

Abraham Lincoln revered Henry Clay. He called the Great Compromiser his "beau ideal" of a statesman, and after Clay died Lincoln played a similarly large role in the prewar sectional conflict. But Lincoln's goal was different from that of Clay or John C. Calhoun or Stephen Douglas. He did not seek a compromise that would placate North and South—he sought a solution. Lincoln believed that the United States had to resolve its contradictory commitments to freedom and to slavery. More than any of the other prominent officeholders described here, he faced the problem squarely, and his solution was to place slavery "in the course of ultimate extinction." Although he specified no timetable, he was categorical that slavery must not expand, nor should it receive any favors from the national government. Instead of an evasive or short-term compromise, he fought for an outcome in the long-term that honored the ideals of the Declaration of Independence.

Yet Lincoln was also a complex, multifaceted, and cautious politician. Ambition and idealism vied for attention in his agenda, and caution or watchful waiting often determined his strategy for the future. The competition between these emotions made him capable of moving appeals, prudent hesitation, or questionable and alarmist tactics to gain office. Contradictions were part of his political career. He led a Republican Party that deepened sectional division, yet he fled from being labeled radical or abolitionist. He cherished the Declaration of Independence and its proclamation that "all men are created equal," but he repeatedly urged colonization of Black people outside of white America. He appealed to northern Democrats and offered many olive branches to southern rebels, but he also acted on the opportunity to impose great change.

Amid unpredictable, disorienting events, President Lincoln's policies alternated between moderation and opportunistic progress. He conducted himself very much as a centrist, yet he ultimately became the agent of historic change. Lincoln rode the storm until the right time to act arrived, and although as president he sometimes kept his ideals largely to himself, he grew in morality and leadership. Lincoln, the cautious politician, remained in touch with the divergent values of the citizenry but also articulated and acted on a higher vision to which later generations could aspire. Tracing the main lines of his policies illuminates the contest between morality and practical politics, between the ideals of the Declaration of Independence and the reality of racism and white supremacy.

ABRAHAM LINCOLN began his political career in the Illinois House of Representatives. There he learned a lot about political competition, but his record was not especially distinguished. He championed an internal improvements scheme that was so wildly ambitious that Illinois had to suspend payment on its bonds and needed decades to retire the debt. In 1837 he made his first comment on the national issue of slavery. After Calhoun and his southern allies imposed the gag rule on Congress, Lincoln and another legislator issued a protest that "slavery is founded on both injustice and bad policy." They paired that moral statement, however, with a condemnation of "abolition doctrines" as "tend[ing] rather to increase than abate its evils."

Several years later Lincoln won election to the US Congress, and his one term there from 1847 to 1849 showed that his concerns about slavery were real but that he was not a radical. In 1849 he introduced a resolution calling for a referendum to end slavery in the District of Columbia. He proposed that the US Treasury would pay "full cash value" to slaveholders who were willing to free their human "property," and that children born to enslaved mothers after 1850 would be free. Once his idea became public, however, criticism arose from both southerners and abolitionists. John C. Calhoun warned his southern colleagues against ideas such as this one from "a member from Illinois." Wendell Phillips, the outspoken abolitionist, called Lincoln "that slave hound from Illinois." Lincoln did not pursue his idea, and more determined northern congressmen regarded him as only mildly antislavery. In the estimate of Representative George Julian, a founder of the Free Soil Party, Lincoln's "anti-slavery education had scarcely begun."

In 1854 the Kansas-Nebraska Act galvanized Lincoln and brought him back into politics. He shared the anger and alarm of many northerners that an immense region from which slavery had been prohibited now had been thrown open to the peculiar institution. Lincoln's protest in his Peoria speech attracted attention and revealed the variety of ways that he could encourage sentiment against slavery's expansion. Lincoln spoke about morality and national purpose, but he also made practical arguments that spoke directly to the self-interest of northerners and white settlers.

His attack on the new law included idealistic sentiments against slavery. Lincoln said that he hated the spread of slavery, not only because slavery was a "monstrous injustice" but also because it "deprives our republican example of its just influence in the world." It soiled "our Republican robe" and made Americans "hypocrites." Stephen Douglas's "*declared* indifference" to the spread of slavery cloaked a "*real* zeal" that Lincoln could "not but hate." He also said that the consensus against the international slave trade and the thousands of slaves who had been freed by their masters testified to people's moral sense that slavery was wrong.

But Lincoln also advanced other kinds of arguments against the Kansas-Nebraska Act. It would allow a few slaveholding settlers who entered the territory first to impose an undesirable institution on all who came to settle later. In addition, the "whole nation," not just a few settlers, was interested in the future of those territories. "We want them for the homes of free white people." The territories could not offer opportunity to northerners "if slavery shall be planted within them," for poor men had to flee slave states in order to better themselves. He also argued that allowing slavery to expand violated the intent of the "revolutionary fathers." Using a telling statistical contrast between South Carolina and Maine, he showed that the Constitution's three-fifths clause gave white men in slave states far more power in Congress than voters in the free states enjoyed. Such a disadvantage to the free states, he said, should not be allowed to grow. In numerous ways, Lincoln told his audience, slavery endangered the Union; in fact, it was "the only one thing which ever" brought danger.

In a clever way Lincoln showed that slavery threatened Douglas's sacred principle of self-government and very possibly wronged Black men. Here he appealed to the growing moral feeling against slavery that Harriet Beecher Stowe and Frederick Douglass had stimulated. Yet he also managed to distance himself from the generally disliked abolitionists. Lincoln insisted that he was *not* "contending for the establishment of social and political equality" between the races. But he suggested that

Douglas's argument for letting territorial settlers govern themselves depended entirely on "whether a negro is *not* or *is* a man."

When white men went beyond self-government to govern "*another* man, that is *more* than self-government—that is despotism." Lincoln asked, "if the negro *is* a man," is it not the "total destruction of self-government, to say that he too shall not govern *himself?*" Then he quoted the "sheet-anchor of American republicanism, Our Declaration of Independence," and its famous words that "all men are created equal." But he continued past the words about equality to put his emphasis on the Declaration's assertion that just power derives "FROM THE CONSENT OF THE GOVERNED." Slavery by its very nature violated that principle. There was no consent, and therefore slavery was dangerous to American democracy.

The Peoria speech raised Lincoln's profile, and he continued speaking and working with others to organize the new Republican Party. But Illinois Republicans did not nominate him for a seat in the US Senate until 1858, when he prepared to challenge Stephen Douglas. By that year the sectional crisis had deepened and intensified in several ways. After "Bleeding Kansas" came the *Dred Scott* decision of 1857, which declared the Missouri Compromise to have been unconstitutional and held that slavery could not be barred from the territories. That Supreme Court decision clearly invalidated the central platform of the Republican Party. But the party survived because many northerners were shocked, and Lincoln and others found ways to fuel the public outrage.

Lincoln criticized the Supreme Court's actions by arguing that the decision contained historical inaccuracies, was not unanimous, and displayed partisan bias. The Supreme Court was supporting the Slave Power rather than American liberty. Again, with great verbal agility, he managed to speak up for the rights of all while also affirming that "there is a natural disgust in the minds of nearly all white people, to the idea of an indiscriminate amalgamation of the white and black races." To Democratic accusations that Republicans favored racial mixing, Lincoln answered that his opposition to having "a black woman for a *slave*" did not mean that "I must necessarily want her for a *wife*." What he did want, and what was right, was that she could enjoy "her natural right to eat the bread she earns with her own hands." In that respect "she is my equal, and the equal of all others."

Then he closed his speech with eloquent words. The authors of the Declaration of Independence meant "to include *all* men" but did not "declare all men equal *in all respects*." They held that all men were equal in their inalienable rights, and "They meant to set up a standard maxim for free society, which should be familiar to all, and revered by all; constantly looked to, constantly labored for, and even though never perfectly attained, constantly approximated, and thereby constantly spreading and deepening its influence, and augmenting the happiness and value of life to all people of all colors everywhere."

The power of these words can move readers today, but by 1858 the battle over a proslavery constitution proposed for Kansas had complicated Lincoln's hopes of defeating Stephen Douglas. The Lecompton Constitution, which would continue slavery in Kansas, was opposed by most settlers, but President Buchanan and southern Democrats favored it. When Douglas broke with his party's president and denounced Lecompton as a violation of the principle of popular sovereignty, he gained substantial ground in the North. Suddenly Douglas appeared as a bold advocate of keeping slavery out of the territories. Some Republican leaders of national stature hoped that Douglas might become a Republican. Others, including New York's Senator William Seward, welcomed the possibility of Douglas's returning to the Senate instead of his Republican challenger, and Lincoln knew it.

To recapture Republican support and shift the terms of the contest against Douglas, Lincoln delivered his most radical, politically opportunistic speech. To the Republican State Convention that had just nominated him for the Senate, he spoke about the "House Divided." The heart of the speech was not its allusion to a biblical passage, however, but a bold charge that Douglas was part of a proslavery conspiracy threatening to take over the country. Allegations of conspiracy always tend to spread alarm. Belief that a conspiracy is gaining power and becoming dominant encourages and tends to justify unusual, even extralegal action. In 1858 Lincoln stoked such fears. He went far beyond a sober assessment of the facts to name Douglas as a key conspirator who was following a careful plan first laid out in 1854.

Lincoln used language that could be understood by all, and not merely in the biblical cadences at the beginning of his speech. Alluding to frontier barn raisings familiar to westerners, he described an odd but telling circumstance. Four men, "Stephen, Franklin, Roger, and James," who came from different places, brought different pieces of timber that somehow, remarkably, fit together perfectly. It was as if there had been "preconcert," action in accord with a "common *plan*." His audience immediately understood him to be talking about Stephen Douglas, Franklin Pierce,

Roger Taney, and James Buchanan. They understood, too, that the plan to which he alluded was the extension of slavery into every territory.

But Lincoln went further and was even more precise. He reviewed legislative events from 1854 forward, linked them to presidential actions and then to the *Dred Scott* decision, and asked "whither we are tending." After this sequence of Democratic leaders' actions, "all that slavery now lacks," charged Lincoln, is one more Supreme Court decision to make it "lawful in all the States. . . . We shall *lie down* pleasantly dreaming that the people of *Missouri* are on the verge of making their state *free*; and we shall *awake* to the *reality*, instead, that the *Supreme* Court has made *Illinois* a *slave* State."

This was the most extreme, most exaggerated attack in Lincoln's political career, and it set the stage for his debates with Douglas. Douglas responded in kind throughout the campaign, raising the stakes by charging repeatedly that Lincoln was an abolitionist, a supporter of Black social and political equality, and a threat to white supremacy. Douglas thundered his unchanging belief that "This is a white man's country." Black people to him were an "inferior and degraded" race, and the American government "was made by white men, for the benefit of white men and their posterity forever, and never should be administered by any except white men." In reply Lincoln charged that today's citizens and future immigrants would lose the chance to better themselves if Douglas prevailed. He warned of the loss of America's moral compass, saying that indifference to slavery risked eradication of "the light of reason and the love of liberty."

On defense, Lincoln had to affirm in detail that he was not "nor ever have been in favor of bringing about in any way the social and political equality of the white and black races." He did not want Black people to be voters, jurors, officeholders, or marriage partners, and he added "that there is a physical difference between the white and black races which I believe will for ever forbid the two races living together on terms of social and political equality." But he also declared in other parts of the debates that slavery was "a moral, a social, and a political wrong," a "cancer" that must not be allowed to grow. The only solution for the nation was to place slavery where the Founding Fathers wanted it to be: "in the course of ultimate extinction."

With his post-1854 rhetoric Abraham Lincoln did a great deal to awaken the North to the dangers of slavery. Yet he and Republicans denied that they were a sectional party. They opposed slavery's extension but granted its right to exist in the slaveholding states. They also opposed social equality or voting rights for Black people or the discarding of white supremacy. Although they raised moral issues, as Stowe or the abolitionists had done, they were careful to separate themselves from abolitionists, and in 1859 that became especially important when John Brown attacked the federal armory at Harpers Ferry. Lincoln, like other Republican leaders, denounced Brown's violence and insisted that Republicans were not abolitionists. Republicans held "to no doctrine" that was not "held to and made by 'our fathers who framed the Government under which we live.'"

When the party approached the 1860 elections, it again was careful to separate itself from abolitionism. The influential editor Horace Greeley noted that this strategy was wise. In 1856 he had written, "It is beaten into my bones that the American people are not yet anti-slavery." Four years later he concluded, "An Anti-Slavery man *per se* cannot be elected." However, "a Tariff, River-and-Harbor, Pacific Railroad, Free Homestead man, *may* succeed *although* he is Anti-Slavery." Republicans championed these measures and were careful to instruct voters on their conservative and constitutional aims. Their party platform declared that the "rights of the States, and especially the right of each State to order and control its own domestic institutions according to its own judgment exclusively, is essential to the balance of power on which the perfection and endurance of our political fabric depend."

Abraham Lincoln and his party carried the free states, and with less than 40 percent of the popular vote, he triumphed in the Electoral College. The danger of secession then became very real. Amid many political discussions and a variety of ideas about last-minute compromises, Lincoln stood firm. Although he was open to some possibilities, he instructed Republicans in Congress to oppose any proposal—such as the Crittenden Compromise—that would allow slavery to expand territorially. He was determined that it must be put "in the course of ultimate extinction." That sealed the decision of southerners like Jefferson Davis to seek independence. By the time Lincoln took office, six Deep South states had seceded, and a seventh was completing the process to do so.

WITH HIS Inaugural Address, President Lincoln began four years of effort to persuade, lure, or ultimately compel the rebellious South to return to the Union. His first words in office show that his priority was to save the Union. At the very beginning of his address he quoted the Republican Party's platform and declared: "I have no purpose, directly or indirectly, to interfere with the institution of slavery in the States where it exists.

I believe I have no lawful right to do so, and I have no inclination to do so." He was sincere in his belief that the Constitution recognized slavery's right to exist where it was already established. At this point and for many months afterward, Lincoln also believed that there was considerable loyalty toward the Union among white southerners. He hoped to reach and engage that loyal feeling.

Although he claimed that northerners believed slavery to be "*wrong*," his Inaugural Address made a variety of appeals to the seceded states. Lincoln argued that a reasonable solution to the issue of fugitive slaves should be possible. He declared that the Union was perpetual and that the idea of secession held within itself the seeds of further schism and anarchy. Lincoln further pledged that he would not begin "bloodshed or violence" and would avoid appointing any "obnoxious strangers" to enforce the law in federal offices or properties in the South. He even went so far as to endorse a constitutional amendment that Congress had proposed and sent to the states for possible ratification. That amendment—which, ironically, might have become the Thirteenth—would have provided "that the federal government, shall never interfere with the domestic institutions of the States, including that of persons held to service."

When the war began six weeks later, Lincoln did not set out to emancipate the enslaved. Rather, he began his work as a centrist president focused on securing as much support as possible in order to preserve the Union. Almost immediately some Republican senators talked to him about abolition, and Lincoln expressed amazement that other northerners seemed "dazzled by the excitement of the hour" and were urging him to arm enslaved Black men in the South. But he had no such intention and at this point regarded his constitutional powers as limited. Militarily, Lincoln believed that he must hold onto the four border slave states—Kentucky, Missouri, Maryland, and Delaware—in order to have the resources needed to win the war. Politically, he was aware that close to half of northern voters had not voted for him and favored the Democrats. Many of those Democrats defended slaveholders' rights and slavery itself. Some editors of Democratic newspapers were willing to give Lincoln a trial, but they would quickly turn against an abolition president.

For these reasons under his administration army commanders returned escaped enslaved people to their enslavers, a practice that did not completely stop until Congress legislated against it in 1862. When Generals John C. Frémont and David Hunter, first in 1861 and then in 1862, declared emancipation in areas they commanded, Lincoln countermanded their decrees. At the end of 1861 he replaced Secretary of War Simon Cameron, who had recommended the arming of enslaved men as soldiers, after Cameron's recommendation became public despite Lincoln's efforts to suppress it. The president was blocking emancipation, but thousands of Black southerners, acting on their own, were seizing freedom. Wherever the Union army appeared in the South, Black men and women surged into the northern military's lines, betting on the prospect of liberation. Their actions would create growing pressure for emancipation as a policy and as a means to win the war.

Lincoln did propose certain actions against slavery during this time, but they were of the most conservative kind, ideas to which most abolitionists and Black people objected. For years Lincoln had favored the colonization movement that Henry Clay had championed, and he worked with members of his administration on schemes to remove Black people to Chiriquí, an area in what is now Panama. In his annual address to Congress in December 1861 Lincoln proposed colonizing both "persons" liberated by war's events and consenting free Black people in some "climate congenial to them." To facilitate this goal he recommended the purchase of new territory and called "this whole proposition" an "absolute necessity, that without which the government cannot be perpetuated."

Around the same time he unsuccessfully urged allies in the Delaware legislature to adopt, on state initiative, a very gradual scheme of emancipation with compensation from the federal government. In March 1862 he urged Congress to encourage such plans by offering financial assistance. He argued that gradual emancipation by loyal states would blast Confederates' hope that more slave states would join them and thereby "substantially en[d] the rebellion." He added that "gradual, and not sudden emancipation, is better for all," and his efforts to promote colonization continued. In 1862 Congress authorized a total of six hundred thousand dollars to support colonization efforts.

Lincoln's movement toward emancipation, on a voluntary, gradual basis, supplemented by compensation and colonization, had been slow and limited in scope. Much northern opinion and the Republican majority in Congress had been progressing much faster. Congress had already passed two confiscation acts aimed at slavery. Many believed not only that slavery was the cause of the war but that its abolition was the key to winning the war. The words of Frederick Douglass—that the *"simple way"* to win the war *"is to strike down slavery itself,* the primal cause of that war"— were having an effect. Events would redouble that effect.

LINCOLN BECAME the Great Emancipator by necessity, not on his freely chosen initiative, however much he sincerely hated slavery. There was precious little progress in the war in 1862, and by July Lincoln decided that he must change his course. To the cabinet he admitted that harsher measures were necessary. "We had about played our last card," Lincoln felt, "and must change our tactics, or lose the game." On July 13, 1862, Lincoln told two of his cabinet secretaries that he "had about come to the conclusion that [an emancipation proclamation] was a military necessity absolutely essential for the salvation of the Union, that we must free the slaves or be ourselves subdued." Eight days later he discussed with the cabinet the idea of issuing a proclamation based on the Second Confiscation Act, which would allow the rebels sixty days to return to the Union or lose those they enslaved. The cabinet discussed the advantage of waiting until there was a Union victory, and there was also talk about the damage this step would do to Republican candidates in the fall elections.

Before acting, Lincoln made a new, heartfelt appeal to the Union's border slave states, telling them that the war was steadily destroying slavery "by mere friction and abrasion." Wasn't it better to adopt programs of voluntary, gradual emancipation and obtain "substantial compensation for that which is sure to be wholly lost?" He emphasized that he was not urging "emancipation *at once*, but a *decision* at once to emancipate *gradually*" and that colonization of Black people in South America could take place. But the legislators from the border slave states rejected his plea and rebuked him, saying that "no one is authorized to question" their "right to hold slaves."

In the end Lincoln waited until September 22 to issue his Preliminary Emancipation Proclamation. With this Proclamation Lincoln entered a revolutionary new phase in his presidency, yet one whose embrace of emancipation did not preclude substantial conciliatory efforts toward Confederates. He promised that efforts for gradual, compensated emancipation with colonization would continue, and at the beginning of December he proposed such a program to Congress, which took no action. The Preliminary Emancipation Proclamation gave rebellious states one hundred days to return to the Union and keep the people they enslaved. If by January 1, 1863, a state sent to Congress representatives chosen through elections in which "a majority of the qualified voters" participated, that state would not be considered in rebellion. If rebellion continued, however, Lincoln promised to declare the enslaved people in rebellious states "forever free."

Lincoln's invitation to the rebels to return to their allegiance and protect slavery created a political defense against critics: if the rebellion continued, he and Republicans could claim that Confederates had brought emancipation upon themselves. But his offer also was sincere. He sent agents into Union-held areas of Louisiana, Tennessee, and Arkansas to encourage elections, and he signaled that he would even accept less than majority participation by voters. White southerners ignored his invitation, however, and various groups in the North were critical. Many Democratic newspaper editors who had defended Lincoln against the Radicals in his party now attacked him viciously as a deceitful abolitionist who had concealed his true colors. As for Radicals and abolitionists, most rejoiced, but some remained skeptical due to colonization and the conservative tenor of his policies.

But on January 1, 1863, Lincoln signed the Emancipation Proclamation, stressing that it was a "necessary war measure" issued "in time of actual armed rebellion" under his authority as "Commander-in-Chief." From this point forward, his government and the army and navy would "recognize and maintain the freedom of said persons." In his proclamation he described emancipation as "an act of justice," and privately he rejoiced that an opportunity to do so much good had come to him.

This major change in policy had rapid and important effects. The flood of formerly enslaved persons into Union lines grew even larger, and the US Army began enlisting thousands of Black men as soldiers. Lincoln recognized that the Black southerners seeking freedom could turn the tide of the war, and by August commanders were telling him that emancipation and "the use of colored troops constitute the heaviest blow yet dealt to the rebellion." He praised the Black soldiers who "with silent tongue, and clenched teeth, and steady eye, and well-poised bayonet" were helping "mankind on to this great consummation," while some northerners "with malignant heart" were striving "to hinder it."

Yet Lincoln still remained open and receptive to ideas that might encourage southerners to return to the Union. In regard to the postemancipation status of the formerly enslaved, his thinking changed slowly. General John McClernand, an old political rival from Illinois, contacted Lincoln to report that some prominent southerners were considering his now-expired offer. Lincoln wrote on January 8 that he would not retract his Proclamation, but he suggested that rebellious states "need not to be hurt by it." They could adopt "systems of apprenticeship" similar to "the most approved plans of gradual emancipation" and receive aid from the government. He then made the striking statement that if McClernand's "friends ... really wish to have peace upon the old terms" that predated the Proclamation, "they should act at once," for they could do so "with entire safety, so far as I am concerned." Evidently, convincing some rebels to rejoin the Union was more important to Lincoln at this point than freedom for those they enslaved.

Another proof that Lincoln's policies on freedom and race were evolving slowly came with the fact that he persisted in authorizing a dubious colonization scheme in 1863. At the end of 1862 Secretary of State Seward had blocked a proposal to colonize up to five hundred Black people on an island off the coast of Haiti. When new, more respectable backers came to the support of the scheme, Lincoln gave his authorization to move it forward, and 453 colonists landed on Île-à-Vache. Conditions there proved disastrous, and supplies for the colonists were inadequate. Many died, and in 1864 the US government had to carry most of the survivors back to the United States.

Lincoln's first plan for Reconstruction at the end of 1863 revealed his evolving priorities in relation to the Union and Black rights. He was aware of the demands of Frederick Douglass and other Black leaders for equal rights, and he appreciated the contribution that tens of thousands of formerly enslaved people were making toward saving the Union. But social progress for Black people would be anathema to defeated slaveholders. Lincoln again moved cautiously, possibly holding different strategies in his mind while waiting to gauge the impact of events. Bringing rebellious states back into the Union remained his priority.

In December 1863 Lincoln announced a Reconstruction plan that placed few demands on white southerners and offered limited benefits to newly freed southerners. It indicated that his policies toward Black Americans had not progressed far beyond emancipation, but Lincoln hoped his proposal would encourage some rebels to start the process of reunification. The "ten-percent plan," as it came to be called, offered amnesty to those who would swear an oath of future loyalty to the United States. High-ranking Confederate soldiers and officeholders were among those who could not take the oath, which also required acceptance of the recent laws and presidential proclamations referring to the enslaved, "so long and so far as not modified or declared void by decision of the Supreme Court." When 10 percent of the qualified voters in a rebellious state had taken the oath, they could organize a new state government with the minimum of necessary changes to the previous code of laws.

Beyond that, Lincoln declared that a new state government should recognize the formerly enslaved's "permanent freedom" and "provide for their education." Other "temporary arrangement[s]" recognizing Black people's "present condition as a laboring, landless, and homeless class, will not be objected to by the national executive." In other words, Lincoln would allow returning rebels to define the status of those they had oppressed people. He explained his reasoning to Congress. "It is hoped," he said, "that the already deeply afflicted people" in the rebel states "may be somewhat more ready to give up the cause of their affliction, if, to this extent, this vital matter be left to themselves." The "deeply afflicted people" were rebellious white southerners, although for the formerly enslaved this, too, was a "vital matter." Lincoln said no more than that the executive retained power "to prevent an abuse."

As was the case with the Preliminary Emancipation Proclamation, President Lincoln truly hoped that some southern white people would respond. He sent one of his personal secretaries and others into the occupied South with ledgers in which to record the names of all who would take the Amnesty Oath. The results were paltry and disappointing. The belief that considerable Union sentiment had existed, even after secession, was slowly surrendering to the fact of hostility or noncooperation. Lincoln also found that Congress had little taste for his plan. In the opinion of the congressional majority, and especially the Radical wing of the Republican Party, it was far too conciliatory toward the rebels and did far too little to protect the loyal Black population of the South. Among most northern voters, however, and Democrats especially, equal rights for Black people threatened white supremacy.

Racist realities demanded attention in 1864, despite evidence that what George Julian had called Lincoln's "education in anti-slavery" was accelerating. On the one hand, Lincoln had contact in the White House with a number of Black activists, both northerners who were agitating for equal rights and southern Black people who were leading the enslaved to freedom and undermining the Confederacy. The chief executive also visited "contraband" camps near the nation's capital and sometimes stopped in to appreciate the singing of those who had escaped from slavery. Lincoln's empathy and humane decency deepened his awareness of injustice and expanded his concern for African Americans. Although his actions still betrayed an interest in the idea of colonization, the prospects for such an idea were small and were fading. Lincoln began to think more profoundly about emancipation and postwar society. Before Republicans met in their convention in June 1864, he urged that the party platform demand a constitutional amendment to put a definitive end to slavery.

On the other hand, Lincoln and his Republican colleagues were also practical politicians who wanted to retain office in a northern electorate that was almost 100 percent white and predominantly racist. The rapid growth of war weariness in 1864 exacerbated their dilemma, for the war dragged on and the Confederacy appeared strong. General Ulysses S. Grant attacked Confederate troops in Virginia without pausing, but the costs in human lives were enormous. It was known that General William Tecumseh Sherman was in Georgia, invading the Confederate heartland, but for months little was heard, and there was no news of decisive progress. When newspaper editor Horace Greeley pressured Lincoln to explore peace with Confederate commissioners in Canada, across from Niagara Falls, Lincoln issued a statement. He said that he would meet with accredited representatives of the rebel government on the basis of "peace, the integrity of the whole Union, and the abandonment of slavery."

To many in the war-weary northern public, these were alarming words. Lincoln and the Republicans had always insisted that the war was fought to restore the Union. Emancipation was only a military measure to win the war, not a war aim in itself. Why, Democrats and others shrieked, was the president now making the possibility of peace and reunion hostage to the interests of Black people? Angry attacks on Lincoln showed that northerners still saw the war as a white person's war, a war for the benefit of white people. The reaction was so severe that Lincoln's advisers on every hand warned him that he was going to lose the election unless he did something to reverse the negative tide.

Under severe pressure and believing that he was going to lose the 1864 election, Lincoln backtracked or obfuscated. He devised a strategy that argued that he had *not* ruled out, and never had denied, that peace could be made on terms *less* than the abandonment of slavery. Lincoln refrained from issuing this statement himself, but his Republican allies and newspapers like the *New York Times* made the argument for him. The *Times*, for example, asserted that Lincoln "has *never* 'prescribed' that abandonment [of slavery] as a '*sine qua non*' of receiving or considering" propositions of peace. "Mr. Lincoln did say that he *would* receive and consider propositions for peace ... *if* they embraced the integrity of the Union *and* the abandonment of slavery. But he did not say that he would *not* receive them even if they embraced neither." Secretary of State Seward declared that once the rebels "laid down their arms, the war will instantly cease." Other questions then would be settled by "courts of law and . . . councils of legislation."

These were shocking and profoundly troubling statements for abolitionists and especially for Black leaders. Frederick Douglass, John Mercer Langston, Dr. John S. Rock, Reverend Henry Highland Garnet, George T. Downing, and others were meeting in Syracuse, New York, at the National Convention of Colored Men. Concluding that the Republican Party was still influenced by "contempt for the character and rights of the colored race," they protested that reelection was more important to Republicans than ending human bondage. It is "very evident," they angrily protested, "that the Republican party . . . is not prepared to make the abolition of slavery, in all the Rebel States, a consideration precedent to the re-establishment of the Union." They feared, and had reason to fear, that "our Republican Administration is not only ready to make peace with the Rebels, but to make peace with slavery also."

What saved Lincoln in the 1864 election was a military breakthrough. Sherman's army captured Atlanta, Georgia, on September 2, and it then was clear that Union victory was certain. The Confederacy would be defeated, Lincoln and the Republicans would triumph, and progress on emancipation and racism would become possible once more. At the beginning of November voters in Maryland approved a new state constitution that prohibited the practice of slavery. Not long after the election a convention in the state of Missouri voted overwhelmingly to abolish slavery there. Once again things seemed to be moving forward not only against slavery but, perhaps as well, against the entrenched forces of racism and white supremacy.

The events of 1864 had illustrated, however, that progress toward "all men are created equal" was difficult and fragile. The enormous war had sobered an overconfident North and convinced its lawmakers that many drastic, even revolutionary methods were necessary. Because the Union faced an existential crisis, that emergency generated a revolutionary dynamic—the same dynamic that Frederick Douglass had called "the logic of events." But outside that emergency the impulse toward progress and equality was weak. It was not robustly developed in the hearts and minds of the white majority. Decades of labor by Black and white abolitionists as well as the crisis of war had not been enough to resolve the conflict between American ideals of freedom, on the one hand, and slavery and white supremacy on the other. For greater progress, presidential leadership was necessary.

ABRAHAM LINCOLN began to confront that challenge to presidential leadership in the last months of his life. His decency and humane concern for individuals and for the nation forced him to reflect on the terrible price that the United States was paying for the sins of slavery and racism. He had always hated slavery and cherished the ideals of the Declaration of Independence. As he signed the Emancipation Proclamation, he remarked, "I never, in my life, felt more certain that I was doing right, than I do in signing this paper." During 1864 his understanding of the aspirations of Black Americans, and his empathy for them, had grown. With the approaching end to the war, his hopes leaped forward, and he began to dream of a nation not just reunited but redeemed. He began to call for forgiveness between enemies and justice for the oppressed—goals that were even more optimistic than they were idealistic, but ones that testified to his generous spirit and moral greatness.

As early as the spring of 1864 Lincoln's correspondence revealed a recognition that freedom, without rights, might be illusory. He prepared, in a quiet way, for the possibility of moving closer to the Radicals in his party. In March he wrote to Michael Hahn, the elected governor of the small, "ten-percent" government that had formed in Union-occupied parts of Louisiana. "I barely suggest for your private consideration," wrote Lincoln, "whether some of the colored people may not be let in" to the ballot. He specifically recommended consideration for "the very intelligent, and especially those who have fought gallantly in our ranks." In a famous phrase, Lincoln noted that he was making only a suggestion, but he believed that this step would help "to keep the jewel of liberty within the family of freedom." Nothing came of this private initiative.

The closing months of 1864, however, brought his instruction to place in the Republican platform a call for a constitutional amendment that would end slavery. Then, after his election, he discussed with some of the Radicals in his party the idea of requiring Black suffrage in southern states. As the year ended Lincoln worked hard to convince Congress to propose the Thirteenth Amendment prohibiting slavery and send it to the states for ratification. To the lame-duck legislators serving out their last weeks before a new Congress assembled, he argued for quick action. Approval was sure to come in March 1865, but it would strengthen the Union, he argued, for Congress to act now. With the assistance of his allies, and with various promises and inducements, enough Democrats in the House voted for the amendment, or refrained from voting, for it to gain the necessary two-thirds majority at the end of January 1865. The historic step of emancipation, begun in the emergency of war, was on its way to permanence within the Constitution.

Lincoln's Second Inaugural reinforced his call for systemic progress and reformation. Its language and cadence suggested a sermon, and its content called the nation to repentance and renewal. If God gave "this terrible war" to Americans because it was "His appointed time" to remove slavery, Lincoln said that God's judgment surely was "true and righteous altogether." That was true even if it meant that "all the wealth piled by the bond-man's two hundred fifty years of unrequited toil shall be sunk, and . . . every drop of blood drawn with the lash, shall be paid by another drawn by the sword." Then Lincoln called on his countrymen to turn away from conflict and hate, to "judge not that we be not judged," and to "achieve and cherish a just and lasting peace." Although his address did not specifically mention freed Black people, its call to act "with malice toward none; with charity for all" was all-encompassing.

The president's concern and empathy grew in March and April 1865 as he visited areas of Virginia that General Grant's army was occupying. His charity extended to soldiers whom he visited on the battlefield and to freed slaves who hailed him in Richmond, the Confederacy's capital. He returned from Virginia, wrote the historian David Donald, "with a new sense of urgency about reconstruction." He wanted a peace that "would ensure his war aims of Union, Emancipation, and at least limited Equality." Looking ahead, Lincoln was pleased that the adjournment of Congress would soon give him an unobstructed opportunity to begin Reconstruction, and he spoke about his hopes for Reconstruction in the final address of his life.

Just two days before John Wilkes Booth fired a bullet into his brain, Lincoln addressed a crowd of happy citizens who were celebrating the war's imminent conclusion. Lincoln told his audience that differing legal theories ought not to slow the process of bringing defeated southern states back into the Union. He defended the progress that his wartime government in Louisiana was making and urged building upon it rather than starting anew. But he recognized that some believed that in Louisiana and elsewhere "the elective franchise" should be given "to the colored man." Lincoln then declared, "I would myself prefer that it were now conferred on the very intelligent, and on those who serve our cause as soldiers." This was the president's first public call for voting rights for Black men, a crucial right that Black leaders and Black citizens, North and South, had been calling for throughout the war.

Lincoln's assassination makes it impossible to know what he might have accomplished in the Reconstruction years. The events of war had brought revolutionary progress that destroyed slavery. But racism and attitudes of white supremacy remained a formidable barrier to equality. It is certain that Lincoln would have employed his proven political talents toward reaching his goal of at least a limited Black suffrage. The likely resistance of southern white people might have given him leverage to make progress. Undoubtedly, he would have done far more than Andrew Johnson, his successor, ever contemplated. Lincoln was aware that many northerners had criticized him for moving too slowly, but he was proud of the progress that he had achieved and asserted that once he moved forward, he did not retreat. Candidate Lincoln, the supporter of slavery where it already existed, had mobilized the North against slavery's extension. President Lincoln, the cautious, centrist savior of the Union, became the liberator of almost four million enslaved people. The victorious Lincoln, in his final acts, pointed the way toward a better, greater society that had abolished slavery and could begin liberating itself from the evils of racism and white supremacy. With eyes set on a more just future, he wanted "free society" constantly to look to, labor for, and more closely attain the ideals of the Declaration of Independence.

Horace Greeley
AMERICAN ENTHUSIAST

~~~

For twenty years or more one newspaper editor became a household word, almost a celebrity, for millions of people in the North. Horace Greeley founded and built the *New-York Tribune*, which through a weekly edition achieved a large readership stretching from New England through the Midwest. Although the paper had a large staff, its editor liked to claim that he was the source of all its distinctive or influential viewpoints. Prominence did not make Horace Greeley inaccessible, however. He made frequent lecture tours throughout the North, and he also answered letters and dispensed advice to strangers. Bespectacled, he had an innocent, youthful face framed by curly whiskers below his chin. His trademark attire was a long white coat, a wide-brimmed hat with a high crown, and dusty boots, all of which reminded many of "Brother Jonathan," the stock fictional character whose image parodied early New England and eventually merged into Uncle Sam. The connection Greeley forged with many of his readers led people to call him Uncle Horace.

Before the Civil War, the middle decades of the nineteenth century were a dynamic, often buoyant time for the nation, and Horace Greeley was a man of his time. The United States was growing in population, economic activity, and geographic extent. Events often seemed to unfold at a dizzying pace, particularly in the North. Many newly arrived immigrants as well as many native-born Americans moved west, in accord with the advice usually attributed to Greeley: "Go West, young man." Farmers expanded their crops, new businesses sprang up, improvements in transportation pulled local economies into regional markets, and ambition fired the hopes of millions. Change could be unsettling, but as individuals adapted, they felt confidence in a better and brighter future. Such assurance gained enormous momentum from national pride, as Americans won a war with Mexico, carried their "Manifest Destiny" to the Pacific, and congratulated themselves for setting a God-ordained example of self-governance for the world. In this expanding, bustling society, many reform causes, even new religions, sprang up in hopes of making a laudable society even better. Horace Greeley's career unfolded in heady times, and he played the role of guide and cheerleader.

Greeley became influential because he embodied and expressed the energy, confidence, and enthusiasm of the years before the Civil War. He was a reflection and champion of the northern spirit in those decades. Horace Greeley was enthusiastic about America—proud of its growth and prosperity, optimistic about its future. He counseled ambition, hard work, virtue, and self-improvement, and he was personally an enthusiast for a variety of reforms, from Sylvester Graham's diet to cooperative utopian communities. In the 1850s his stirring prose played an important role in strengthening northern resistance to aggressions by the Slave Power.

But after 1860 his temperament revealed weaknesses that were both personal and societal. Greeley was a man who discerned serious problems but preferred to discount conflict and promote harmony. As a result, he was erratic—unreliable in a crisis and an inconstant guide to the future. His enthusiasm for American progress blotted out awareness of racial inequities and profound sectional differences. His abundant energy and indefatigable labors often ended in inconsistencies, shallow analysis, and an unjustified, blithe optimism. Like his countrymen, he wanted to "go ahead" in a time of progress. Assuming that harmony and unity would somehow prevail, Greeley ignored southern realities, minimized racism, and backed away from other reforms that he endorsed in theory. In his ambition and his haste to put difficulties in the past, he proved to be very American.

BORN IN New Hampshire in 1811, the young Horace Greeley loved reading newspapers and books and studied Caleb Bingham's *Columbian Orator* just as Frederick Douglass had done. He quickly gravitated toward the printing and newspaper business. At the age of fifteen he became an apprentice for a Vermont printer. Five years later he went to New York City to seek his fortune. There he found jobs working for printers and lived in one of Sylvester Graham's boardinghouses, where he met his future wife, Mary Young Cheney.

In 1833 the *New York Sun* began to achieve success as a penny daily, a cheap journal on smaller-size paper that entertained the workingman with colorful or scandalous local stories. This innovation attracted Greeley but also troubled his conservative, moralistic streak. There were too many shocking stories of crime, scandal, or "humbug," and he thought that newspapers should not be a "force for evil." He launched a daily paper that failed before publishing a weekly journal "of politics and intelligence" called the *New-Yorker*. But he still looked forward to founding a daily newspaper. Greeley decided that he could publish sensational stories, such as an account of the lurid murder of a prostitute, but give them a moralistic treatment that would better suit the expectations of respectable middle-class readers. In this way a newspaper could be "the guardian of public taste." This orientation to virtue and respectability was personal to him as well, for he categorically opposed divorce despite the fact that his own marriage was quite unhappy.

The *New-Yorker* never became a great success, but it attracted the attention of two leaders of the state's Whig Party—Thurlow Weed and William H. Seward. Greeley formed a close relationship with them that would last until nearly the Civil War. Greeley was ideologically a Whig, a believer in protective tariffs, internal improvements, and the American System of Henry Clay. He shared with Whig leaders a great confidence in the market economy and a future of free enterprise, growth, and social harmony. When the slavery issue flared up in the mid-1830s, he took positions that were progressive, but in the mildest sense—he viewed slavery as a blight that the southern public would eventually abandon, and he was harshly critical of abolitionists, including women, who, in his judgment, should not be forming antislavery societies. More important to Greeley's budding career was Thurlow Weed's proposal that the young, struggling editor edit a new campaign sheet designed to promote Seward for governor. With increased salary and extremely demanding working hours, he added that new assignment to his work at the *New-Yorker*. After Seward was elected, in 1840 Greeley headed another partisan paper, the *Log Cabin*, to boost the Whig candidate for president, William Henry Harrison. Patterns of frenzied work and Whig loyalty now characterized a rising editor whose *Log Cabin* had reached eighty thousand subscribers. In 1841 Greely was ready to pursue his personal goal and ambition. He launched the *New-York Tribune*.

The *Tribune*'s success in the next twenty years was a tribute to Horace Greeley's energy, journalistic insight, and skill in hiring staff. Early on he decided that a weekly edition could expand his readership, and it was through the weekly edition that thousands of people far from New York City became part of his readership. Greeley himself often wrote three columns per day. He also hired talented reporters and editors. Henry Raymond went on to become Greeley's rival as editor of the *New York Times*. Charles A. Dana became managing editor after several years, while Thomas McElrath effectively managed the growing paper's finances. The *Tribune* ran contributions from Henry David Thoreau, the Transcendentalist George Ripley, and intellectuals like George William Curtis, Margaret Fuller, and even Karl Marx (who initially was hired to cover the 1848 revolutions in Europe).

Intelligent book reviews and reprinted lectures enhanced the paper's content. Essayists, editorials, and reviews tended to emphasize morality, character, harmony, and paternalism. Greeley was realizing his desire to elevate and inform, and the *Tribune* became very influential, not just in New York City but also in small towns and rural areas throughout the North. One journalist described the respect it enjoyed as second only to the Bible. Clarence Darrow remembered that the paper "was the political and social Bible of our home." By 1850 the *Tribune* had the largest national circulation of any newspaper, with twenty-nine thousand subscribers and more than two hundred thousand readers. In 1853 it employed 183 persons, including thirteen editors and twenty foreign correspondents. By 1861 subscriptions reached forty-five thousand, and readership was probably more than three hundred thousand.

During the 1840s, as Greeley sought to be a "guardian of public taste," the *Tribune* spoke out in favor of a variety of reforms: temperance, the Graham diet, vegetarianism, agrarianism, land reform, and Fourier's association movement. But Greeley's agenda was one of moderate progress, not radicalism. Charles Fourier's theories of cooperative living involved revolutionary change to marriage and sexual relations, ideas that Greeley never mentioned and wholly rejected. He hoped merely that citizens might band together in cooperative enterprise, through shared labor or joint stock companies, in order to avoid class conflict. He gave some encouragement to the women's movement, speaking positively about the Seneca Falls Declaration and praising Margaret Fuller's book *Women in the Nineteenth Century* as an able assertion of "what are termed Women's Rights." But he viewed women's suffrage as unwise and felt it should not be "conceded" until a majority of women desired it. At times he described suffrage as a natural right, but he also contradicted himself, arguing that the right to vote could be restricted for many valid reasons. When tenants in upstate New York protested burdensome rents on land, he sympathized with their plight but opposed all violence. In his autobiography

Greeley described himself as "conservative by instinct, by tradition, and disinclined" to risk modest gains in search of larger goals. Harmony between the classes in America seemed to be a matter of faith with him, an inevitable part of American progress. Receptive to change, he didn't want it to go too far.

Soon the slavery issue brought undeniable conflict to national politics and forced Greeley to take some stands. He would become a leader of free-soil opinion during the 1850s, but he also showed some of the vacillations and contradictions that would subvert his influence during the Civil War and Reconstruction. Like most Whigs, he had opposed the war with Mexico, and he discerned in its promoters "a determination to uphold and fortify Slavery." The Wilmot Proviso, calling for the prohibition of slavery in any territory taken from Mexico, had his strong support, but soon he decided that the safest solution to conflict over the territories was to advocate "No Territory." Loyal to the Whigs, he opposed abolitionists and the Free Soil Party in 1848 and 1852. Yet he penned some powerful condemnations of human bondage. Slavery, he said, was in a "deadly feud" with "the conscience of mankind," and Congress had no more right to legalize slavery than to recognize cannibalism or "any other iniquity condemned by . . . the civilized and Christian world."

After the booming population of California demanded statehood, explosive controversies over slavery and the newly acquired territories became unavoidable. In 1850 Horace Greeley began by supporting Henry Clay's proposals for compromise. But after Stephen Douglas steered the somewhat amended proposals through Congress, Greeley reversed himself and denounced the compromise. He condemned it as "flagrant treachery" and "gross incompetency" because slavery was not explicitly barred from the lands taken from Mexico. Then, after Millard Fillmore, a New York Whig, replaced the deceased Zachary Taylor as president, Greeley contradicted himself, calling the compromise a "fair and equal" settlement of the questions dividing North and South. Worried that the Whigs would lose the 1852 presidential election, Greeley opposed the Free Soil Party. But he condemned the decision of the national Whig Party to accept the compromise as final, saying of that position, "We defy it, execrate it, spit upon it." He was inconsistent, but he had sensed that if the conflict over slavery's expansion intensified, many northern voters would abandon the Whigs to support the cause of free soil.

That was exactly what happened, with northern anger mounting first over the compromise's fugitive slave law. Greeley spoke out strongly, denouncing the law as unconstitutional, immoral, and "a criminal outrage upon the inalienable rights of man." Like many northern voters, he could not countenance reenslaving someone who had escaped from bondage. Violent resistance to the law, however, alarmed him, and instead he urged a peaceful process of trial by jury for fugitives. Then, in 1854, the Kansas-Nebraska Act aroused the North, gave birth to the Republican Party, and sealed the decline of the Whig organization. Greeley's editorial of June 1, 1854, echoed "The Appeal of the Independent Democrats." Douglas's law was "an act of deliberate bad faith," born of "sordid motives and threatening the most calamitous results." Greeley condemned the Kansas-Nebraska Act for throwing open to slavery "one million miles of Territory, heretofore shielded Forever from slavery." Douglas, he said, was a "lying little villain," a man of "impudent, brazen Sophistry," and Greeley called for "a desperate struggle of Freedom against Slavery." He endorsed calls for free-soil men to emigrate to Kansas, helped purchase a howitzer for the territory, and serialized in the *Tribune* an antislavery novel, *The Kansas Emigrants*, by abolitionist Lydia Maria Child. The "only policy," he believed, was to unite to "resist the aggressions of Slavery." Thus, through his journalistic and personal efforts he helped to launch the Republican Party. In fact, he suggested the name "Republican" as appropriate for a party that would champion liberty.

Through the rest of that decade, Greeley effectively, even eloquently voiced the positions of the new Republican Party. He explained that the Republicans were an antislavery party, not abolitionist—"defensive, not aggressive," he declared. Congress had no power to interfere with slavery in the states where it existed, but all remaining territories must be "consecrated to Free Labor and Free Men," and the Republican Party would assure that end. Greeley contrasted the "growing prosperity, universal education, and continual advancement" of the free-labor North with the "decay, dilapidation, sterility, ignorance, brutality, [and] pauperism" of southern slave society. His paper published "accounts of Negroes burned at the stake, of slave hunts and slave tortures." He criticized the slave system as "essentially, necessarily aggressive" and blasted the Democrats for supporting the "subjugation of Freedom."

Like many of the Republicans, however, and like the majority of northern white people, Greeley was hardly a champion of the interests of Black citizens. He viewed slavery as "far more fatal" to white people "than it ever could be" to Black people. That was a major reason why "we would fain see it swept out of existence." In the *Tribune* in 1855 he described

African Americans as "indolent, improvident, servile, and licentious," although he admitted there were individual exceptions. Two years later he modified his judgment rather modestly, saying that "there is no reason to believe that, if afforded fair play, the protection of the laws, and opportunities for industry and education, free Negroes might not make useful citizens." But clearly his concern was more for a liberty-loving nation and its white majority than for Black people. He even believed in 1856 that most white southerners favored a restoration of the 1820 Missouri Compromise line.

Greeley's attitudes toward the Irish were similar. He opposed the anti-immigrant Know-Nothings, or American Party, because ethnic or religious prejudice violated the basic principle of political equality. But his opinion of Irish Catholic newcomers was decidedly negative. "Our immigrant population is deplorably clannish, misguided, and prone to violence," he wrote. "Irish associations to influence elections, Irish clanship, Irish claims to office, are all wrong, and Irish browbeating and club-handing at the polls are atrocious." Foreigners who came to America needed to assimilate the Protestant, middle-class values that Greeley held, and these were, in his mind, essentially white attributes. Citing religion, Greeley also argued against divorce with Robert Dale Owen and Elizabeth Cady Stanton. The *Tribune*'s editor roundly condemned divorce as contrary to Christian doctrine and destructive of America's progress.

In 1856 John C. Frémont made a strong showing as the Republican Party's first nominee for president. Horace Greeley was encouraged and declared, "we have made a great beginning." Thereafter his newspaper helped the party grow by championing its policies and excoriating the Democrats. The evil Slave Power had captured the Democratic Party, Greeley warned, and Democratic officeholders were working to acquire countries to the south in order to spread slavery there. President Buchanan's support of the Lecompton Constitution for Kansas was another indefensible betrayal. In opposition to slavery's expansion Greeley recommended sending free-soil emigrants to Border States, such as Missouri or Virginia, so they could undermine slavery there. When the *Dred Scott* decision was announced, Greeley repudiated it as "entitled to just so much moral weight as would be the judgment of a majority of those congregated in any Washington barroom." The Supreme Court had made an "attack on the rights of human nature." After John Brown seized the federal armory at Harpers Ferry, Greeley denied that Republicans had any connection to the insane plan, but he defended the motives of Brown—a man who wanted to "deliver from bitter bondage and degradation those whom he had never seen." In memorable language Greeley predicted that "John Brown dead will live in millions of hearts." The staunch and vigorous support of the *Tribune* did much to make Republican victory possible in 1860. Abraham Lincoln had not been Greeley's first choice among Republican candidates for the presidency, but the *Tribune* had done much to build the Republican Party and to send Lincoln to the White House.

THE NEXT four years were torturous and difficult for Horace Greeley as well as for Abraham Lincoln. Greeley had hoped for a post in the cabinet or the Senate, and the crisis of war seemed to overwhelm him. His positions and recommendations shifted wildly, and at one point he suffered an attack of "brain fever," or what would now be called a nervous breakdown. Many began to question the wisdom of his counsels, and President Lincoln once asked, "What in the world is the matter with Uncle Horace?" Two factors explained Greeley's shocking inconsistencies during the war. Emotionally, he proved to be unstable in a crisis. Dangers unnerved him, and he overreacted to near-term events and was incapable of taking a long view amid uncertainty. Second, his desire for unity was such an article of faith for him that unpleasant facts could not negate it. He could convince himself that strong steps were necessary, but soon he would regret their consequences. The American enthusiast was adrift, tossed about in the storm of war.

In the weeks before Lincoln's inauguration southern states threatened secession, and some began taking legal steps to leave the Union. Horace Greeley's response was to let them "go in peace." He was not in favor of "coercive measures." He even wrote to Abraham Lincoln recommending that if seven or eight contiguous slave states wanted to leave the Union, the president should allow them to do so. But once six states actually declared that they were out of the Union, Greeley reversed direction and opposed any compromise. By April 1861 he had become more warlike, and after the firing on Fort Sumter he was as aggressive and bellicose as anyone.

The Union defeat at Bull Run in July 1861, however, unmanned Greeley. He was unable to sleep for seven days, and a bout with "brain fever" forced him to absent himself from the *Tribune* and from his role as oracle for six weeks. Believing that he saw "sullen, scowling, black despair" on every brow, he wrote what one historian called a "half-crazed" letter to Lincoln in which he urged peace "at once and on their [the Confederates'] own terms." Yet toward the end of 1861 Greeley changed and began to view the North's cause not as preservation of the Union but as ending slavery. To Gerrit Smith he confided that he felt himself to be an instrument of God for that purpose. Greeley praised General Frémont's declaration of emancipation in Missouri and criticized Lincoln for overruling it. In September 1861 he complained that the war would have been "triumphantly ended" within months if Lincoln had acted against slavery. The *Tribune* suggested Florida as a future home for the entire, freed Black population of the United States. He hoped emancipation might bring a sudden end to an enormously expensive war.

In the first half of 1862 Greeley continued to assert that if slavery were abolished, "there would be no reason for conflict among us." Ecstatic about Lincoln's call in March 1862 for compensated emancipation, he increased pressure on the chief executive by publishing in August "A Prayer of Twenty Millions." Claiming to speak for Republicans and loyal Unionists, Greeley charged Lincoln with being "strangely and disastrously remiss in the discharge of his duties" because he was not freeing slaves under Congress's Confiscation Act. Greeley demanded that the president "EXECUTE THE LAWS," ignore "fossil politicians," discard "timid counsels," and strike immediately at slavery. Lincoln replied, in a letter that became famous, that his "paramount object" was to save the Union, and therefore his actions on slavery would be in accord with that goal. The next month, when Lincoln acted, Greeley was not satisfied. He criticized the Preliminary Emancipation Proclamation as a limited and cautious measure.

Then a statement near the end of 1862 seemed to veer in the opposite direction. Although for months Greeley had emphasized the vital importance of emancipation, his *Tribune* suddenly declared that the North had always been ready for "a peace that would restore 'the Union as it was.'" Those five words summed up the Democratic Party's position, which Greeley now seemed to respect. The *Tribune*'s editor wanted emancipation, but he seemed to see it as a benefit for the nation more than for the enslaved. He described the nation's "black step-children" as "humble, ignorant, timid, distrustful.... They are not, let us frankly admit, the equals in prowess, capacity, or opportunity, of four millions of Whites," even though they are "human beings." At the same time that he welcomed emancipation, Greeley called on Lincoln to proclaim universal amnesty for southern rebels and to assume the Confederate debt.

Social progress, Greeley seemed to assume, would come easily despite the ingrained nature of slavery and racism. He claimed that Lincoln's

Emancipation Proclamation brought "a State sunk in the semi-barbarism of a medieval age to the light and civilization of the Nineteenth Christian Century." As if the South's transformation had been accomplished, he contacted the French ambassador and Clement Vallandigham, the Ohio Copperhead, in January 1863 to suggest that they arrange a mediation that would bring peace. When the war dragged on, Greeley again became despondent and said that disunion would not be the worst possible outcome for the conflict. Then another reversal of attitude came after the Union victories at Vicksburg and Gettysburg in July 1863. Buoyed for a while by this news, Greeley became supportive of President Lincoln for several months.

His positive mood did not last, however. In 1864 he joined an effort to prod several governors into jettisoning Abraham Lincoln as the Republican Party's nominee for reelection to the presidency. Salmon Chase, John C. Frémont, Ulysses S. Grant, or even Benjamin Butler seemed to Greeley to be superior candidates. Only when such efforts failed did the *Tribune*'s editor fall in line behind the party's renomination of the president. Then, in the summer of 1864, Greeley experienced another crisis. Grant's army was wearing down and depleting Robert E. Lee's Army of Northern Virginia. The battlefield losses were heavy, however, and they dismayed many in the northern public. Greeley panicked and lunged at any chance for peace. In a letter to Abraham Lincoln, Greeley reported a rumor that Confederate commissioners at Niagara Falls, Canada, had "full powers" to make peace. "Our bleeding, bankrupt, almost dying country," Greeley insisted, "longs for peace—shudders at the prospect of fresh conscriptions, of further wholesale devastations, and of new rivers of human blood." Moreover, he asserted that there was "a wide-spread conviction that the Government . . . are not anxious for Peace." That conviction, he warned, was "morally certain, unless removed," to damage Lincoln's hopes for reelection. Before closing, Greeley suggested that Lincoln did "not realize how intently the people desire" what he vaguely described as "any peace consistent with the national integrity and honor."

This letter was in essence a threat designed to force Lincoln to act lest the possibility of negotiations became known. But Lincoln had a far sounder grasp of two essentials: the course of the war, which was leading to Union victory; and the determination of Jefferson Davis to achieve independence. Taking advantage of the fact that Greeley had promoted contact with the Confederates in Canada, the president sent him to Niagara Falls to talk with them. As Lincoln expected, there was no delegation with "full powers" to make peace and no interest on the part of the Confederacy in returning to the Union. Greeley's initiative came to nothing. Instead, General William Tecumseh Sherman captured Atlanta, and Lincoln was reelected. Those events ensured that the "bleeding, bankrupt, almost dying country" would be reunited through a Union victory early in 1865.

As the war neared its end, Greeley impatiently envisioned a complete reconciliation between North and South. Late in 1864 he called for "Magnanimity in Triumph." Union victory should bring a peace with no treason trials, no executions, and a speedy reunion. Lincoln's Second Inaugural Address, famous for its invocation of "malice toward none . . . charity for all" and a "just and lasting peace" was neither peaceful nor conciliatory enough for the *Tribune*'s editor. He believed that the southern masses were loyal at heart and that nonslaveholders would quickly be "undeceived" about the reasons for the conflict. On the day after Lee surrendered at Appomattox, Greeley called for universal amnesty for Confederates. "The Southern mind is now open to kindness," he declared, "and may be magnetically affected by generosity." In this highly optimistic spirit, Greeley began to address the issues of Reconstruction, which embraced the meaning of freedom for the formerly enslaved as well as the steps toward reunion of North and South.

HORACE GREELEY'S actions in Reconstruction, stretching from 1865 to his death in 1872, again involved inconsistencies, retreats from principled stands, evasion of hard truths, and an unfounded, blithe optimism that all would turn out well. Ambition for public office, which almost always had been denied him, also influenced his course. Racial attitudes that were all too widely shared throughout the North exerted a quiet but effective force, making it easy for him to abandon policies that his intellect had identified as necessary. In the years of Reconstruction Horace Greeley traveled from supporting strong, necessary measures to yielding to the South's position on vital issues. The optimistic, conflict-averse Greeley made a transition from American enthusiast to negligent Pollyanna.

As Reconstruction began Greeley called for amnesty *and* equal rights, reunion *and* justice. On racial matters he seemed to be almost at one with the abolitionists and Radical Republicans who were insisting that those formerly enslaved must now enjoy their rights. Greeley counseled that reunion with the rebellious states should be withheld until there was evidence of a "manifest and rapid increase and diffusion of good will between Whites and Blacks at the South." He called on southern leaders to deal justly with the freed people. "There is no civilized country on earth," declared his *Tribune*, "whose constitution excluded Blacks, as such, from office or denies them the Right of Suffrage.... Four Millions of Americans ... shall not be doomed to hopeless, perpetual impotence and pupilage in the land of their nativity and the home of their affections," especially when "blacklegs" are allowed to vote. Even under impartial rules of qualified suffrage many southern Black people "*are* qualified, while others will make haste to be like them if properly encouraged."

Greeley's paper in 1865 presented a long list of reasons why Black suffrage was a right. The reasons included the following points: "1. Because they are human; 2. Because they are rational, accountable beings; 3. Because they are required to pay taxes and fight to uphold the Union ... ; 4. Because they are required to obey the laws, and punished, at least equally with the whites, whenever they break them; 5. Because it is proved that they can never be shielded from crying injustice and abuse unless they are enfranchised; 6. Because it is not *right* to tax away their money to educate white children, yet not let them send their own children to neighboring schools." He also pointed out that enfranchising the freedmen would make "several States preponderantly loyal," whereas denying them the ballot would leave all "political power in the hands of a caste preponderantly DISloyal." Greeley also scorned the idea that southern white men could represent the interests of Black southerners just as they represented the interests of their wives. Such "virtual" representation had been rejected in the American Revolution, and Greeley accurately noted that it was especially invalid for a people who were "shunned, despised, detested." Due to rebel "hate" and "persecution," it was essential to establish "Equal Rights for All" and make "the enfranchisement of the loyal Black ... the corner-stone of successful Reconstruction." In this same vein Greeley told a friend in 1866 that if, at the end of Reconstruction, "the negro [is] still a serf, we shall be a beaten, bankrupt party, and shall have richly deserved our fate."

Through part of 1866 Greeley's actions lived up to his words. He opposed President Andrew Johnson's vetoes of the Civil Rights bill and an extension of the Freedmen's Bureau and was glad that Congress overrode those vetoes. But another change of direction was soon forthcoming. Hopeful that New York's Republican Party might nominate him for the US Senate, Greeley editorialized that a policy of universal amnesty for rebels would be desirable even *without* a system of impartial suffrage that would enfranchise some Black men. That effort to broaden his appeal for a state race failed, however, to get him the nomination, and he returned to themes of reconciliation. In September 1866 he urged that three leading men from each section be invited to the White House for "free and friendly conference and discussion." He believed that such a conference could "find a common ground whereon the North and South should not merely be reconciled, but made ever more fraternal and harmonious." Belief in such "common ground" required a willful rejection of realities North and South. President Johnson felt no need for outside advice on his policies. He commented that Horace Greeley ran "to goodness of heart so much as to produce infirmity of mind."

In 1867 Greeley made additional, notable efforts to assuage the white South, while giving vulnerable Black people reason to wonder about his support. He called for the pardoning of Jefferson Davis and took action to make that happen—appearing before a court to give bond for the former Confederate president. Many northern newspapers roundly condemned this action and wondered about Greeley's motives. The Union League Club of New York City considered expelling him. Perhaps, said the rival *New York Times*, Greeley hungered for "notoriety" or some new "title to fame," but whatever his motive he was guilty of a "blunder" that "deserves almost as severe punishment as if it were a piece of sheer baseness." Greeley also spoke at the African Church in Richmond and delivered a decidedly mixed message. He criticized the Black Codes that were restricting the freed people and declared that the riots in southern cities during 1866 had proved that "guaranties for the rights of the colored people of the South" were necessary. If ignorant white people were allowed to vote, Greeley felt that ignorant Black people should have the ballot as well. But he also said that Black people "are and must remain, to some extent, a separate and peculiar people in the land." His view that their numerical importance would "steadily decline" suggested weakness in his commitment to them.

For a time, Greeley remained supportive of many significant Republican policies. He backed the Fourteenth and Fifteenth Amendments, the 1867 Military Reconstruction Act, and the impeachment of President Johnson. Greeley argued to his readers that the Republican Party was the guarantor of the nation's future. But he rejected the Radicals' call for confiscation of land from the former large slaveholders. Instead, he urged making public lands available to the freedmen at favorable prices. Where Radicals saw the need for stronger measures, Greeley began to move in the opposite direction. He declared that there should be no preferential treatment of the formerly enslaved, and in 1868 he predicted that Ku Klux Klan violence would soon die out. Indeed, as the outrages of the Ku Klux Klan increased, Greeley's response was to call again for universal amnesty. His insight that rebel "hate" made "Equal Rights" and Black suffrage necessary had been forgotten.

As Reconstruction continued, Greeley showed greater concern for southern white people than for Black southerners. In 1869 he wrote: "The Colored People of this country are called to evince eminent Self-Reliance. They must trust God and help each other, asking of the Whites naked justice, and that only." In harsher tones, a *Tribune* editorial declared: "If negroes will not work, they must starve or steal. And, if they steal, they must be shut up, like other thieves." Any freed Black people who assume that they "can live in comfort without work, . . . have now entered a school" where "they will certainly and speedily be taught better." Too much government aid for African Americans would be "pernicious" and "certain to injure those [it] intended to benefit." Greeley now declared his opposition to the Freedmen's Bureau and "all manner of coddling devices." The "negroes [should] take care of themselves."

When the Fifteenth Amendment was ratified early in 1870, Greeley seemed to feel that a new day had dawned, with impartial suffrage guaranteed thereafter. Black men in the South would have access to the ballot, and as a result all the needs of the freed people were satisfied. He seemed unable to imagine the ways in which their right to suffrage could be nullified. Clearly, Greeley had grown more indifferent to the challenges they faced. That year he referred to Black people as "an easy, worthless race, taking no thought for to-morrow." In 1871 Robert Brown Elliott, the Black congressman from South Carolina, called attention to a rising tide of Ku Klux Klan violence and, under these conditions, condemned the idea of amnesty for former rebels. Promptly the *Tribune* blasted Elliott for doing "his race lasting harm." Many white people, the newspaper said in unjustified alarm, would take Elliott's words as proof that Black people's claims of goodwill and kindly feeling were a lie. White citizens would conclude, "Only give them [the Black people] power, and they would disfranchise all who are not Black." This editorial went on to make the false claim that Klan violence was the work of "wild youngsters" acting out of resentment over the political restrictions on their social betters. Congressman Elliott responded that the *Tribune* was defending "masked murderers," Klansmen who were "living realities, who show no mercy."

Elliott's words had no effect on Greeley, who continued to believe, against the evidence, that harmony and cooperation were within reach.

He asked the South's natural leaders to "call the ablest, most intelligent Blacks around [them]" and to "inspire the negro to work, and plan, and save, by proffering the Right of Suffrage to all who shall prove worthy of it and capable of exercising it intelligently, safely, and usefully." To Greeley "mutual kindness and trust" could prevail between the races and between the propertied and the landless. Like many conservatives in the North, he had decided that the South needed the influence of traditional white leadership. A failed bid by Greeley to obtain the nomination for governor of New York intensified his ambition but did not change his opinions.

Greeley's vanishing concern for the formerly enslaved and increasing sympathy with former rebels were expressive of trends within the North. Just as his powerful editorials in the 1850s had mirrored and encouraged the North's growing support for the Republican Party, his attitudes now reflected the reality that a long-prejudiced public was tiring of the quest for racial justice. In the deadly crisis of civil war, events had pushed northerners toward revolutionary measures and viewpoints. Necessity had convinced a majority to take unexpected steps demanded by the emergency. But the feeling of revolutionary change and progress faded. After the war, mundane concerns, personal priorities, and deep-rooted prejudices steadily became more prominent. The North was losing its determination to win the peace or democratize the South, and the ever-popular and ambitious Horace Greeley was leading the way.

In 1871 Greeley undertook a speaking trip through the South. His motive was to enhance his political position with white southerners and northern opponents of Radical Reconstruction, as well as to promote harmony and sectional unity. Traveling from New Orleans into Texas and then along the Mississippi River, he stopped at many towns and cities. Farming, which he claimed to love, was his supposed subject, but he had more to say about Reconstruction and reunion. He told southerners that goodwill toward the former rebel states was growing in the North. "The general sentiment of the North," he claimed, was to "let bygones be bygones." He regretted the treatment white southerners had received and told audiences that the Ku Klux Klan would never have appeared had there been an immediate amnesty. A good many southern newspapers welcomed his comments and spoke well of him. But at one Louisiana plantation, where Greeley complimented enlightened former slaveholders, a Black listener concluded that Greeley was the "whitest man in America."

Meanwhile, back in New York City, his staff at the *Tribune* added words of regret that "the most intelligent, the influential, the educated, the really useful men of the South"—elite white people, that is—had been deprived of power. As a result, "rascally foreign adventurers" and "the ignorant class, which only yesterday hoed the fields and served in the kitchen," were taxing and swindling the southern people. This was precisely the interpretation that leaders of the white South were presenting about Reconstruction. After finishing his tour, Greeley published a book that credited the South with being ready to embrace the nation once more, despite the "idleness and improvidence" of former slaves. His comments about reconciliation and "local control" surely encouraged racist white southerners.

On his return to New York City Greeley addressed a gathering in his honor and signaled that he was available for higher office. He was, after all, an ambitious man in an age of ambition. "I shall never decline any nomination that has not been offered to me," he coyly remarked. Saying that the purpose of his trip had been to "promote clearer understanding," he made the preposterous assertion that if a "representative Northern man could have traversed the South . . . and openly asserted the convictions of the North," the "terrible Civil War might have been averted." Greeley's campaign for the presidency was now underway.

A strange coalition of disparate interests was beginning to come together in support of a candidate like Greeley who would promote reconciliation and amnesty. A significant fraction of the Republican Party was disillusioned with President Ulysses S. Grant and the corruption that had blossomed in his administration. Many of these men came from old elites who were out of power and resentful of patronage politics. Ironically, they were devotees of free trade rather than the protective tariffs that Greeley always had advocated, most recently in a four-hundred-page book published in 1870. Other white Republicans and conservative business interests saw Reconstruction in the South as a chaotic mess and wanted to resume commercial and political ties with former elites. Members of the anti-Grant faction called themselves Liberal Republicans and emphasized civil service reform, an end to corruption, and magnanimity toward the South in addition to free trade.

Horace Greeley proved ready to accept an evasion on his principled opposition to free trade if the Liberal Republicans would accept him. When the Liberal Republicans met in Cincinnati, opponents of Greeley found themselves outmaneuvered, and Greeley readily accepted a platform that avoided a clear position on tariffs. The party's platform left its position on free trade or tariffs up to local units, thus avoiding open disagreement. After braving some criticism, Greeley accepted the

Liberal Republicans' nomination and resigned his editorship in order to campaign. He called for America's "long-estranged people" to "reunite and fraternize." His reiteration of the motto "Universal Amnesty and Impartial Suffrage" lost much of its meaning when he also promised to restore "local self-government." Less than two months later the Democrats held their convention and reluctantly swallowed the *Tribune*'s editor and founding Republican as their best chance to defeat Grant. Although Greeley had devoted all of his career to savaging the Democrats, he now welcomed "a genuine New Departure from outworn feuds" and a new day of "Progress and Reform."

From the start there was abundant and well-aimed criticism of the Liberal Republican/Democratic nominee, whose record displeased a variety of voting blocs. It also was easy to put a spotlight on all the contradictions in Greeley's previous statements and positions. Many who had launched the Liberal Republican movement recognized that he was not truly a believer in their core principles. He had not been enthusiastic even about civil service reform. Republican voters, if they were to support Greeley, would have to forgive the way he had forgotten all the party's trials during the Civil War, his warmth toward recalcitrant rebels, and his payment of Jefferson Davis's bail. The freedmen's prospects under a Greeley presidency seemed grim. Benjamin Butler provided a blunt summary of that point for Republicans: "Go vote to burn school houses, desecrate churches and violate women, or vote for Horace Greeley, which means the same thing." Abolitionists called Greeley a "turncoat & traitor." When people asked Frederick Douglass if he was going to desert Horace Greeley, his response was, "No, but Horace Greeley has deserted us." Thomas Nast, the popular cartoonist for *Harper's Weekly*, penned many devilishly effective anti-Greeley cartoons. To win the votes of Democratic voters, whom Greeley had always denounced, scorned, and described as "lewd, ruffianly, criminal and dangerous," was another major challenge. The candidate faced such an uphill battle that he suffered another spell of "brain fever" and spent most of the campaign on his Chappaqua farm, where his wife was seriously ill. After discouraging early returns arrived, he made a demanding, exhausting tour through New Jersey, Pennsylvania, Ohio, Kentucky, and Indiana, appealing for a "common platform of American Nationality."

The results were not a surprise. Grant won in a landslide, as Horace Greeley received less than 44 percent of the popular vote and carried only six states, all of which had formerly allowed slavery. In the North hundreds of thousands of Democrats voted for their party's candidates for state offices but withheld their support from Greeley, the Democrats' longtime opponent. Shattered and despondent, the defeated candidate went back to his farm at Chappaqua, where soon he joined his wife in death.

Horace Greeley's desire for harmony and unity had collided with harsh realities. Union victory had not erased all the conflicts between North and South. National unity and fraternity were an illusion, as divisions in the country over Reconstruction remained deep and enduring, with a legacy that extended far into the twentieth century. Nevertheless, the fact that he had gained the nomination, aided by the views on race and Reconstruction that he had expressed, revealed important facts about the American public.

During the presidential campaign, Greeley's supporters had touted him as a representative man, the American who could realize through his leadership the feelings and desires of the population. They presented him as the archetype of a hardworking, virtuous American who patriotically believed in the nation's unity, progress, and bright future. His leadership was supposed to reunite the country and restore harmony. That proved not to be a convincing argument, as the failure of Greeley's candidacy demonstrated.

But in some ways Horace Greeley *was* representative of major attitudes, forces, and trends in American life. He was ambitious, always eager to succeed, and though he worked hard, he also was willing to put success ahead of firm adherence to principle. Greeley was patriotic, but so eager to believe in national greatness and promise that he did not face squarely some of society's defects. Such optimism became blindness. For him and others it proved easier to look past deep conflicts and assume that problems would disappear. Like most white people, he embraced racist ideas, and even when aroused to consider justice for African Americans, his concern for their plight proved modest and easily overridden by other interests.

Moreover, Greeley's accommodation to the views of former slaveholders and rebels reflected the waning of support for Reconstruction. During the Civil War many northern Democrats had defended slaveholders' right to enslave Black people and had criticized the war as unnecessary. Even among Republicans there were many officeholders and voters who were deeply racist and saw little place for African Americans in the nation's future. Fortunately, as the Civil War and Reconstruction unfolded, growing numbers of citizens awoke to the humanity and rights of those who had been enslaved. But for all too many the "traitors" and "rebels" who had seceded and caused a bloody, destructive war quickly became, in peace, "our southern brethren" or "our erring sister states" once more. More than four million African Americans, loyal to the Union and ready to contribute to democracy, somehow did not count as part of "we the people." For Horace Greeley and for millions of other Americans, the ties of race and the traditions of white supremacy were more powerful than the nation's founding principle of equality.

Albion Tourgée

Civil War as a Sustained Clash of Cultures

~

Most of the men who fought in the Civil War were young. Albion Tourgée, born in 1838, was representative not only of them but also of many of the cultural forces behind the conflict. He sprang from elements of northern society that had been deeply touched by currents of reform. He also embodied a conviction that crystallized during the war for a minority of northerners. Individuals like him drew inspiration from a revolutionary momentum that developed as the Union fought for its existence. The racial progress achieved during the war convinced Tourgée and others that preservation of the Union was not enough, that military victory must produce a better, reformed nation. American democracy required not just the abolition of slavery but the abolition of racial prejudice and white supremacy as well. Union victory should mean equal rights for all and color-blind justice under the law in a nation that lived up to its democratic ideals.

The pursuit of equal rights and color-blind justice became the central theme of Albion Tourgée's contentious life. He was not a mild-mannered person; his personality was neither hesitant nor half-hearted. Confrontation was often more characteristic of him than congeniality. He proved to be a bold, assertive, and fearless advocate for democratic values and racial equality, and he practiced his convictions in hostile territory, against belligerent opponents, and through decades of unfavorable social change. His life reflected the dangers faced by northern reformers in the postwar South as well as the subsequent discouraging struggle against northern society's retreat from Reconstruction and equality. For racism was endemic among a large portion of the North's population, and citizens like

Tourgée were a minority. Still, with energy and unflagging determination, Tourgée advanced democratic ideals through his careers in politics, law, and literature.

As an activist Tourgée influenced Reconstruction politics, and as a novelist he laid bare the depths of the nation's racial problem and the reasons for the failure of Reconstruction. He experienced success as well as failure and made many southern enemies and numerous Black friends and allies. As a writer, editor, and columnist he never stopped challenging the Republican Party to address its unfinished agenda. Through his fiction and nonfiction writing he called on members of his race to practice equality, discard racist theories, and resist the influences of the Gilded Age and social Darwinism. Through his literary and journalistic efforts, he bridged the color line more fully than virtually any influential white man in the final twenty years of the century. Despite achievements during his lifetime, his record and example in unsuccessful efforts would prove most important for the future. Often his fate was to struggle against the tide. Nevertheless, his legal arguments in the *Plessy v. Ferguson* case of 1896 left a record to which the United States would repair in its slow progress against racism.

DIVERGING SOCIETAL cultures were a major cause of the Civil War, because culture exerts a powerful and persistent, if sometimes unnoticed, influence. The opinions and beliefs of individuals never arise in a vacuum—they are deeply influenced by the values and conventions of society. In the decades before the Civil War, the economies and social systems of North and South moved steadily apart, and diverging economies and cultures led to conflict. Whereas in the South booming profits from cotton created southern aristocrats like Jefferson Davis and entrenched slavery as a core institution, many northern communities experienced quickened commerce, widespread prosperity, and discussion of egalitarian social reform. Albion Tourgée spent his youth in one of the regions of the North most receptive to reformist ideas.

The Western Reserve, that area of northern Ohio that once had been called Connecticut's Western Reserve, consisted of a dozen or so counties, including some that bordered Lake Erie. Settlers from New England had brought their values to the area, leading many to label it the "last footprint of Puritanism." It resembled New England in its distribution of small farms and towns, in its religious activism, and in an openness to vigorous democratic discussion. More than many other parts of the North, the Western Reserve had been affected by the revivalism of the Second Great Awakening. Many viewed it as an extension of the "burned-over district," and as one historian has put it, the area "was a veritable cauldron of radicalism on political, religious, and social issues." Politics in Ohio divided between the reformist north, with antislavery centers such as Oberlin, and the conservative south, where early settlers had arrived from slaveholding Virginia or Kentucky.

Albion Tourgée's hometown in Ashtabula County was one site where runaway slaves on their journey to Canada received welcome and assistance. A little farther west, in Oberlin, aroused citizens of both races prevented the capture of a person fleeing from slavery in 1858. In the aftermath of their actions, the federal government indicted thirty-seven individuals for resistance to the fugitive slave law. Enormous publicity and controversy surrounded the subsequent trial and further radicalized opinion. Only two of the defendants received prison sentences, and those were rather short. Legal action against the remaining thirty-five was dropped. But antislavery activism was only one of many reform causes that found support in the area.

The great majority of the Western Reserve's residents enjoyed substantial economic equality, and there was a vigorous democratic atmosphere that encouraged religious toleration and public education. Temperance, prison reform, educational reform, and women's rights were among the variety of reform movements that attracted attention. Thus, Tourgée grew up in an area where discussion of society's structure and its future was the political birthright of every citizen and where participation in democratic decision-making was encouraged. The local culture schooled him in love for democracy and hostility toward inequality. Not long after the war ended, he recalled that "The Reserve never knew an Aristocracy." Its democratic openness contradicted the South's aristocratic practices, which many northerners believed were a fundamental cause of sectional conflict. On another occasion he described the Western Reserve as a "synonym for intelligence and freedom of thought."

It was this atmosphere of equality and open democratic participation that first motivated Albion Tourgée. He had a strong idealistic but independent streak in his character, suggested, for example, by the fact that he frequently attended church services but aligned himself with no one denomination. Persistent conflict with his father also inclined him to an outspoken individualism. When the young woman whom he loved and later married, Emma Kilbourne, urged him to try to charm and cultivate her parents, he replied, "I would not sail under false colors, or win love by false pretenses." He was fortunate to receive a good education and showed an interest in writing while he attended the University of Rochester.

With the outbreak of war, Tourgée cut his education short and volunteered for the army. In service he suffered physical injury but gained a new awareness of the wrongs of slavery and the potential of African Americans. After fighting at the Battle of Bull Run, he was disabled during the Union retreat when the wheel of a gun carriage ran up against his back. Serious damage to his spine left his legs paralyzed for months, and in August 1861 the army declared him unfit for duty. Tourgée then tried to work as a recruiter and studied law on the side. One year later he had recovered almost full use of his legs, although recurrent problems with his back plagued him at times throughout his life. He reenlisted and joined his local Ohio unit, which had been sent to Kentucky to form part of the Army of the Cumberland.

On the march to Frankfort, the tired and heavily laden soldiers encountered scores of enslaved people in Kentucky who were eager to help the Union cause and its army. The men brought water or food and insisted on carrying the soldiers' knapsacks or equipment. The weary troops gladly accepted this help and became acquainted with the Black men who stayed with them to be of service. Tourgée became friendly with "our faithful Negro man" and noted how devoted the enslaved people were to the Union cause. In Kentucky Tourgée also had occasion to see some of the punishments and cruelties of slavery. Within a few months he wrote to his fiancée that he was "sick at heart" over realities of slavery that made his "blood boil!" The policy of the US government also outraged him, since commanders in the slaveholding but Union state of Kentucky ordered their troops to return to bondage those who escaped from slavery. His fellow soldiers and several of the officers resisted these orders, sometimes with success. These experiences prompted Albion Tourgée to apply to lead Black troops. Although he never received that assignment, a dedication to Black equality joined his ingrained belief in democracy and opposition to aristocracy.

In January 1863 Tourgée was captured and sent to Libby Prison in Richmond. After being released he rejoined the army and participated in resistance to what he felt was the "tyranny" of military discipline. His back problems reemerged on long marches, however, and rather than go into the invalid corps, Lieutenant Tourgée resigned his commission. Back in Ohio he found himself at loose ends, and even marriage could not supply him with a sufficient sense of purpose. He tried practicing law and teaching, but with the end of the war he considered the possibility of moving to the defeated South. After learning that William Holden, the provisional governor of North Carolina, was encouraging northern immigration, Tourgée investigated that possibility. He even managed to meet with Holden and in August 1865 moved to Greensboro in the Tar Heel State. There his career began as a tireless advocate of racial equality, as a political activist, and as a writer.

IN NORTH CAROLINA the culture of the Western Reserve and the culture of a conservative, tradition-bound, slaveholding society collided. Naively certain of the superiority of his New England–inspired values, Tourgée acted on them without hesitation. Always outspoken and assertive, he promptly found himself in public confrontations with antidemocratic attitudes and the local power structure. Along with members of his wife's family and two fraternity brothers from college, he purchased land from a local Quaker and established the West Green Nursery. As workers he hired local Black people at favorable wages and arranged to sell land to some of them on time. He also helped a woodworking factory with many Black employees find new markets for its products. In addition, he and his wife opened a school for the freed people, invited Black people to dine with them in their home, and even adopted a formerly enslaved child.

All these actions, though proper and commendable in Tourgée's eyes, were outrageous and offensive to most white North Carolinians and especially to the elite who controlled government. Officials of the Freedmen's Bureau reported "an almost universal determination expressed to make [the Negroes] politically and socially an inferior and degraded caste." Many white people insisted that corporal punishment was essential to the labor system, and others spoke of extermination of the Black race. Jonathan Worth, elected governor under Andrew Johnson's plan of Reconstruction, declared of equality, "This will not be tolerated."

Energetic and active, eager to advance American democracy to a fuller realization, Tourgée quickly involved himself in politics. In 1866 he headed the North Carolina delegation to an anti-Johnson convention of Southern Unionists in Philadelphia. Speaking there he assailed rebel aristocracy and serfdom and defended the "American birth right of impartial suffrage and equality before the law." That fall he campaigned in North Carolina for candidates of the newly formed state Republican Party. The local Quaker community, including some who had aided the

Underground Railroad, was often supportive, but Tourgée's manner of acting and expressing himself shocked many. Robert Dick, a man who would become a Republican ally, initially thought that Tourgée was "crazy" or "a bad man." Opponents listened to his public oratory "in speechless disgust" and believed he was making himself "the most hated man" in the community. But, ironically, Tourgée's assertive manner, boldly calling attention to himself and his views, echoed the masculine belligerence common to the southern leadership style. As a result, the same man who was shocked and disgusted said, "I couldn't help admiring the persistence and pluck of the little devil."

What Tourgée experienced as an immigrant to North Carolina translated directly into characteristic scenes in the two novels that he published immediately after leaving the South. In *A Fool's Errand, By One of the Fools*, which would appear in 1879, the main character, army veteran Comfort Servosse, attends a public meeting early in Reconstruction. Called upon to speak because some local white people thought he might be a "spy . . . sent down here . . . to assist in overturning our institutions," Servosse at first establishes his independence by "coolly" refusing to cooperate or be intimidated. But after winning the "admiration" of the crowd, he readily instructs the audience about some unwelcome truths. In regard to questions such as allowing the freedman's testimony in the courts, he asserts, "The logic of events has settled these things." The Black man "was allowed to testify on the battle-field, and will be allowed to testify in courts of justice." To white southerners who declared that they "would never submit to 'nigger suffrage,'" he explained that they had "nothing to do" with that issue. Although "not yet recorded in the statute-books," Servosse baldly predicted that "it is in the book of fate. . . . If you will give the elective franchise to every colored man who owns a hundred dollars' worth of real estate, and every one who can read and write, the nation will be satisfied. Refuse, and all will be enfranchised without regard to your wishes or your fears." The plucky, confrontational Servosse, like Tourgée himself, even seized the occasion to make fun of a local braggart who exaggerated his accomplishments.

Similarly, in *Bricks without Straw*, which would appear in 1880, local white people echoed Governor Worth's determined hostility to equality. They described the principal Black character, Nimbus Ware, as an "industrious, thrifty, and honest" man destined for "trouble." Nimbus Ware was "too sassy . . . he ain't respectful," says a local man. He "talks as independent as if he was a white man," and "our people won't stand a nigger's puttin' on such airs." Another offense was that Ware owned "a good house, and a terbacker-barn . . . and stock, and one of the finest crops of terbacker in the county." He was "better fixed up than lots of white men in the county," and such violations of slavery's caste system were not permissible, explained the sheriff. "If they were all like him, a white man couldn't live in the country. . . . [W]e'd have to kill the last one of 'em to have any peace."

Fighting against these attitudes, Tourgée won election in 1867 as a delegate to the constitutional convention that Congress required after it took control of Reconstruction policy. There his principles and his energetic, even bellicose advocacy gave him a prominent role. Tourgée fought for equal civil and political rights for all, abolition of property qualifications, elections for all offices, public schools, and reform of the criminal code, which still allowed public whippings. True to his taste for open debate and argument, he also backed opportunities for the outnumbered white conservatives to voice their opposition to "dangerous innovations." In fact, he relished the chance to contest their arguments for white supremacy and racial distinctions. For example, when they demanded the exclusion of Black people from holding any executive office, Tourgée demanded to know why white people would want to single out a group with whom they had so often mixed their blood.

Given Congress's Reconstruction program and the progressive majority in the convention, Tourgée helped to bring about a real democratic revolution to North Carolina's politics. Traditionally the state had enforced property qualifications for office, had until 1857 kept roughly half the white men in the state from voting for their state senator, and had relied on a system of local government that was controlled by members of the elite who were appointed for life. In contrast to that, the new constitution did away with property qualifications for holding office, established a democratic system of elected county commissions, reformed the criminal code, and expanded the rudimentary system of public education. In much of the state, especially in piedmont counties where Black people were a sizeable minority of the population, these changes attracted biracial electoral majorities that included many white voters. Virtually all Black voters favored the Republicans, and more than 30 or 40 percent of the eligible white people voted with them. People of both races who long had felt shut out of opportunity now became active, as local governments involved scores of citizens in surveying the need for more schoolhouses or other civic improvements. These changes were essentially revolutionary in what had been a reactionary, elite-dominated social system. A culture of open democracy, equal rights, and more equal opportunities confronted its opposite, and local officials lost the positions of power that had been theirs for decades.

The violent reaction was not slow in coming. In 1868 Ku Klux Klan violence erupted in the Tar Heel State, and especially in the piedmont counties where Tourgée worked. There the margins of victory for Republicans were small, so that violence against and intimidation of Black and white voters could return power to the Conservatives (or Democrats, as they soon called themselves). Local elites who had controlled the old county court governments, often for decades, became the leaders and organizers of the Klan. They were able to recruit many, though not all, of the lower-class white people who objected to the loss of white supremacy as racist norms were challenged. Soon violence became common across the middle of the state as Republicans of both races were threatened and attacked. Between 1868 and 1872 the Klan's reign of terror accounted for at least one or two hundred whippings in Rutherford County alone, and many more in a dozen counties across the piedmont. Klansmen snatched Republicans from their houses at night, beat, stabbed, or killed them, and attacked symbols of Black progress. Schoolhouses and churches for Black people were burned, and newly acquired property was threatened or destroyed.

Among the scores of murders, there were two that directly affected Albion Tourgée because he was close to the victims. The Klan kidnapped Wyatt Outlaw, a local Black leader, and hung him from a tree near the Alamance County Courthouse. John Stephens, a white leader and Republican state senator, met his fate in nearby Caswell County. Albion Tourgée called for federal action against the Klan's violence. He wrote to the state's Republican US senator, Joseph Abbott, saying that Stephens had bravely stood by his constituents though "warned of danger." Tourgée declared that "any member of Congress who ... does not support, advocate, and urge immediate, active, and thorough measures to put an end to these outrages ... deserves to be damned."

Tourgée himself expected to "be one of [the Klan's] next victims," for "my steps have been dogged for months." His lobbying of Congress helped secure passage of the 1871 Ku Klux Klan Act, and he also traveled to Washington to consult with investigators about the Klan. But national leaders whom he later satirized as the "wise men" were not willing to mount or sustain the major effort that would have been necessary to safeguard the freed people and their Republican allies in the South. Comfort Servosse in *A Fool's Errand* commented that the North's Republican leaders left newly freed, uneducated, and propertyless people defenseless against the "hate" of white neighbors who monopolized "the wealth, the intelligence, [and] the organizing skill" of the South. There were too few Republicans who shared Tourgée's convictions, and racism and white supremacy remained strong among much of the northern electorate.

Tourgée courageously resisted the Klan, standing guard at times to defend local Republicans. In 1868 he won election to a superior court judgeship, and he not only refused to suspend court under threats but confronted hostile juries in actions against Klansmen. His courage and impartial application of the law won him respect, as did his important work on a three-man commission to revise the state's civil code. Always active and energetic against aristocratic and racist forces, he briefly published a newspaper and continued fighting for equality. He never retreated from the stand he had taken soon after his arrival in North Carolina—that "there is no color before the law." But Democrats steadily regained power in North Carolina during the 1870s. After Tourgée's judgeship ended in 1874, he managed to support himself as a federal pension officer while writing political articles for his Republican allies. But it was clear that Reconstruction was ending, as the North abandoned efforts to change the South's culture. In the elections of 1878 Tourgée lost a doomed attempt to win a seat in Congress. After his wife and child returned to the North, he fought depression and forced himself to complete writing projects, which included *A Fool's Errand*. Then he, too, left North Carolina.

TOURGÉE DID not expect a great success for *A Fool's Errand*, but the book became a publishing sensation in 1879 and 1880. Within six months it had sold more than 43,000 copies, and within a year sales reached 150,000. Tourgée quickly followed up on that success with *Bricks without Straw* in 1880, and it, too, had a favorable reception. His long postwar career as a writer was off to a good start. Many other novels and essays would follow, and in 1883 Tourgée launched a high-quality magazine called *Our Continent*, for which he wrote in addition to commissioning many well-respected contributors. Unfortunately, this effort may have been ahead of its time, since publications like it became very popular within a decade or so. For Tourgée, the magazine's failure in 1884 was a serious financial blow. But he kept writing and never abandoned his political activism.

In 1880 he had come close to having a major impact on national policy. Tourgée knew and was friendly with Ohio's James Garfield, who won the Republican Party's nomination for president that year. Tourgée campaigned energetically for the party, and his writings and his previous novels helped Garfield to victory. Tourgée also shared with Garfield his ideas on how to overcome the failure of Reconstruction. At the end of *A Fool's Errand* his protagonist, Comfort Servosse, had admitted that Reconstruction was a failure, even if it had advanced the claim for "the universality of manhood." The North and South remained "two distinct, hostile, and irreconcilable ideas—two civilizations" locked in conflict. For serfdom to end and liberty to triumph, said Servosse, the nation must "educate those whom it made ignorant, and protect those whom it made weak.... Make the spelling-book the scepter of national power. Let the Nation educate the colored man and the poor-white man *because* the Nation held them in bondage, and is responsible for their education; educate the Voter *because* the nation can not afford that he should be ignorant." The novel suggested that education was the essential, if long-term, solution to the clash of freedom-loving and slaveholding cultures in the United States.

In 1880 Tourgée developed these ideas in conversation with James Garfield and presented them to a wider public in 1881 in the *North American Review*. In that article he argued that Garfield's nomination had coincided auspiciously with "a new idea," the notion that "the general government—the American nation or the American people" should change its relation "to the illiterate voters of the several States." Acknowledging that education was basically a state responsibility, Tourgée asserted that "it is the duty of the national government to aid that to the extent of its constitutional ability." He showed that although 20 percent of voters in the nation were illiterate, 45 percent of southern voters were illiterate, compared to only 9 percent in the former free states. The "sixteen Southern States contain about one-third of our voting population, and *almost three-fourths of our* illiteracy." All seemed to agree that a better-educated populace was desirable, and therefore he proposed a solution—a national fund "in aid of primary schools ... to be administered under the supervision and control of the national government." By distributing supplementary money "on the basis of illiteracy" and ensuring that it went directly to teachers and schools where it was most needed, the South would gain two-thirds of the funds and the whole nation would benefit from a better-educated populace. His plan was also a way forward when more direct political measures had been abandoned.

Tourgée described his proposal as "not only good policy, but the highest justice. Slavery was the parent of ignorance," and the nation had encouraged slavery. Its destruction in the Civil War imposed on the South a huge task of "making the freedman a citizen." He also believed that this program must be pro-Union; it should not allow a pro-Confederate curriculum or lessons teaching that secession and war were right. Federal aid to education in this manner would encourage prosperity, promote manufactures, discourage Black exodus from the South, and increase national unity. President Garfield, in his inaugural address, devoted a great deal of attention to the kind of ideas Tourgée advocated, and after Garfield's assassination the initiative did not fade away. Throughout the 1880s Congress debated an education bill sponsored by Senator H. W. Blair of New Hampshire. Tourgée remained engaged on the issue and pressed for provisions that would ensure that the money went where it was most needed. Eventually, however, Senator Blair's bill failed to win passage.

Lack of action on his education proposals did not stop Tourgée from striving in many other ways to help African Americans. During the 1880s and 1890s he developed personal and working relationships with more Black leaders than probably any other prominent white person. Through his journalism he formed ties with many Black editors and writers. Among them were T. Thomas Fortune, the influential editor of the *New York Age*; William H. Anderson, a novelist and editor of the *Detroit Plaindealer*; Harry C. Smith, editor of the *Cleveland Gazette*; Ferdinand L. Barnett, a lawyer and newspaper editor in Chicago; and Barnett's wife, Ida B. Wells, the prominent leader of campaigns against lynching. Tourgée supported Wells and eventually succeeded in getting Ohio to adopt an antilynching law. That law became the model for legislation approved by nine other states. Tourgée also corresponded with and advised Charles W. Chesnutt, Black America's foremost novelist of that era, and debated emigration with Bishop Henry McNeil Turner of the African Methodist Episcopal Church. He worked most closely with Louis A. Martinet, editor of the *New Orleans Crusader*.

For many of these individuals, Tourgée offered a forum and publicity for their ideas during his almost ten-year career as a columnist for the *Chicago Daily Inter Ocean*. The *Inter Ocean* was a respected and staunchly Republican newspaper with two hundred thousand subscribers, and from 1888 to 1898 (with a few interruptions) it featured a column by Tourgée on its editorial pages. His weekly piece, "A Bystander's Notes," treated a wide variety of political, social, and cultural topics, but matters of race and white supremacy were repeatedly prominent. Tourgée used his column to advance his own views, but he also used it to present Black perspectives and interracial discussions. He invited and printed letters and comments from Black readers of high or low status. In turn, many Black newspapers reprinted his column for the benefit of their readers who did not see the *Inter Ocean*. In this way Tourgée reached a substantial Black audience and educated many white readers about the views and needs of the Black community. His early dedication to open democratic discussion and debate was a lifelong priority, and he sometimes debated Black spokesmen on the merits of certain legislation or proposals.

As the "Bystander," Tourgée argued that southern Black people had accumulated significant property, advanced in literacy, and flocked to churches and should be seen as a valued ally to Republicans. Moreover, if Republicans permitted the suppression of the Black vote, they would forfeit a majority of the electorate in three southern states. He called on the Republican Party to resist "violence, intimidation, and fraud," whether in the South or in northern states such as Ohio. Frequently he publicized atrocities against Black citizens in southern states and called on the nation to act. In addition, he criticized unfair labor contracts and serf-like conditions, sometimes documenting his complaints through letters from suffering southern Black people. Supposedly "scientific" racists such as Harvard's Nathaniel Southgate Shaler, or the British academic James Bryce, came in for criticism and refutation as Tourgée continued to defend equality, democracy, and "simple justice and Christian teaching." He urged white readers to subscribe to Black newspapers, including the *Richmond Planet*, the *Indianapolis World*, and the *Southwestern Christian Advocate*.

In 1890 Louis Martinet of the *New Orleans Crusader* formed an American Citizens' Equal Rights Association in reaction to "caste" legislation—a law requiring separate railroad cars for Black and white passengers. Promptly Tourgée backed the organization's protest, denounced the "'Jim Crow' car law" as unconstitutional, and called on white readers to join a movement for equal rights. To his surprise, letters began pouring into his office, and in a subsequent column he asked readers if they were ready to form a Citizens' Equal Rights Association. Again the response was unexpected and surprisingly strong; he had tapped into a vein of belief that the purpose of the Union victory was being forgotten and discarded amid the Gilded Age and ideas of social Darwinism. The nation's founding ideals of equality had been ignored but continued to inspire part of the population.

By the fall of 1891 thousands of white and Black citizens had responded to Tourgée's invitation to join the National Citizens' Equal

Rights Association (NCERA). In less than a year the organization had more than one hundred thousand members. Its membership totals eventually reached a quarter million. News about it and letters printed in the "Bystander" columns and in other sympathetic papers revived concern for equal rights, but the organization did not endure. Tourgée was busy with a variety of projects, including a looming challenge to the "Jim Crow car" legislation, and he seemed to hope that local chapters would initiate further action. He did go to the 1892 Republican National Convention and used the organization's numbers to argue that the party should adopt a bold, reformist course. Instead, the party nominated Benjamin Harrison on a conservative platform. Without active and effective leadership, the members of the NCERA lost interest in an organization that was not making practical gains toward the goal of equal rights. But it demonstrated a potential that progressives set out to tap when they organized the National Association for the Advancement of Colored People in 1909.

In 1891 Tourgée had already begun his work in the legal case for which he would often be remembered. *Plessy v. Ferguson*, which would be decided by the Supreme Court in 1896, had its beginning with Louis Martinet in 1890. The New Orleans editor denounced the new law requiring a separate car for Black railway passengers and organized opposition to it. Tourgée followed the issue in his "Bystander" columns and the next year offered to serve pro bono in a legal challenge to the legislation. The two men agreed on another counsel to assist Tourgée locally, in the Louisiana courts, but put their hopes on carrying the case to the US Supreme Court. Tourgée probably hoped that, while the case developed, agitation by the National Citizens' Equal Rights Association could influence the Court to be more supportive.

The prospects for success were not favorable. In recent Court precedents Tourgée faced more evidence that society had been turning away from the progress made during the Civil War and Reconstruction. The Thirteenth, Fourteenth, and Fifteenth Amendments of that era had promised to write equal justice into the nation's Constitution. The Fourteenth Amendment, with its prohibition of hostile state legislation, its language to protect life, liberty, and property, and its promise to provide equal protection under the laws, seemed especially important. But in a series of significant decisions, the Supreme Court had been narrowing the scope and application of the amendment.

The ruling in the *Slaughterhouse Cases* in 1873 began that process. In that decision the Court acknowledged that slavery had brought about the war and that the three amendments were designed to provide "additional guarantees of human rights, additional powers to the Federal government, [and] additional restraints upon those of the States." It also declared that the Thirteenth Amendment prohibited both slavery and "all shades and conditions of African slavery." Admittedly, the "one pervading purpose" of the Civil War and Reconstruction amendments was to give freedom to "the slave race," establish that freedom on a firm basis, and protect "the newly made freedman and citizen from the oppression of those who had formerly exercised unlimited dominion over him."

But the Court then proceeded to emphasize the distinction between state and national citizenship. It interpreted the "privileges and immunities" of citizens of the United States very narrowly, whereas the "privileges and immunities" of citizens of the several *states*, on the other hand, are "those privileges and immunities which are *fundamental*; which belong of right to the citizens of all free governments." The crisis of secession and civil war had forced changes and proved the need for a "strong National government," said the Court, but it held that "our statesmen ... still believed" that "regulation of civil rights" by state and local governments "was essential to the perfect working of our complex form of government." The justices refused to be "a perpetual censor upon all legislation of the States, on the civil rights of their own citizens." This decision denied that Congress had "intended to bring within the power of Congress the entire domain of civil rights heretofore belonging exclusively to the States."

U.S. v. Cruikshank, handed down in 1876, reinforced the idea that protection of a citizen's rights lay primarily with the states and added that the guarantees of the federal Bill of Rights did not limit the states. Then in 1883, in the *Civil Rights Cases*, the Court struck down the Civil Rights Act of 1875. The Court's decision asserted that the Fourteenth Amendment had not given Congress "plenary power" to protect individual rights. Under the amendment Congress had power to pass "corrective legislation" but not "to adopt direct and primary" laws protecting individual rights. The Court said that even if the Fourteenth Amendment gave Congress the power to pass "all necessary and proper laws for the obliteration and prevention of slavery" and all of slavery's "badges and incidents," that did not authorize a law covering public accommodations in an inn, theater, or public transport. Denial of equal accommodations, claimed the Court, did not constitute a "badge of slavery" or entail "any slavery or servitude." If a denial of public accommodations violated any right, the injured individual would have to appeal to state law or to some "corrective legislation" of Congress. But "it would be running the slavery argument into the ground to make it apply to every act of discrimination" relating to "matters of [social] intercourse or business." Jim Crow discrimination did not trouble the Court's majority.

In dissent, Justice John Marshall Harlan argued that since slavery was the cause of the amendment, and since slavery "rested wholly upon the inferiority, as a race, of those held in bondage," freedom "necessarily involved immunity from, and protection against, all discrimination against them, because of their race." He believed that Congress had power, through the Fourteenth Amendment's enforcement clause, to "enact laws to protect that people against the deprivation, *because of their race*, of any civil rights granted to other freemen in the same State." Such legislation, Harlan claimed, "may be of a direct and primary character."

Tourgée needed to move the Court in the direction of Justice Harlan's dissent. He knew that would be a difficult task, but his convictions were strong. In an 1892 essay in the *Inter Ocean* he argued that "free speech, peaceful assemblage, unrestricted discussion of all questions affecting the public welfare, party organization, the nomination and support of candidates are inalienable rights of every citizen of the United States." The federal government, he believed, had a duty to "assert and maintain" those rights "in every part of the National domain." As he had asserted in 1889, "the past has shown conclusively that the white man of the South is not a fair or just guardian of the interests of the colored man."

Tourgée and Martinet agreed to challenge Louisiana's separate car act through the denial of equal seating to a light-skinned individual. Discrimination against such a person had the added benefit of inviting arguments against the idea of racial identity and what constituted blackness or whiteness. Accordingly, Martinet and his associates arranged such a trial, and Homer Plessy, a man whose appearance did not suggest African ancestry, boarded a "whites only" railroad car. He was detained when he refused to go to the separate car for Black people, and his attorneys then challenged the Louisiana statute in state court. As they expected, they lost their suit at every state level, but thereafter Tourgée and Martinet were ready to appeal in 1893 to the US Supreme Court. Their case would not be heard until 1895, and the decision would be handed down in 1896. By that date the atmosphere in society had not improved, and all knew that challenging racially discriminatory southern laws was an uphill battle.

Tourgée took a comprehensive approach in his briefs and oral arguments. He attempted to refute the narrow view in the *Slaughterhouse* decision that the protection of civil rights was a state function. He emphasized the broad language of the Fourteenth Amendment, which spoke of "every person," "no person," and "no state shall." The amendment, he said, "*creates a new* citizenship of the United States embracing new rights ... controlled by a *new* authority." It protected all citizens, Black and white, and sought to establish "universal equality whereby the rights of life, liberty, and property are secured to all—the rights which belong to every citizen in every free country and every republican government." Since slaveholding states had used their "exclusive jurisdiction" to "protect and perpetuate slavery," that state power "should disappear with slavery.... As it was intended to promote injustice, it should not be perpetuated, in the hope of establishing justice."

Tourgée ridiculed the law's attempt to use social definitions of race. If a slight admixture of African ancestry made a white man Black, "why not count every one as white in whom is visible any trace of white blood?" In reality, he argued, it was "impossible" to classify US citizens by race, because "in all parts of the country, race-intermixture has proceeded to such an extent" that many people could not be easily classified. The whole purpose of racial classification in law was to protect "the domination of the white race." The separate car law was not designed for the mutual convenience or comfort of people of all races, as its defenders claimed. If separation were necessary and important, why did the law allow white people to bring a child's nonwhite nurse into the whites-only car? Clearly, the law was "intended to 'keep the negro in his place,'" for "the exemption of nurses shows that the real evil lies not in the color of the skin but in the relation the colored person sustains to the white. If he is a dependent it may be endured; if he is not, his presence is insufferable." Having exposed the law's true purpose, Tourgée added a comment that would become influential. "Justice," he said, "is pictured blind, and her daughter, the Law, ought at least to be color-blind."

Tourgée put forward many additional arguments, including the interesting assertion that white identity was a form of property. To a Court that was increasingly defending property rights, this unusual line of argument perhaps could prove useful, and it exposed the racism at the heart of the law. To buttress his claim, he made direct appeals to the professional and personal experience of the members of the Court. All of them had practiced law. "How much," he asked, "would it be *worth* to a young man entering upon the practice of law, to be regarded as a *white* man rather than a colored one?" He pointed out that white people were in the majority, owned "nineteen-twentieths" of the nation's property, and controlled "ninety-nine hundredths of the business opportunities." Racism and racist laws advantaged white people at the expense of Black citizens. "Probably most white persons if given a choice," said Tourgée, "would prefer death to life in the United States *as colored persons.*" The separate car law defended white supremacy, and Tourgée boldly declared that if "a member of this court" mysteriously became Black overnight, to be ordered into a "'Jim Crow' car" would "fill the judicial mind" with "rage."

Tourgée did not win his case. His direct assault on recent precedents from the Court may have indicated that he knew he was fighting not for his day but for an American future in which equality might prevail. The Supreme Court's decision stated: "The object of the [Fourteenth] amendment was undoubtedly to enforce the absolute equality of the two races before the law, but in the nature of things it could not have been intended to abolish distinctions based on color, or to enforce social, as distinguished from political equality." The words "in the nature of things" essentially authorized racism and gave judicial sanction to attitudes of caste. The Court then claimed that segregation laws "do not necessarily imply the inferiority of either race to the other." American society had accepted many discriminatory practices, including school segregation, which had been upheld "even by courts of States where the political rights of the colored race have been longest and most earnestly enforced." Louisiana, ruled the Court, was justified in following "the established usages, customs and tradition of the people"—that is, the customs of the dominant white population. The Court added, in words that ring patently false today, that the "fallacy of the plaintiff's argument" was its assumption "that the enforced separation of the two races stamps the colored race with a badge of inferiority." Such an idea, if it existed, supposedly resided solely in the Black mind. "Legislation," the Court concluded, "is powerless to eradicate racial instincts."

Albion Tourgée's life had been a refutation of ideas of racial inequality and racial instincts. Unfortunately for him, his devotion to equality and to the ideals of the Declaration of Independence ran up against the social trends of what historian Rayford Logan called "the nadir" period in American race relations. Tourgée fought many losing battles. His principles did not prevail in Reconstruction, in federal aid to education, in *Plessy v. Ferguson*, or in his efforts to renew the revolutionary momentum of the

Civil War years. He dealt with the reality that despite the monumental achievements of the Civil War era, the North and the nation had not been ready to extinguish racism and white supremacy. The nation's contrasting cultures shared an often-virulent racism, coupled with substantial indifference to Black interests. Not until 1954 would the Supreme Court overturn its 1896 ruling and hold that segregated schools were *inherently* unequal. The traditions of the Civil War period are relevant today because the nation still grapples with those demons. Today's citizens, when consulting history, can draw some inspiration from Tourgée's example and apply it to the serious challenges that remain. He set a standard for dogged pursuit of equality in an imperfect democracy.

Elizabeth Cady Stanton
Profound Radical

~

She did not look the part. In fact, through the last half of a long public career, her appearance was that of a kindly, portly grandmother instead of one of the most incisive, far-reaching critics of United States culture in the nineteenth century. An ordinary citizen who glimpsed her at a public event might have assumed that he would hear from a respectable, thoroughly conventional lady. The observer could not have been more wrong.

Elizabeth Cady Stanton was a veteran crusader for women's rights when the Civil War began. At age forty-five in 1860, she had given birth to seven children. Forty years of agitation, lecturing, writing, and organizational leadership lay in front of her. As the years went by, her figure became rounded, her face filled out, and a thick cap of fluffy white curls crowned her head. She seemed to fit the image of a cheerful older lady ready to embrace and cuddle her grandchildren. But in fact, she steadily and progressively attacked the dominant values of society with a penetrating intellect that saw to the bottom of multiple issues. Fearless and defiant in the face of criticism, Elizabeth Cady Stanton assailed ways of thinking and forms of prejudice that were the foundation of social practice. In her critiques and demands for change she traveled farther and drilled deeper than any of the other reformers discussed in this book. Her convictions about feminism, the law, and religion remain vital to controversies today.

Elizabeth Cady Stanton's keen intelligence, determination, and abundant energy probably would have carried her far no matter what circumstances she encountered. But, in fact, significant events in her life almost conspired to make her a feminist and reformer. She was born in 1815 into a well-educated, respected family with reformist connections in New York's Mohawk Valley. Her father was a lawyer and judge, esteemed by his colleagues and the community and socially conservative in his views. Beyond her immediate family, she had cousins and acquaintances who were deeply involved in abolition and political activism. Her childhood was happy, and the love she felt for her father was deep and very important to her. Even as a girl she loved to linger around his office, reading legal texts or listening to discussions among his law students.

When she was only eleven, an older brother, who had just graduated from Union College, "came home to die." His death was a tragedy that plunged the family into deep sorrow. Young Elizabeth tried to comfort her devastated father by climbing onto his lap. After many moments had passed, his response was as brief as it was telling: "Oh, my daughter, I wish you were a boy." Hoping to ease her father's pain, she resolved to become well educated and courageous, as an outstanding boy might be. She studied Greek, Latin, and mathematics and learned to leap a fence on horseback. She hoped, "Now my father will be satisfied with me," only to find that, instead of praising her success, his comment again was, "Ah, you should have been a boy!" Soon she discovered that, despite impressive academic achievement, she was not allowed to enter Union College. Her hard work at Emma Willard's college preparatory school for girls in Troy, New York, could not overcome the prohibitory handicap of female gender.

Two other youthful experiences left a mark on her character and thinking. While she was a student at Troy, she attended a six-week protracted meeting at which Charles Grandison Finney preached repeatedly on the depravity of human beings. The experience so strongly affected the conscientious, impressionable young girl that she fell into a weeks-long depression, one that only a lengthy visit with supportive relatives was able to alleviate. Turning toward science and rationality, she rejected the dark but popular religious theology that, she concluded, did "incalculable harm to the very souls" it sought to save. Already she was questioning both male dominance and established religion.

Immersion during the 1830s in the social circle of her older cousin Gerrit Smith inspired in her a deep interest in social justice and change. Smith was a wealthy landowner who was also a prominent abolitionist, reformer, and sometime congressman. While visiting Smith's home in Peterboro, New York, she heard or met abolitionists such as England's George Thompson and America's James Birney, William Lloyd Garrison,

Wendell Phillips, Samuel May, Abby Kelley, Lucretia Mott, Frederick Douglass, and others. Temperance advocates who also visited argued against the evils of alcohol. Gerrit Smith made his home a stop on the Underground Railroad, and Elizabeth Cady witnessed the anxiety and desperation of a young woman who had run away from slavery, an experience that strengthened her support for abolitionism. The atmosphere of the Smith estate inspired in her a zeal for reform and progress. Social life seemed "tame and profitless elsewhere," she recalled.

It was at Gerrit Smith's that she also met Henry Brewster Stanton, an abolitionist ten years older than she who had studied at Lane Seminary and who wrote for Garrison's *Anti-Slavery Standard* and the *Liberator*. Stanton was already renowned as an orator, one whose antislavery speeches could make people laugh or cry. Frederick Douglass once called him "unquestionably the best orator in the anti-slavery movement." Abolitionist discussions led to more personal conversations until one morning Stanton surprised Elizabeth Cady with a declaration of his feelings. After some hesitation on her part, they married in 1840, when she was almost twenty-five. Judge Cady, like most of society's "respectable" leaders of the time, scorned abolitionists and disapproved of the match, but he later welcomed Henry Brewster Stanton to his home to study law.

No sooner had Elizabeth Cady Stanton married than she again encountered the Western world's ingrained prejudice against women. For their honeymoon, she and Henry Stanton embarked on a voyage to Europe, with their first stop to be at the World's Anti-Slavery Convention in London. Women who arrived there to represent various antislavery societies found that they were excluded because of their sex. Well-known leaders such as Lady Byron, Ann Green Phillips, Lucretia Mott, and others were denied any opportunity to participate. It was another humiliating, enraging experience. Henry Stanton made "a very eloquent speech" in favor of admitting the women, but they were relegated to a low, curtained area, permitted only to observe in silence. William Lloyd Garrison protested for the "sacred rights of women" and refused to take part in the convention, thus winning Elizabeth Stanton's admiration. In fact, she favored the Garrisonians' principled determination to shun politics over the political abolitionism favored by her husband.

That divergence was one of many differences over reform causes that appeared in the long and mainly happy marriage of Elizabeth and Henry Stanton. She later told a friend that her husband was the kind of intelligent, well-informed man with whom she could always have satisfying conversations over breakfast. They shared a commitment to reform and social improvement. Although their views sometimes differed, Henry Stanton did not interfere with his wife's activism. As the years went by, her lecturing and campaigning, as well as his travels and legal business, often kept them apart for many weeks, but they lived together until his death in 1887, fifteen years before she died. The marriage apparently was free of bitter conflict. More importantly, it did not impede Elizabeth Cady Stanton's personal growth and activism. Upon her return from their honeymoon tour, she felt a determination to work for women's rights. Formative experiences had combined with her strong character to create a woman determined to attack patriarchy, even as she entered on several busy years as a wife and young mother.

The next decade involved motherhood, a move to Boston, another move back to New York State for Henry Stanton's work and health, and activism as well. At first Elizabeth Cady Stanton read law and history as her husband studied with the judge, but three children came within five years. Their new mother found herself on "seas of doubt without chart or compass." Discovering that little was authoritatively known about child-rearing, she struggled to find the right methods and argued with the nurses she was financially privileged to employ. Characteristically, she applied her intelligence, asserted herself, and became satisfied with the decisions she imposed. She also took pride in overseeing and planning the renovations of a house when the couple moved to Seneca Falls, New York. Such domestic responsibilities bolstered in her a sense of accomplishment, but as the decade advanced, the "novelty of housekeeping" faded and "domestic life was now irksome."

Elizabeth Cady Stanton's immersion in currents of reform continued, especially during the family's residence in Boston between 1843 and 1845. There she visited frequently with William Lloyd Garrison and met a constellation of leading reformers, both female and male. Among the women were Lydia Maria Child, Abby Kelley, Paulina Wright, and Maria Chapman, and the men included Theodore Parker, Wendell Phillips, John Greenleaf Whittier, Ralph Waldo Emerson, Louisa May Alcott, Nathaniel Hawthorne, Parker Pillsbury, Frederick Douglass, and others. In 1843, when the New York State Legislature was considering a Married Woman's Property Bill, she seized opportunities to lobby the lawmakers, both in committee rooms and in social settings. This modest legal reform had been under consideration since 1836 and would finally become law in 1848. (It gave New York's women the right, for the first time, to control real and personal property, be parties to contracts and lawsuits, and make wills.)

Through antislavery conventions and fairs, Cady Stanton's interests in reform intensified, and after the family moved to Seneca Falls, New York, in 1847 she enjoyed the presence of many nearby activists. Despite the press of domestic duties, she began to become more active in reform. Frustration fueled an important initiative when her maternal duties became especially onerous, due to malaria that afflicted all her children and her servants. Exhausted by the practical difficulties that oppressed married women and mothers, and longing also for intellectual stimulation, she remembered in anger the treatment of women at the World's Anti-Slavery Convention in London. "All elements," she recalled, "conspired to impel me to some onward step." In a visit to Lucretia Mott's home, she poured out her frustration, and her "vehemence and indignation" struck a chord in Mott and the other women there. They issued a call for a Woman's Rights Convention to be held only five days later. Despite the short notice, and despite widespread "sarcasm and ridicule" from editors and male leaders, a crowd of women filled a church in Seneca Falls. A number of male reformers, such as Frederick Douglass, also attended and gave their support. The stands taken by that convention inspired similar meetings elsewhere.

Elizabeth Cady Stanton wrote most of the Seneca Falls Declaration of Sentiments. She famously took as her model Thomas Jefferson's Declaration of Independence, revising it to insist that "all men and women are created equal," endowed with "inalienable rights," and entitled to "equal station." But her text included harsh words as well as soaring ideals. It summed up "the history of mankind" as one "of repeated injuries and usurpations on the part of man toward woman," all with the goal of establishing "an absolute tyranny over her." Chief among the evidences of this despotism was denial of woman's "inalienable right to the elective franchise," the cause that would take center stage for most of Elizabeth Cady Stanton's career. But just as her penetrating analysis of society's wrongs would go far beyond the suffrage, the Seneca Falls Declaration also arraigned woman's degraded status in American law—without rights to property or legal existence when married, and subject to unjust "laws of divorce." It went on to denounce the exclusion of women from education, profitable employments, and careers that would allow them to develop their minds and abilities. It also condemned the moral codes and religious doctrines that sought "in every way . . . to destroy her confidence in her own powers, to lessen her self-respect, and to make her willing to lead a dependent and abject life." Thus, suffrage and the whole system of "social and religious degradation" appeared on the agenda in 1848. It foreshadowed the broad range of issues that Stanton would address, boldly and controversially, throughout her life.

The Declaration also challenged its critics, whether male or female. It commanded America's women to educate themselves on their subordination and not to "publish their degradation, by declaring themselves satisfied with their present position" or reveal "their ignorance, by asserting that they have all the rights they want." Yet "most" of the women who had attended the convention and signed the document withdrew their support when newspapers and ministers everywhere reacted in horror. Only antislavery papers such as Douglass's *North Star* or Horace Greeley's *New-York Tribune* were supportive. This was only the first of many times that allies of both sexes would criticize Elizabeth Cady Stanton for going too far. She responded with disdain for the backsliding women and defiance toward the all-too-predictable men. Already she had achieved a truly courageous independence of mind, a strength that would sustain her through the next fifty-four years. Her own explanation for this remarkable characteristic was uncomplicated: "I was always courageous in saying what I saw to be true, for the simple reason that I never dreamed of opposition." The truth of her reasoning seemed to her to be so "plain" that she was "only surprised" by hostile opposition.

The 1850s brought her four more children but increased and outspoken activism as well. In 1854 New York's Woman's Rights Convention adopted Elizabeth Cady Stanton's address to the state legislature, which she delivered in person. She demanded a new code of laws and argued that women deserved the right to vote since they were citizens, property holders, and taxpayers. Despite their admitted morality, virtue, and intelligence, women were classed "with idiots, lunatics, and negroes," she complained; in fact, their position was lower, since some Black men could vote. The denial of the right to vote was "rank usurpation," and she appealed to national ideals of equality. But in addition, she detailed abuses that women suffered due to biased laws and violent or drunken husbands. She appealed to the lawmakers to consider how their daughters were degraded by custom, how they suffered "instant civil death" once they were married, and how unfairly the law treated them if they were widowed. "By your laws, the child is the absolute property of the father, wholly at his disposal in life or at death," she said. Legislators and slaveholders were alike in the way they dismissed the feelings of those they dominated. The problem was that lawmakers "cannot take in the idea that men and women are alike.... Would to God you could know the burning indignation ... the humiliation" that women felt at their treatment. On this occasion, even Elizabeth Cady Stanton's conservative father was impressed by her arguments.

Susan B. Anthony, who became Stanton's lifelong ally and partner in reform, distributed twenty thousand copies of the address, and some men from the abolition movement spoke out in support. Several thousand citizens signed petitions for equal rights and women's suffrage. But the disapproval of respectable editors and journals was thunderous. Such "performances" were a "joke," "ludicrous," and disgusting, declared the *Albany Register*. The "unsexed women" had left their "true sphere" and endangered both "existing institutions and ... all the social relations of life." American women needed to shun such "insane teachings." Even more exasperating was the hostile reaction of most women, who slammed the door in the face of Susan B. Anthony or others circulating petitions. Others charged that the feminists were neglecting their children to pursue their dangerous notions. Society women accused Stanton of immodesty. The breadth of disapproval was evidence of the immense challenge that lay ahead. As Frances Seward, Senator William H. Seward's wife, remarked, "custom and prejudice ... are stronger than truth and logic."

Undeterred, Elizabeth Cady Stanton persisted in her radicalism. She continued to support abolitionism and wore and defended bloomers as a sensible garment for women's lower bodies. She concentrated much of her attention on the defective laws governing marriage. Her relentless legal and logical analysis naturally carried her to positions that most, even reformers, found unacceptable. Before the startled National Women's Rights Convention in 1860 she attacked marriage, which social custom regarded as sacred. Marriage, she contended, must be "a contract made by equal parties to live an equal life, with equal restraints and privileges on either side." What the law upheld was merely "man marriage," a type of contract in which women bore "all the penalties and sacrifices." Too many virtuous women were trapped in marriages "of force and endurance," and separation from a debased husband only brought stigma and hardship to the wife. Man's "entire control" of a woman in marriage made her a "toy ... for his special use—to meet his most gross and sensual desires."

Logically, she continued, reform of the laws of marriage must allow divorce—an intensely controversial and truly radical idea for that time.

Stanton insisted that unsuitable marriages should be easily dissolved, like other contracts. Many women at the convention objected strongly, and male allies, who feared that discussion of this issue would weaken the abolitionist cause, hesitated or faltered. Garrison wanted the issue postponed, and Wendell Phillips favored removing all mention of Stanton's speech from the minutes. Others who had been strong supporters in the past completely rejected her ideas. Horace Greeley, for example, proclaimed that marriage was "*a union for life*, indissoluble," as decreed by Jesus. Moreover, argued Greeley, "this Christian doctrine of Marriage is a chief reason for the moral, intellectual and even material supremacy of Europe over Asia in our day." Couples who were not ready to have children engaged in a "shameful and unblest" union, said Greeley. Divorce would "invite the sensual and selfish to profane" the marriage tie "whenever appetite and temptation may prompt." He further warned that divorce had "debauched and ultimately ruined" Rome. The disappointing defections by male reformers continued a few months later, when Garrison and Phillips commented on a celebrated case in which a woman had fled with her daughter from an abusive husband. These leading male abolitionists condemned the woman as a fugitive from the law; to Stanton and Anthony, she was as deserving of support as a runaway from slavery. In the next decade such differences of opinion would have major consequences.

THE CIVIL WAR was so great a crisis that it temporarily suppressed these fissures within the ranks of abolitionism and women's rights. The preservation of the Union and the emancipation of the enslaved became paramount. Elizabeth Cady Stanton, Susan B. Anthony, and others threw themselves into the wartime cause. They supported efforts to create hospitals for the wounded and to generate needed medical supplies, and they put their organizational abilities to work to create the Woman's National Loyal League in 1863 and the American Equal Rights Association (AERA) in 1864. Stanton was the president of the Loyal League; Anthony was secretary. They helped others such as Lucy Stone, Abby Kelley, and Frederick Douglass to establish the AERA, whose president was Lucretia Mott. The war years were a time of intense activity.

The work of Stanton's Woman's National Loyal League was key to abolition. She consulted and coordinated with Horace Greeley, William Lloyd Garrison, and other men prominent in abolition efforts, and then her organization launched a campaign with Senator Charles Sumner. To strengthen his efforts in Congress, they canvassed churches and neighborhoods and delivered a petition for emancipation that contained more than three hundred thousand signatures. In addition, they promoted dozens of lectures on the necessity of freedom for the enslaved. Suddenly, in the context of wartime crisis, they won fulsome praise from the same publications that had ridiculed their demands for suffrage or divorce. This was evidence of a critical cultural fact: although emancipation and equality for African Americans were enormous challenges, society was more willing to consider emancipation than equal rights for women.

Elizabeth Cady Stanton was determined that women must gain their equal rights along with African Americans. She had inserted that demand for equality into the resolutions that founded the Woman's National Loyal League, and she remained vigilant as victory approached. By 1864, when the AERA was active, politicians began discussing the need for amendments to the Constitution. Promptly and repeatedly she warned that if the word "male" were attached to constitutional guarantees of rights, it would block the path to equality for women. Stanton and Anthony sent out petitions demanding that states should not be allowed to disfranchise "any of their citizens on the ground of sex." To do so would "turn the wheels of civilization backward." At the same time, she and other women's leaders faithfully supported the rights of Black people. When William Lloyd Garrison proposed to disband the Anti-Slavery Society, Stanton backed Wendell Phillips and others who insisted that its work would not be done until African Americans gained equality.

As Reconstruction moved forward, Stanton confronted a bitter truth, similar to one that Black abolitionists had experienced when support from white abolitionists weakened. "It is impossible," Stanton wrote, "for the best of men to understand women's feelings or the humiliation of their position." Gender, like race, was a division that ultimately made allies unreliable. The loyalty that champions of women's rights had given to Black interests and needs was not going to be repaid by the male abolitionists who had influence. Ahead lay schism between male abolitionists and women like Stanton, and also among women's rights advocates over Stanton's outspoken challenges to respectable opinion.

In 1866 Stanton and Anthony pressured the US Senate to debate female suffrage, as well as ballots for males freed from slavery. The results were distressing. Most men in the Senate believed not only that women were not repressed and should be shielded from the dirty world of politics but also that woman's suffrage undermined God's plan on which "the whole theory of government and society proceeds." In response

Stanton and Anthony transformed the National Woman's Rights Convention into an organization explicitly dedicated to suffrage for Black people *and* women. To their dismay, most of the abolitionists whom they had vigorously supported during the war now refused to back suffrage for women. Repeatedly women were told that it was "the Negro's hour." Stanton continued to lobby Washington's politicians, and in 1867 she, Anthony, and other leaders went to Kansas, where a women's suffrage amendment was on the ballot. For more than three months they crisscrossed the state, enduring harsh conditions of transport and lodging, and speaking in mills, farms, churches, and cabins. With no support from major eastern newspapers, they struggled against the tide, and Stanton concluded that her decision to prioritize emancipation during five years of wartime crisis had been a blunder.

That same year New York held a constitutional convention, and Elizabeth Cady Stanton went before legislative committees to demand suffrage "irrespective of race, color, or sex." She offered well-informed arguments based on legal authorities, provisions in the existing state constitution, and principles from the American Revolution. In addition, she argued that New York's politics needed "the moral power of wise and thoughtful women." Urging continued progress on rights for all individuals, she challenged the lawmakers: "Where did *you* get the right to deny the ballot" to women or to Black people? The nation needed to embrace "higher ideas of justice and equality" for "the world has never yet seen, a GENUINE REPUBLIC." In making her case she also rejected property or educational requirements and categorized male suffrage as "another violation of the republican idea." Such a limited suffrage she often described as an "aristocracy of sex."

Horace Greeley was chair of the lower House's committee on elections. Stanton and Anthony presented to his committee a petition from many women, with the signature of Mary Cheney Greeley, his wife, at the top. For added emphasis, they had her sign as "Mrs. Horace Greeley." The influential editor was unmoved and evidently angered. Despite his previous statements in support of female suffrage in theory, and despite the space he previously had given in the *New-York Tribune* to women's advocates, Greeley ignored their pleas and closed the columns of his paper to Stanton. Thereafter he referred to her as "Mrs. Henry B. Stanton." This was another sign, one of many, that the male allies of women's rights could not be trusted. They were allies in words, not deeds. For Stanton this issue was reaching a breaking point, but not all female reformers shared that degree of frustration or were comfortable with her outspoken views on related issues, such as divorce.

In 1868 Stanton and Anthony founded a Workingwoman's Association and the Woman's Suffrage Association of America, aiming to strengthen the campaign for women's right to vote. They petitioned both the Republican and the Democratic presidential nominating conventions to add female suffrage to their platforms, but without success. Concentrating their lobbying efforts on Congress, they focused on the proposed Fifteenth Amendment, arguing that it must be written so as to bar discrimination in voting rights on the basis of gender as well as race. But by February 1869 Congress had rejected the broader language that would have protected women's rights. Within a month, Stanton and Anthony succeeded in getting allies in Congress to introduce a proposal for a Sixteenth Amendment that would specifically guarantee the ballot for women.

But 1869 proved to be a year of confrontation and division. In May the Equal Rights Association met, with Elizabeth Cady Stanton in the chair. Her anger at the "odious and unnatural" exclusion of women from suffrage led her into some invidious comparisons based on race or class. The nation needed the influence of women and feminine virtues, she argued. Why were women's rights ignored "when millions of ignorant foreigners" were allowed to vote, along with Chinese who had "low ideas of womankind" and "the ignorant African just from his own land or the southern plantation, in whose eyes woman is simply the being of man's lust." The proposed Fifteenth Amendment, she said, made women "the political inferiors of unlettered and unwashed ditch-diggers, boot-blacks, butchers, and barbers, fresh from the slave plantations of the South and the effete civilizations of the old world." Such insensitive and racist remarks inflamed a debate that was centering on the question of whose rights deserved priority—those of Black people or of women.

Stanton and Anthony proceeded to criticize the Fifteenth Amendment, as they had done before, but now they were attacked and accused of racism. Some delegates booed them, and others demanded that they leave the Association. By majority votes the Association decided not to censure Stanton or Anthony but also endorsed a resolution, submitted by Frederick Douglass, to support the Fifteenth Amendment. Bitterly disappointed over their failure to win support for women's suffrage, Stanton and Anthony decided that they must act. They launched a new National Woman Suffrage Association to work for a Sixteenth Amendment. Five months later other women, led by Lucy Stone, organized the American

Woman Suffrage Association. Not until 1890 would these organization unite.

Stone and other female leaders supported the Fifteenth Amendment and were less radical in outlook. They also feared that Elizabeth Cady Stanton's bold, outspoken opinions on divorce were endangering progress. To men and women who viewed marriage as sacrosanct—and they were the norm at that time—her views were positively alarming. Others suspected that she favored immoral ideas of free love and promiscuity. The latter charge was not true, but Stanton did not shrink from controversy. She had opposed a bill in New York to outlaw prostitution, and she did not criticize advocates of free love because she believed the nature of marriage had to be discussed. To a relative she explained that if free love meant a "woman's right to give her body to the man she loves and no other, to become a mother or not, as her desire, judgment, and conscience may dictate . . . to be absolute sovereign of herself," then she supported free love.

Often Elizabeth Cady Stanton spoke out in defense of some woman who, in desperation, had defied conventions and met with public condemnation. In 1868 she defended a woman, suffering from puerperal fever and close to starvation, who was found with her dead infant. Although there was no evidence that this woman had killed her baby, an all-male jury and judge found her guilty of homicide. Stanton's campaign for a pardon was controversial but ultimately successful. Then, in 1870, she and Susan B. Anthony organized public protests in the case of Abby Sage, a woman who had obtained a divorce in Indiana in order to marry a *New-York Tribune* reporter, whom Sage's divorced husband then murdered. Not only did the courts excuse the killing as temporary insanity, but they also awarded custody of Sage's child to the murderer. Stanton called that verdict the *Dred Scott* decision for women's rights and concluded that women "must first be emancipated from . . . a divinely ordained allegiance to man" before their "pride of sex can be so roused as to demand the rights of citizenship." She resolved thereafter not only to fight for suffrage but also to spend her days "in teaching woman her duties to herself." That included a woman's "physical and intellectual education" as well as changes in the law. For the next three decades she worked tirelessly toward suffrage and much broader cultural goals.

THE CONFLICTS of the late 1860s had separated Elizabeth Cady Stanton from former allies but strengthened her independence of thought. Male reformers had proved unreliable, and in 1872, when Horace Greeley ran for president on the Liberal Republican and Democratic Party tickets, she opposed him and supported President Grant. "I had rather see Beelzebub president than Greeley," she remarked. The split with Lucy Stone and other conservative leaders was so deep that Stanton's National Woman Suffrage Association remained independent for twenty years. Stanton and Anthony knew that women had to fight for suffrage on their own, against prominent female opponents or against ordinary women who accepted traditional ideas. The educational reformer Catherine Beecher, for example, opposed women's suffrage, and Harriet Beecher Stowe parodied Stanton in a novel titled *My Wife and I*. Stowe wrote that book to defend her mendacious brother, Henry Ward Beecher, who denied an affair with the wife of abolitionist Theodore Tilton. None of these facts slowed Elizabeth Cady Stanton's energetic pace of organizing or proselytizing, and in the next phase of her career she broadened her attack on the institutions and beliefs that blocked gender equality.

Late in 1869 Stanton had made a lecture tour in the Midwest, speaking at lyceums, the popular forums of that era that featured a variety of speakers. Lecturing to lyceums was a way to reach grassroots audiences and spread her ideas, and in addition it was a source of funds that she valued as her husband's income declined. Until 1880 Stanton traveled far into the Midwest and New England on the lecture circuit, often spending eight difficult months on the road and speaking to church or reform groups as well. Her situation was a strange one. She advocated for a wide range of ideas that were distinctly unpopular and violative of social conventions. Yet she was a popular speaker and even became celebrated by much of the press. Her benevolent, grandmotherly appearance caused journalists to compare her to Martha Washington or Queen Victoria. Audiences enjoyed listening to a personable, unflappable, quick-witted speaker who used humor and could be clever with a retort. She was entertaining, a sensation, and her popularity grew despite the arguments that one woman described as "bayonet thrusts" and "gun shots."

Elizabeth Cady Stanton was fortunate to enjoy robust health, because her travels also included efforts in support of suffrage campaigns. With Susan B. Anthony she made a speaking trip to California and the Far West, where Mormon women in Utah showed surprising interest in their ideas. Wyoming had been the first territory to grant the ballot to women, and Utah did the same to ward off federal interference with its marriage practices. Western states proved to be the first to enact voting rights for women—Wyoming, Colorado, Utah, and Idaho all gave women the ballot by 1896—and Elizabeth Cady Stanton's efforts as a lecturer, writer, and organizer undoubtedly helped to make this possible. She went to Michigan in 1874 as part of a National Woman Suffrage Association campaign to support a state amendment on suffrage.

Speaking frequently, Stanton continued to demand women's rights and to denounce the laws and customs that subjected women. In 1875, for example, she argued that the state should enable women to be "self-reliant and independent instead of weak and helpless." She objected that "the church" taught that "woman is the weaker vessel, unworthy to enter the presence of God, to preach and pray" and that subjection to a husband was woman's "heaven-ordained condition." Women sought and deserved "the same advantages, opportunities, and codes of laws man claims for himself," and without them twenty million women were "in chains." For the celebration of the nation's centennial in 1876, Stanton wrote her association's declaration and spotlighted America's failure to apply its founding values of equal rights to half the population. Although women had shown "equal devotion with man to the cause of freedom," they still suffered taxation without representation and the denial of basic rights such as suffrage and trial by a jury of their peers. The "aristocracy of sex," she wrote, was "a more absolute and cruel despotism than monarchy." She asserted "our full equality with man in natural rights; that woman was made first for her own happiness, with the absolute right to herself—to all the opportunities and advantages life affords for her complete development." Justice involved "all the civil and political rights" of American citizens.

In 1878 she addressed the Senate Committee on Privileges and Elections, instructing the lawmakers on the broad language of the Constitution and calling for protection of women's rights through a Sixteenth Amendment. How, she asked, could the United States guarantee to every state a republican form of government if "one-half the people are forever deprived of all participation in its affairs?" She charged that the judiciary had "uniformly proved itself the echo of the party in power" and declared that national protection of rights was necessary. All citizens should be declared "equal before the law," not only the "four million negroes" but also the "twenty million women" defrauded "of their inalienable rights." In addition to using words of the Founders, she quoted President Rutherford B. Hayes, who one year before had declared, "Equality under the laws for all citizens is the corner-stone" of the reunited nation. Her speech was a small part of the lobbying and writing that she did in later years, and she served as president of the National Woman Suffrage Association from 1878 to 1890.

During the last thirty years of her life Elizabeth Cady Stanton developed ideas that have contributed to the foundations of feminist thought. In speeches and articles, she deepened her arguments about woman's nature, marriage and divorce, women's education and development, and religion. Radical at the time, many of these ideas are still controversial in some quarters today. When editors decried the growing number of divorces, Stanton defended them as a sign of the "new woman's" aspirations for personal liberty. Alexander Hamilton had written that if another person controlled one's subsistence, that other person has "a power over my whole moral being." Thus, "the moral status of woman," wrote Stanton, "depends on her personal independence and capacity for self-support," and in a "true civilization, the masculine and feminine elements in humanity must be in exact equilibrium." Increased numbers of divorces were "the result of higher moral perceptions as to the mother's responsibilities to the race." They showed that society has "not yet reached the ideal marriage state."

Her defense of divorce broadened to describe more fully what marriage ought to be. Men and women, she argued, "must stand as equals," and suffrage, by elevating women, would help to establish the proper basis for family life. Instead of the law's "unjust, unequal" approach to marriage, society should embrace an equal relationship based on "loving companionship . . . mutual help and happiness . . . the development of all that is noblest in each other." There could be no "holy relation," she said, "no not even a desirable one,—when love and mutual respect are wanting." She even quoted Milton on the danger to society of families "where love is not the law." Children suffered in unhappy marriages and should be raised to value the true relations based on equality and love.

Believing as she did that political equality for women required far-reaching changes in society, it was natural that Stanton turned her attention to religion. Working with others to develop a commentary on the Bible was one of her large publishing projects, along with compiling a history of the women's suffrage movement. In *The Woman's Bible* Stanton and her collaborators advanced ideas that were, by turns, perceptive and convincing or totally unconventional and shocking in her time. Her overall approach to the Bible and established Christianity was quite critical. The Bible taught "that woman brought sin and death into the world" and that marriage should be "a condition of bondage, maternity a period of suffering and anguish." All these things she flatly rejected. She had educated herself in modern biblical criticism and urged her readers "to understand the Bible better than to worship it as an idol." It should be read with "reason" and "common sense." In characteristically blunt language, she praised the Bible's "bright jewel[s]" that frequently were "buried under some rubbish." Her mind could not regard "contradictory records of the same event" or "miracles opposed to all known laws, [or] customs" as the sacred "Word of God."

One example of an insightful and persuasive argument was her treatment of the creation stories in Genesis. She pointed out to her readers that there were two creation narratives in the Bible, not just the story of woman being formed from man's rib in order serve him. In the first account of the appearance of women, Scripture declared that "God created man in his *own* image, in the image of God created he him; male and female created he him." Thus, wrote Stanton, "in the Godhead ... the masculine and feminine elements were equally represented." God was feminine as well as masculine, His own image "*male and female*. Thus, Scripture, as well as science and philosophy, declares the eternity and equality of sex." Stanton asserted that masculine and feminine elements were equally essential to the universe, and woman was not "an afterthought." Theories that man was first in creation "have no foundation in Scripture." She asserted, too, that the Bible's language gave man and woman dominion over other living things, but that "not one word is said giving man dominion over woman."

She further argued that the apostle Paul recognized equality as "the very soul and essence of Christianity" when he said, "There is neither male nor female; for ye are all one in Christ Jesus." From the simultaneous creation of woman and man to this New Testament principle, the Bible recognized "the feminine element in the Godhead." She then wondered, given "this declaration of equality of the sexes in the New" Testament, how a "contemptible status" for women could be justified "in the Christian Church of to-day." Some "wily writer," she concluded, had introduced the idea of man's dominion and "to do this a spirit of evil must be introduced." Woman was not the "origin of sin," as so many ministers proclaimed.

In other parts of *The Woman's Bible* she made reasonable and persuasive arguments, noting for example that "the Christian Church admitted women into her regularly ordained ministry during the first two hundred years of Christianity." Similarly, she argued that Jesus was usually patient and appreciative of women. In one passage she took a malleable position toward miracles by saying that "human power" was "developing in so many remarkable ways" that Jesus's gifts might prove attainable to others. But in many other places her commentaries probably overtaxed the patience of any but her already convinced readers. She directly questioned the doctrine of the virgin birth as irrational and declared that if Jesus was divine, "then there was nothing remarkable in his career." As a man, however, Jesus's life revealed "the possibilities of human nature" and furnished "a constant inspiration, our hope and salvation." With approval she cited the opinion of one minister in Boston who judged that "millions" had lived who were as good as Jesus.

Other statements, though thought-provoking or convincing today, scandalized many conventional, "respectable" women and men of her day. The New Testament, Stanton declared, relegated women to an "inferior position ... more clearly and emphatically" than the Old Testament. Nunneries had "disgraced and distorted and demoralized ... womanhood for a thousand years." Commenting on the parable of the poor widow who contributed her two mites to charity, Stanton drew the lesson that "when women learn the higher duty of self-development, they will not so readily expend all their forces in serving others." In relation to another parable about virgins waiting for a wedding feast, she concluded that women who "sacrifice themselves to educate the men of their households," instead of developing their own intellects, were like the foolish virgins who let their lamps run out of oil.

Elizabeth Cady Stanton insisted on the full development of women's intellectual, social, and physical capacities. Elected president in 1890 of the National American Woman Suffrage Association (NAWSA), which after twenty years reunited the two women's suffrage organizations, she made this the theme of her farewell address in 1892. Stepping down from the presidency, she spoke uncompromising truths. The "voyage of life," she said, is made alone, no matter what one wishes: "In the long, weary march, each one walks alone." As an individual, each woman must be "the arbiter of her own destiny," equipped with equal rights to seek "individual happiness and development. . . . As an individual, she must rely on herself." For that reason, "We ask for the complete development of every individual." Women needed a broad education, knowledge of business to gain "pecuniary independence," development of their "muscular system," and knowledge of self-defense and "the use of weapons." Men could not insulate a woman from the solitude "that at time must come to everyone. . . . Man's love and sympathy enter only into the sunshine of our lives." Her valedictory advice to her fellow champions of women's rights was to prioritize concern for "our inner being which we call ourself." Lucy Stone and many others praised this address, but Elizabeth Cady Stanton's views continued to provoke criticism. Although *The Woman's Bible* was a best-seller, some female activists harshly condemned it, and in 1896 the NAWSA pointedly voted not to endorse it.

Elizabeth Cady Stanton was, of course, far from perfect, for she was human. She was repeatedly guilty of ugly prejudice. In the 1860s her biased diatribes may have sprung largely from frustration, anger, and resentment that educated women like herself were denied a right that was granted to illiterate Black men, just freed from slavery. But it also was true that the racial and class prejudice that she sometimes voiced had roots in her background. She was economically and socially privileged throughout her life, a member of an elite class of reformers. She lost touch with the poor and tended to look down on immigrants, working-class families, and uneducated Black people. The latter part of her career also unfolded in a time of social Darwinism, growing economic inequality, and hostility to those recently arrived on US shores. She did not escape their influences. Ironically, as early as 1869 she had recognized that the entitlement to "Manhood Suffrage" fostered prejudice among "educated, refined women" toward "the lower orders of men." In a similar and deplorable way, New York's Democratic Party, she noted, had used white supremacy to encourage Irish voters to hate and attack Black people. But she herself indulged in rhetoric that created racial and class prejudice.

Nevertheless, throughout a long and energetic career Elizabeth Cady Stanton championed and advanced many reforms. Despite enormous disapproval and discouragements, she persisted and continued to fight. She was a thinker far ahead of her time, especially in regard to the wrongs of patriarchy, and she was someone who did much good during her lifetime. She accomplished much that deserves respect today, and many of her ideas seem more relevant to issues now, more than a century after her death, than they did when she was alive. Her place in the ranks of reform and feminist thought is deservedly secure.

A BRIEF GUIDE TO FURTHER READING

THE ESSAYS in this book are based on my previous research and publications, on major works by other historians, and on primary sources that are readily available through the internet. This concise guide to further reading includes secondary sources I have used as well as works that are important in themselves and valuable for further investigation.

The introduction discussed the different paths to economic development that were occurring in the North, the South, and the "middle border." Those different paths obviously had political and cultural implications, and for further reading the following books are valuable: George Rogers Taylor, *The Transportation Revolution, 1815–1860* (New York: Harper Torchbooks, 1968); Charles R. Morris, *The Dawn of Innovation* (New York: Public Affairs Press, 2012); Daniel Walker Howe, *What Hath God Wrought: The Transformation of America, 1815–1848* (New York: Oxford University Press, 2007); Sven Beckert, *Empire of Cotton: A Global History* (New York: Knopf, 2014); James L. Huston, *Calculating the Value of the Union: Slavery, Property Rights, and the Economic Origins of the Civil War* (Chapel Hill: University of North Carolina Press, 2003); and Aaron Astor, *Rebels on the Border: Civil War, Emancipation, and the Reconstruction of Kentucky and Missouri* (Baton Rouge: Louisiana State University Press, 2012). Eugene Genovese was a leading proponent of the view that the slave system impeded industrialization, for example in his book *The Political Economy of Slavery: Studies in the Economy and Society of the Slave South* (New York: Vintage, 1965). Recently a number of historians have been reexamining the extent of industrial progress in the Old South. For examples, see Aaron Marrs, *Railroads in the Old South: Pursuing Progress in a Slave Society* (Baltimore, MD: Johns Hopkins University Press, 2009); and William G. Thomas, *The Iron Way: Railroads, the Civil War, and the Making of Modern America* (New Haven, CT: Yale University Press, 2011). A brief but balanced perspective on southern industrialization by Gavin Wright, an eminent economic historian, can be found in the foreword to Susanna Delfino and Michele Gillespie, eds., *Technology, Innovation, and*

Southern Industrialization: From the Antebellum Era to the Computer Age (Columbia: University of Missouri Press, 2008). Wright's *The Political Economy of the Cotton South* (New York: Norton, 1978) is outstanding.

Henry Clay has been the subject of many studies through the years. The best recent, thoroughly researched work is David S. Heidler and Jeanne T. Heidler, *Henry Clay: The Essential American* (New York: Random House, 2010). Other valuable studies, old and new, include James C. Klotter, *Henry Clay: The Man Who Would Be President* (New York: Oxford University Press, 2018); Glyndon G. van Deusen, *The Life of Henry Clay* (Boston: Little, Brown, 1937); and Merrill D. Peterson, *The Great Triumvirate: Webster, Clay, and Calhoun* (New York: Oxford University Press, 1987). The University Press of Kentucky has published in eight volumes *The Papers of Henry Clay* (Lexington: University Press of Kentucky, 1959–91). A study of the early development of Clay's Kentucky is Stephen Aron, *How the West Was Lost: The Transformation of Kentucky from Daniel Boone to Henry Clay* (Baltimore, MD: Johns Hopkins University Press, 1996). For greater insight into the early role of slavery in sectional politics and the brief Era of Good Feelings, see John Craig Hammond and Matthew Mason, eds., *Contesting Slavery: The Politics of Bondage and Freedom in the New American Nation* (Charlottesville: University of Virginia Press, 2011). Studies of the compromises and sectional crises in which Henry Clay played a major role include Robert Pierce Forbes, *The Missouri Compromise and Its Aftermath: Slavery and the Meaning of America* (Chapel Hill: University of North Carolina Press, 2007); William W. Freehling, *Prelude to Civil War: The Nullification Controversy in South Carolina, 1816–1836* (New York: Oxford University Press, 1965); Richard E. Ellis, *The Union at Risk: Jacksonian Democracy, States' Rights, and the Nullification Crisis* (New York: Oxford University Press, 1987); David M. Potter, *The Impending Crisis, 1848–1861* (New York: HarperCollins, 1976, 2011); Stephen E. Maizlish, *A Strife of Tongues: The Compromise of 1850 and the Ideological Foundations of the American Civil War* (Charlottesville: University of Virginia Press, 2018); and Holman Hamilton, *Prologue to Conflict: The Crisis and Compromise of 1850* (Lexington: University of Kentucky Press, 1964). A recent study that details the various motivations behind the colonization movement is Beverly C. Tomek and Matthew J. Hetrick, eds., *New Directions in the Study of African American Recolonization* (Gainesville: University Press of Florida, 2017).

John C. Calhoun, like Henry Clay, has attracted many biographers and historians. Among the works that focus on him and on his thought are Margaret L. Coit, *John C. Calhoun* (Englewood Cliffs, NJ: Prentice-Hall, 1970); Charles M. Wiltse, *John C. Calhoun*, 3 vols. (Indianapolis, IN: Bobbs-Merrill 1944–51); Robert Elder, *Calhoun: American Heretic* (New York: Basic, 2021); and John G. Grove, *John C. Calhoun's Theory of Republicanism* (Lawrence: University Press of Kansas, 2016). Also reflective of his importance are *The Papers of John C. Calhoun*, 25 vols. (Columbia: University of South Carolina Press, 1959–99). Two outstanding books about proslavery thought and politics are Larry E. Tise, *Proslavery: A History of the Defense of Slavery in America, 1701–1840* (Athens: University of Georgia Press, 1987); and Lacy K. Ford, *Deliver Us from Evil: The Slavery Question in the Old South* (New York: Oxford University Press, 2009). Insightful works on southern proslavery interests are Edward B. Rugemer, "Caribbean Slave Revolts and the Origins of the Gag Rule: A Contest between Abolitionism and Democracy, 1797–1835," in *Contesting Slavery: The Politics of Bondage and Freedom in the New American Nation*, ed. John Craig Hammond and Matthew Mason (Charlottesville: University of Virginia Press, 2011); and Matthew Karp, *This Vast Southern Empire: Slaveholders at the Helm of American Foreign Policy* (Cambridge, MA: Harvard University Press, 2016). In the past historians sometimes asked, why did southern leaders feel that slavery had to expand? But that is probably the wrong question. Expansion was the dominating mindset of most Americans at that time, both North and South, and southern leaders were prospering, were in control of the presidency during the 1850s, and were optimistic about the future of the slave system. Accordingly, they were eager to expand their influence to the South and the West. Important works that reveal this reality include Robert E. May, *The Southern Dream of a Caribbean Empire, 1854–1861* (Gainesville: University Press of Florida, 2002) and *Manifest Destiny's Underworld: Filibustering in Antebellum America* (Chapel Hill: University of North Carolina Press, 2002); and Kevin Waite, *West of Slavery: The Southern Dream of a Transcontinental Empire* (Chapel Hill: University of North Carolina Press, 2021).

Biographies of Harriet Beecher Stowe and studies of her influence include David S. Reynolds, *Mightier Than the Sword: "Uncle Tom's Cabin" and the Battle for America* (New York: Norton, 2011); Joan D. Hedrick, *Harriet Beecher Stowe: A Life* (New York: Oxford University Press, 1994); and Noel B. Gerson, *Harriet Beecher Stowe: A Biography* (New York: Praeger, 1976). Another very useful study of *Uncle Tom's Cabin* and its impact is Thomas F. Gossett, *"Uncle Tom's Cabin" and American Culture* (Dallas, TX: Southern Methodist University Press, 1985).

The most recent, impressive biography of Frederick Douglass is David W. Blight, *Frederick Douglass: Prophet of Freedom* (New York: Simon and Schuster, 2018). Other valuable examinations of Douglass's life and thought include William S. McFeely, *Frederick Douglass* (New York: Norton, 1991); Waldo E. Martin, *The Mind of Frederick Douglass* (Chapel Hill: University of North Carolina Press, 1984); and D. H. Dilbeck, *Frederick Douglass: America's Prophet* (Chapel Hill: University of North Carolina Press, 2018). The most recent, comprehensive study of the abolition movement is Manisha Sinha, *The Slave's Cause: A History of Abolition* (New Haven, CT: Yale University Press, 2016). Also very useful in relation to the abolition movement are James M. McPherson, *The Negro's Civil War* (New York: Ballantine, 1965, 1982, 1991); and Hugh Davis, *"We Will Be Satisfied with Nothing Less": The African American Struggle for Equal Rights in the North during Reconstruction* (Ithaca, NY: Cornell University Press, 2011). Douglass's autobiographies are Frederick Douglass, *Narrative of the Life of Frederick Douglass, an American Slave* (Boston: Published at the Anti-Slavery Office, 1845); *My Bondage and My Freedom* (Auburn, NY: Miller, Orton and Mulligan, 1855); and *The Life and Times of Frederick Douglass* (Hartford, CT: Park Publishing, 1882). The autobiographies are available in various reprints.

The most respected biography of Stephen A. Douglas is Robert W. Johannsen, *Stephen A. Douglas* (New York: Oxford University Press, 1973). Also valuable is Johannsen's *The Frontier, the Union, and Stephen A. Douglas* (Urbana: University of Illinois Press, 1989). Other studies of Douglas and his career include Fergus M. Bordewich, *America's Great Debate: Henry Clay, Stephen A. Douglas, and the Compromise That Preserved the Union* (New York: Simon and Schuster, 2012); Damon Wells, *Stephen Douglas: The Last Years, 1857–1861* (Austin: University of Texas Press, 1971); Michael E. Woods, *Arguing until Doomsday: Stephen Douglas, Jefferson Davis, and the Struggle for American Democracy* (Chapel Hill: University of North Carolina Press, 2020); and Robert E. May, *Slavery, Race, and Conquest in the Tropics: Lincoln, Douglas, and the Future of Latin America* (New York: Cambridge University Press, 2013). A recent study that focuses on racial attitudes in the states of Illinois, Indiana, Ohio, and Kentucky is Matthew E. Stanley, *The Loyal West: Civil War and Reunion in Middle America* (Urbana: University of Illinois Press, 2016).

Studies that focus on Jefferson Davis include William J. Cooper Jr.'s standard biography, *Jefferson Davis: American* (New York: Knopf, 2000); Paul D. Escott, *After Secession: Jefferson Davis and the Failure of*

Confederate Nationalism (Baton Rouge: Louisiana State University Press, 1978); and Paul D. Escott, *Military Necessity: Civil-Military Relations in the Confederacy* (Westport, CT: Praeger Security International, 2006). For understanding of why Davis never faced a trial for treason, see Robert Icenhauer-Ramirez, *Treason on Trial: The United States v. Jefferson Davis* (Baton Rouge: Louisiana State University Press, 2019). All recent works on the Confederacy owe a great debt to Emory M. Thomas's books *The Confederate Nation* (New York: Harper and Row, 1979) and *The Confederacy as a Revolutionary Experience* (Englewood Cliffs, NJ: Prentice-Hall, 1970). The problems faced by the Confederacy have received additional, recent attention in Barton Myers, *Rebels against the Confederacy: North Carolina's Unionists* (New York: Cambridge University Press, 2014); William W. Freehling, *The South vs. the South: How Anti-Confederate Southerners Shaped the Course of the Civil War* (New York: Oxford University Press, 2001); Robert Mackey, *The Uncivil War: Irregular Warfare in the Upper South, 1861–1865* (Norman: University of Oklahoma Press, 2004); and Stephanie McCurry, *Confederate Reckoning: Power and Politics in the Civil War South* (Cambridge, MA: Harvard University Press, 2010). Recent studies of Confederate aspirations include John D. Majewski, *Modernizing a Slave Economy: The Economic Vision of the Confederate Nation* (Chapel Hill: University of North Carolina Press, 2009); Michael Bernath, *Confederate Minds: The Struggle for Intellectual Independence in the Civil War South* (Chapel Hill: University of North Carolina Press, 2010); and Adrian Brettle, *Colossal Ambitions: Confederate Planning for a Post–Civil War World* (Charlottesville: University of Virginia Press, 2020). For more on the Confederate debate on emancipation, see Robert F. Durden, *The Gray and the Black: The Confederate Debate on Emancipation* (Baton Rouge: Louisiana State University Press, 1972); Bruce C. Levine, *Confederate Emancipation: Southern Plans to Free and Arm Slaves during the Civil War* (New York: Oxford University Press, 2005); and Philip D. Dillard, *Jefferson Davis's Final Campaign: Confederate Nationalism and the Fight to Arm Slaves* (Macon, GA: Mercer University Press, 2017).

The best single-volume biography of Abraham Lincoln is David Donald's *Lincoln* (New York: Simon and Schuster, 1995). Despite being only one volume, Donald's work is very comprehensive, penetrating in its insights, and free of mythology. Michael Burlingame deserves great credit for the indefatigable research behind *Abraham Lincoln: A Life*, 2 vols. (Baltimore, MD: Johns Hopkins University Press, 2008). The most recent of the major studies of Lincoln is David S. Reynolds, *Abe: Abraham Lincoln in His Times* (New York: Penguin, 2020). Other studies that help to illuminate issues touched on in this book's essay include Daniel W. Crofts, *Lincoln and the Politics of Slavery: The Other Thirteenth Amendment and the Struggle to Save the Union* (Chapel Hill: University of North Carolina Press, 2016); William W. Freehling, *Becoming Lincoln* (Charlottesville: University of Virginia Press, 2018); and Paul Escott, *"What Shall We Do with the Negro?": Lincoln, White Racism, and Civil War America* (Charlottesville: University of Virginia Press, 2009), and *Lincoln's Dilemma: Blair, Sumner, and the Republican Struggle over Racism and Equality in the Civil War Era* (Charlottesville: University of Virginia Press, 2014). A sound discussion of the question of who deserves credit for emancipation is Ira Berlin's essay "Who Freed the Slaves? Emancipation and Its Meaning," in *Union & Emancipation: Essays on Politics and Race in the Civil War Era*, ed. David W. Blight and Brooks D. Simpson (Kent, OH: Kent State University Press, 1997). An important addition to our understanding of the colonization movement is Phillip W. Magness and Sebastian N. Page, *Colonization after Emancipation: Lincoln and the Movement for Black Resettlement* (Columbia: University of Missouri Press, 2011). See also Page's *Black Resettlement and the American Civil War* (Cambridge: Cambridge University Press, 2021). For an understanding of the depth of white supremacist attitudes in the North, see Paul D. Escott, *The Worst Passions of Human Nature: White Supremacy in the Civil War North* (Charlottesville: University of Virginia Press, 2020). Always valuable on the larger story of white racial attitudes is George M. Fredrickson, *The Black Image in the White Mind: The Debate on Afro-American Character and Destiny, 1817–1914* (New York: Harper and Row, 1971).

Horace Greeley's career has attracted a good many biographies. Among the most insightful or thorough are James M. Lundberg, *Horace Greeley: Print, Politics, and the Failure of American Nationhood* (Baltimore, MD: Johns Hopkins University Press, 2019); Glyndon G. Van Deusen, *Horace Greeley: Nineteenth-Century Crusader* (Philadelphia: University of Pennsylvania Press, 1953); and Robert C. Williams, *Horace Greeley: Champion of American Freedom* (New York: New York University Press, 2006). A compact but useful study is Mitchell Snay, *Horace Greeley and the Politics of Reform in Nineteenth-Century America* (Lanham, MD: Rowman and Littlefield, 2011). A detailed account focusing on his journalistic career is Lurton Dunham Ingersoll, *The Life of Horace Greeley* (New York: Beekman, 1974). It also is helpful to read *The Autobiography of Horace Greeley,* or *Recollections of a Busy Life: to which are added Miscellaneous Essays and Papers* (New York: E. B. Treat, 1872).

There are three major studies of Albion Tourgée (who did not use the acute accent on the *e* at all times in his life): Otto H. Olsen, *Carpetbagger's Crusade: The Life of Albion Winegar Tourgee* (Baltimore, MD: Johns Hopkins University Press, 1965); Mark Elliot, *Color-blind Justice: Albion Tourgee and the Quest for Racial Equality from the Civil War to* Plessy v. Ferguson (New York: Oxford University Press, 2006); and Carolyn L. Karcher, *A Refugee from His Race: Albion W. Tourgée and His Fight against White Supremacy* (Chapel Hill: University of North Carolina Press, 2016). For background on the potentials and problems of Reconstruction in Tourgée's North Carolina, see Paul D. Escott, "White Republicanism and Ku Klux Klan Terror: The North Carolina Piedmont during Reconstruction," in *Race, Class, and Politics in Southern History*, ed. Jeffrey J. Crow, Escott, and Charles L. Flynn Jr. (Baton Rouge: Louisiana State University Press, 1989). A valuable commentary on Tourgée's arguments in the case of *Plessy v. Ferguson* is Michael Kent Curtis, "Reflections on Albion Tourgee's 1896 View of the Supreme Court: 'A Consistent Enemy of Personal Liberty and Equal Right,'" *Elon Law Review* 5 (2013): 19–87. Eric Foner contributed a recent analysis of the significance of the three constitutional amendments that came out of the Civil War and Reconstruction in *The Second Founding: How the Civil War and Reconstruction Remade the Constitution* (New York: Norton, 2019).

Interest in Elizabeth Cady Stanton, her deeds and her ideas, is growing, and there are many valuable studies available for further reading. Stanton's own memoir, *Eighty Years and More: Reminiscences, 1815–1897,* has been reprinted by Boston's Northeastern University Press in 1993 and is an introduction to her personality and career. Fortunately for the student, a great many of her speeches, addresses, and other writings are now available online, and these should be studied by anyone interested in her career. It also is easy to obtain reprints or online versions of *The Woman's Bible*, which was first published between 1895 and 1898, as well as commentaries on it. Among the growing number of biographies and more focused studies are Elizabeth Griffith, *In Her Own Right: The Life of Elizabeth Cady Stanton* (New York: Oxford University Press, 1985); Lori D. Ginzberg, *Elizabeth Cady Stanton: An American Life* (New York: Hill and Wang, 2009); Lois W. Banner, *Elizabeth Cady Stanton: A Radical for Woman's Rights* (Boston: Little, Brown, 1980); and Sue Davis, *The Political Thought of Elizabeth Cady Stanton: Women's Rights and the*

American Political Traditions (New York: New York University Press, 2008). Ann D. Gordon, *The Selected Papers of Elizabeth Cady Stanton and Susan B. Anthony* (New Brunswick, NJ: Rutgers University Press, 2000), is a good place to start in examining the long and fruitful working partnership between these two key feminists. An outstanding book of analytical essays, with some useful documents, is Ellen Carol DuBois and Richard Cándida Smith, eds., *Elizabeth Cady Stanton, Feminist as Thinker: A Reader in Documents and Essays* (New York: New York University Press, 2007).

INDEX

Abbott, Joseph, 155
abolition, 14, 34, 42, 45, 167
abolitionists: denounced and disliked, 16, 34, 168; in 1850s, 65; mentioned, 6, 33, 34, 45, 77, 112, 113, 121, 145; oppose expansion of slavery, 21; oppose Texas statehood, 20; views of Garrisonians, 61
Adams, John Quincy, 17, 28–29
Africa, 14, 15, 42
African Americans: enslaved, 4, 13, 151; free, 13, 15; grow in numbers, 24, 95; laborers for Confederacy, 104; mentioned, 6, 87, 88, 168; oppose colonization, 15; as soldiers, 69, 121, 151; speak out in South in 1865, 67; voters, 13, 39, 70. See also *Dred Scott* decision
Alcott, Louisa May, 169
American Antislavery Society, 70, 71
American Colonization Society, 14, 15, 45
American Equal Rights Association, 173, 174
American Revolution, 6
American System, 17, 18, 29, 30, 31, 131
American Woman Suffrage Association, 176–77
Anderson, William H., 158
Anthony, Susan B., 172, 173, 174, 175, 177, 178
antislavery, 17
Appalachian Mountains, 4, 10, 95
Appeal of the Independent Democrats, 82
Assing, Ottilie, 75
Atchison, David, 86, 99

Bagby, George William, 92
Bank of the United States, 11, 27–28
Barnett, Ferdinand L., 158
Beecher, Catherine, 42–43, 178
Beecher, Henry Ward, 86, 178

Bell, John, 90, 101
Birney, James, 167
Black Convention Movement, 67, 70, 125
Blair family, 15
"Bleeding Kansas," 86, 114
Border South, 15
Border States, 16, 90, 135
Boyce, W. W., 106
Bragg, Thomas, 96
Breckinridge, John, 89, 101
British West Indies, 39
Brown, Albert Gallatin, 89
Brown, John, 66, 86, 100, 117, 135–36
Brown, Joseph E., 103–4
Buchanan, James, 68, 86, 99, 115–16, 135
Butler, Benjamin, 138, 145
Byron, Lady, 168, 169

Cable, George Washington, 54
Calhoun, Floride, 26, 31
Calhoun, John C.: abandons nationalism, 18, 29–31; becomes aggressive champion and defender of slavery, 18, 32, 34, 35, 36–37, 39, 40, 41; breaks with Jackson, 30–31; champions nullification, 31–32; declares slavery a "positive good," 33–34; demands gag rule, 33; *A Disquisition on Government*, 40; example to other southern leaders, 26, 35, 37, 41, 95; influences Democratic Party, 32; leads in nationalist measures, 26–28, 29; mentioned, 5, 10, 12, 81, 92, 97, 111, 112; opposes Compromise of 1850, 39–40; personal qualities, 25, 27, 28, 29, 30, 33, 37, 38, 39–40; praises stability of slave society, 34, 35; predicts class conflict in North, 35; role in annexation of Texas, 35–37; secretary of state, 36; secretary of war, 28; seeks presidency, 29;

193

Calhoun, John C. (*continued*)
seeks southern unity, 35, 37, 38–39; seeks western support, 38; *South Carolina Exposition and Protest*, 30, 40; on southern rights in territories, 37; supports Clay's plan in nullification crisis, 19; supports national bank, 11; theory of concurrent majority, 40–41; vice president, 29; views on slavery, 31–32, 33–34; warns of North-South conflict, 34, 37, 39, 40–41
California, 21, 22, 80, 133
Cameron, Simon, 119
Cass, Lewis, 37, 79, 80
Chapman, Maria, 169
Chase, Salmon, 82, 138
Chesnutt, Charles W., 158
Child, Lydia Maria, 134, 169
Clay, Henry: arranges Missouri Compromise, 12–13; backtracks on Texas, 20; becomes secretary of state, 17; criticizes abolitionists, 16; death of, 24; devotion to Union, 10, 19, 24; early career, 9; fame of, 9, 22; health of, 22; important role in American Colonization Society, 14, 16; important role in Compromise of 1850, 21–23, 80; mentioned, 4, 29, 37, 119, 131; nullification crisis, 19, 32; personal qualities, 9–10, 19, 23–24; presidential candidate, 17, 18, 19–21; proposes elements of his American System, 11, 27; racism of, 15–16, 24; as slaveholder, 14–15; views on slavery, 14–16
colonization, 15, 17, 42, 52, 53, 54, 72, 111
Compromise of 1850, 21–23, 39, 44, 64, 80, 81, 82, 133
Constitution, 5, 13, 22, 27
Constitutional Union Party, 89
Cooke, John Esten, 92
Crittenden, John, 90
Crittenden Compromise, 90–91, 102, 117
Cuba, 98
culture, 2, 3, 6, 130, 149–50, 152, 172
Curtis, George William, 132
Cushing, Caleb, 100

Davis, Jefferson: agrees with Douglas's Freeport Doctrine, 100; dedication to Confederate independence, 103, 107, 108, 110; demands territorial expansion of slavery, 22, 97, 98, 99, 100, 101; faces intense criticism as president, 105–6, 108, 109; health problems, 100, 109; helps Douglas on Kansas-Nebraska Act, 82, 99; mentioned, 117, 138, 141; military career, 93–94, 96–97, 102; nonstereotypical background, 92–93, 94; opposes Compromise of 1850, 97–98; personal qualities, 95–96, 97, 102; policies as strong Confederate president, 102–5; position on Kansas, 99; position on secession, 101–2; postwar reputation and influence, 109–10; proposes arming and freeing slaves, 107; secretary of war, 96, 98; views on race and slavery, 94, 97, 107, 109, 110; views on the Union, 98, 100, 101; wealth, 94; works to deny Douglas nomination for president, 101
Davis, Joseph Emory, 93, 94
Davis, Varina Howell, 95–96
De Bow, J. D. B., 38
Declaration of Independence, 4, 6, 10, 24, 48, 65, 88, 111, 114, 126
Deep South, 16
Delany, Martin, 63–64
Democratic Party, 20, 69, 77, 78, 79, 83, 86, 87, 89, 100, 101, 121, 123, 124, 134, 135, 137, 145, 146
Disquisition on Government, A (Calhoun), 40
Dixon, Archibald, 82
Doolittle, James, 15
Douglas, Stephen A.: Compromise of 1850, 22–23, 80–81; denounces abolitionists, 83; dominates committee on territories, 80, 86; early career, 78; Kansas-Nebraska Act, 81–83, 86; mentioned, 5, 111, 113, 114, 115; personal qualities, 77, 78, 85, 90, 91; and popular sovereignty in territories, 22, 79, 83, 85, 86–87, 88; presidential ambitions,

77, 88, 89, 90, 101; racist views, 77, 85, 87–88; rivalry with Lincoln, 84, 85, 87–88, 90, 91; as slaveholder, 84–85; split with Buchanan and southern leaders, 86–87, 88–89; support for white supremacy, 77, 88; supports North and Union, 77, 89, 90–91; supports southern interests, 79, 81–82

Douglass, Frederick: autobiographies, 61, 65; briefly favors emigration, 65; criticizes Republicans and Republican Party, 65–66, 67, 69, 70; criticizes United States, 62; demands equal rights and ballot, 69, 70, 71, 72; early life, 58, 59–60; endorses John C. Frémont, 65; escape from slavery, 60; gains legal freedom, 61; holds federal offices, 73, 74, 76; joins Garrisonians as lecturer, 60–61, 62; leads call for wartime emancipation, 66–67, 68; marriages, 60, 75–76; meets with John Brown, 66; mentioned, 6, 87–88, 113, 119, 125, 130, 145, 168, 169, 170, 171, 173; minister to Haiti, 73; personal qualities, 58–59, 61, 62–63, 76; post-Reconstruction career, 71–74; publishes newspapers, 62, 63, 64, 72; reacts to Gilded Age, 74; recruits Black soldiers, 69; relationship with Lincoln, 66, 68, 69, 73–74; religious faith, 59, 64, 65; rumors about, 62, 64, 75; on Santo Domingo, 73; sees violence as justified, 65; on social equality, 70–71, 74; split with Garrison, 62–63, 64; suffers violence, 60–61; tour of British Isles, 61; views on Constitution and Declaration of Independence, 59, 64, 65; views on different races, 72–73; views on women's rights, 63, 72

Downing, George T., 71, 125
Dred Scott decision, 65, 87, 99, 114, 116, 135

Eaton, John, 31
Eaton, Peggy, 31
economy: northern developments, 3–4, 6, 12, 16, 24, 129, 149–50; southern developments, 4, 6, 12, 16, 24, 94–95, 149; in West, 10

Elliott, Robert Brown, 142
emancipation: gradual, 17; mentioned, 5, 15, 36, 51, 54, 56
Emerson, Ralph Waldo, 64, 169
enslaved people. *See* slavery; slaves; slave trade
equality, 2, 5, 56

Federalists, 12
Fifteenth Amendment, 72, 141, 142, 160, 176
Fillmore, Millard, 133
Finney, Charles Grandison, 167
Foote, Henry S., 95
Foote, Shelby, 5
Force Bill, 32
Fortune, T. Thomas, 158
Founders, 1, 3, 10, 12, 14, 16, 17, 24, 83, 87, 88, 116
Fourteenth Amendment, 72, 131, 160, 161, 162, 163
Freedmen's Bank, 75
Freedmen's Bureau, 142, 152
Free Soil Party, 63, 64, 65, 112, 133
Frémont, John C., 65, 69, 118, 135, 137, 138
fugitive slave law, 22, 23, 39, 44, 64, 65, 81, 118, 133–34
Fuller, Margaret, 132

Garfield, James, 76, 156–57, 158
Garnet, Henry Highland, 67, 125
Garrison, William Lloyd, 33, 45, 60, 71, 167, 168, 169, 173, 174
Giddings, Joshua, 82
Gold Rush, 21, 80
Graham, Sylvester, 13
Grant, Ulysses S., 73, 74, 124, 138, 144, 178
Great Britain, 10, 27, 36
Greeley, Horace: builds *New-York Tribune*, 131–32; changing views on Lincoln and the war, 136–39; criticizes abolitionists, 131, 133; criticizes Douglas and Kansas-Nebraska Act, 134;

Greeley, Horace (*continued*)
  criticizes Irish immigrants, 135; criticizes slavery's influence, 133, 134; early career, 130–31; helps build Republican Party, 117, 134–35, 135–36; mentioned, 171, 173, 175, 178; personal qualities and enthusiasms, 129, 130, 131, 132–33, 136, 137–38, 139, 142, 144, 145, 146; presidential candidacy, 143–46; proposes peace negotiations, 124, 138; publicizes various reforms, 132; vacillating positions on Reconstruction, 139–43; views on divorce, 131, 135, 173; views on race, 134–35, 137, 139, 140, 141, 142, 144, 146; views on slavery, 131; views on southerners, 135, 139, 141, 142–43; views on women's rights, 131, 132, 175
Greeley, Mary Cheney, 175
Griffiths, Julia, 63–64
Gulf region, 4, 36, 93, 94, 95

Hahn, Michael, 126
Haiti, 122
Hamilton, Alexander, 11, 180
Harlan, John Marshall, 162
Harper's Magazine, 89
Harrison, William Henry, 20, 35, 131
Hartford Convention, 12
Hawthorne, Nathaniel, 169
Hayes, Rutherford B., 74, 179
Hofstadter, Richard, 1, 2
Holden, William, 152
Hunter, David, 118

Illinois, 9, 13, 17, 80, 83
immigrants, 3
immigration, 5, 24, 45, 129
Indiana, 17
industrialization, 5
internal improvements, 11, 27, 30, 38

Jackson, Andrew, 12, 17, 18, 19, 20, 29, 30, 31, 32, 78
Jefferson, Thomas, 11, 12, 14, 32, 92
Johnson, Andrew, 72, 142

Johnson, Reverdy, 89
Jones, J. B., 96
Julian, George, 112, 123

Kansas-Nebraska Act, 65, 81, 84, 112, 113
Kelley, Abby, 168, 173
Kentucky, 4, 9, 11, 14, 15, 16, 17, 93, 95, 150
Ku Klux Klan, 142, 143, 155

Lane Seminary, 42, 168
Langston, John Mercer, 67, 125
Lecompton Constitution, 86, 99, 135
Lee, Robert E., 92, 107, 138
Liberal Republicans, 144–45
Liberty Party, 20–21, 61, 63, 65
Lincoln, Abraham: appeals to northern Democrats, 111, 118; charges a Slave Power conspiracy, 115–16; criticizes Supreme Court, 114; favors gradual, compensated emancipation, 112, 119, 120; holds out incentives to rebels, 117–18, 120–21, 122–23; issues Emancipation Proclamations, 68–69, 120–21; mentioned, 2, 4, 6, 43, 58, 64, 73, 77, 84, 85, 87, 90, 93, 101, 102, 136, 138, 139; personal qualities, 111, 112, 121, 122, 123, 126, 127–28; praises Clay, 9, 111; priority on preserving Union, 118, 124, 137; response to secession, 117, 118; on rights for Blacks, 122, 123; shares views of middle border, 17; slow to move against slavery, 67; supports colonization, 15, 111, 119, 120, 122, 123; supports some Black suffrage, 126–27; urges Thirteenth Amendment, 126; views on race, 113–15, 116–17, 123, 126; views on slavery, 112, 113, 116, 117–18, 123–24, 127
Lost Cause myth, 92, 93, 102, 109, 110
Louisiana Purchase, 13, 21
Lowndes, William, 11

Madison, James, 10, 11, 14, 92
Manifest Destiny, 77, 78, 130
Martinet, Louis A., 158, 159, 160, 162
Marx, Karl, 132

Maryland, 125
Mason, James, 39
Mexico, 19, 20, 21, 22, 35, 36, 38, 78, 79, 80, 83, 130
"middle border" area: defined and discussed, 16, 17; political views in, 17
Midwest, 17
Minor, B. B., 38
Mississippi, 93
Mississippi River, 38, 93
Mississippi Valley, 38, 80
Missouri, 125
Missouri Compromise, 13–14, 17, 29, 39, 65, 79, 82, 83, 97, 99, 114
Monroe, James, 14, 28, 92
Mott, Lucretia, 168, 170, 173

Nashville Convention, 97
National American Woman Suffrage Association: formed, 182; refuses to endorse Stanton's valedictory address, 183
National Citizens' Equal Rights Association, 159–60
National Era, 43
National Woman's Rights Convention, 175
National Woman Suffrage Association, 176, 178, 179
Native Americans, 3, 32, 80
New England, 12, 21, 29, 149
New Mexico, 22
New York, 21
New-York Tribune, 129, 136, 171
northerners: fear expansion of slavery, 21
Northwest Ordinance, 82
nullification, 18, 19, 30–31, 32

Oberlin, Ohio, 150
Oberlin Collegiate Institute, 42
Ohio, 17, 149–50
Ostend Manifesto, 98
Outlaw, Wyatt, 155
Owen, Robert Dale, 135

Packenham, Richard, 36
Page, Thomas Nelson, 92

Parker, Theodore, 169
Pennington, J. W. C., 66
"petticoat affair," 31
Phillips, Ann Green, 168
Phillips, Wendell, 71, 112, 158, 169, 173, 174
Pierce, Franklin, 82, 98, 99, 101, 115
Pillsbury, Parker, 169
Pitts, Helen, 75
Plessy v. Ferguson, 160–64
Polk, James K., 20, 21, 78, 79
popular sovereignty, 22, 37, 79, 80, 81, 83, 87, 88, 89
population, 12
proslavery theories, 17

Quitman, John, 98

racism, 2, 3, 6, 55, 56–57, 59, 61, 67, 69, 71, 73, 76, 77, 83, 87, 91, 108, 112, 128, 130, 146, 148, 155, 156, 164, 165, 176
Randolph, John, 11, 32
Reconstruction, 5, 7, 41, 71, 109, 110, 122, 127, 139, 146, 148, 153–56
Remond, Charles Lenox, 66, 71
Republican Party: mentioned, 17, 56, 64, 65, 82, 87, 100–101, 111, 114, 125, 135, 144, 156, 159–60; prewar position on slavery, 117
Ripley, George, 132
Rock, John, 67, 125

Sage, Abby, 177
Scott, Winfield, 96
Second Great Awakening, 44, 150
Seddon, James, 96
Seneca Falls Convention, 63, 132, 170
Seward, Frances, 172
Seward, William, 9, 115, 122, 124–25, 131
Sherman, William Tecumseh, 124, 125, 139
slaveholders, as planters, 3, 16
slavery: growing southern concern to defend, 18, 29, 84, 86; mentioned, 4, 5, 6, 7, 9, 10, 12, 13, 16, 21, 26, 41, 77, 89, 91, 95, 133; as source of prejudice, 74; in Texas annexation, 19

slaves: flood into Union lines, 68, 119, 121
slave trade, 12, 22
Smith, Gerrit, 63, 64, 82, 137, 167
Smith, Harry C., 158
Smith, James McCune, 66
South: antislavery societies in, 12; as economic region, 17; Texas and expansion intensify fears for slavery, 20, 21, 22, 23, 29, 39, 84
South Carolina, 17, 18, 19, 29, 30, 32, 33, 92
South Carolina Exposition and Protest, 30, 40
"Southern Address," 38–39
Southern Literary Messenger, 38
Spooner, Lysander, 64
Stanton, Elizabeth Cady: addresses New York legislature, 171–72; argues for divorce and equality in marriage, 135, 172–73, 176, 177, 180; criticizes religion, 179, 180–82; early, formative years, 166–68, 169, 170; fights for emancipation during Civil War, 173–74; fights for married women's rights, 169–70; fights for suffrage and women's rights in Reconstruction, 174–75; launches and leads National Woman Suffrage Association, 176, 179, 180; leads Woman's National Loyal League, 173; lecturer, 178, 179; marriage, 168–69, 178; mentioned, 56; motherhood, 169, 170, 171; personal qualities and beliefs, 166, 168, 169, 170–71, 175, 176, 177, 178, 180, 183; racist remarks, 176, 183; splits with American Woman Suffrage Association, 176–77; valedictory address, 182–83; works for a Sixteenth Amendment, 176, 179; writes most of Seneca Falls Declaration, 170–71
Stanton, Henry Brewster, 168
states' rights, 26, 30–31, 32, 79, 92, 103
Stephens, Alexander, 106
Stephens, John, 155
Stone, Lucy, 173, 176, 178, 183
Stowe, Harriet Beecher: family background, 42–43; family involvement in reforms, 42; influence in England, 43, 56; life pattern and publications, 43; mentioned, 63, 85, 113, 117, 178; motives in writing *Uncle Tom's Cabin*, 45–46; personal qualities, 43, 56, 57; racial views, 56–57, 73; on women's rights, 56. *See also Uncle Tom's Cabin*
Stuart, J. E. B., 92
Sumner, Charles, 73, 82, 174
Supreme Court, 5, 23, 75, 87, 88, 89, 160–64, 165

Talmadge, James, 13
Taney, Roger, 115–16
tariffs: attacked by Calhoun, 30–31; championed by Calhoun, 27; mentioned, 36, 38; protective, 11, 18, 19
Taylor, Zachary, 96, 133
technological advances, 12, 17, 38, 77, 80
Tennessee, 4, 95
Texas, 19–20, 21, 22, 35–36, 78
Texas v. White, 5
Thirteenth Amendment, 124, 126–27, 160, 161
Thompson, George, 167
Thoreau, Henry David, 132
Tilton, Theodore, 178
Toombs, Robert, 91
Tourgée, Albion: in army, 151; assails aristocracy, 153; assails white supremacy, 163–64; campaigns for equal rights, 153, 156, 159–60; cultural background, 149–50, 152; journalist's career, 158–59, 160, 162; and Ku Klux Klan violence, 155; mentioned, 6; personal qualities, 148, 149, 150–51, 152, 154, 156, 158, 164; *Plessy* case, 160–64; Republican in Reconstruction, 152, 154, 155–56; views on education, 156–58; views on race, 148, 151, 152, 154, 158–59, 162, 163, 164; views on slavery, 151; writing success, 153–54, 156
Turner, Henry McNeal, 66, 158
Tyler, John, 20, 21, 36

Uncle Tom's Cabin: appeals to Christian values, 47–48, 49, 50–51, 52–53, 54; appeals to motherhood and family values, 46–47, 48; attitudes on race, 47, 53, 54, 55; criticism of Constitution and government, 47–49; depiction of Black people, 49–50, 53; depiction of northerners and racism, 51–52, 53, 55–56; depiction of southern whites, 55; role of women, 47–48; slavery's corrupting effects on whites, 51–52, 55; slavery's treatment of women, 46, 50, 55; success and influence, 43; support of colonization, 52, 53, 54–55; views of Africa, 52, 54
Union: danger to, 21, 40–41, 78, 80, 89; idealism about, 3, 4, 10, 77, 89
Unionists in South, 10, 17
Upshur, Abel, 36
Utah, 22

Vallandigham, Clement, 138
Van Buren, Martin, 20, 35, 63
Virginia, 29, 32, 36, 39, 64, 92, 94, 100, 150

Walker, William, 98
War Hawks, 10, 27, 28
Washington, Bushrod, 14
wealth: aspirations for, 3, 6, 24–25, 45, 59, 94
Webster, Daniel, 10, 14
Weed, Thurlow, 131
Wells, Ida B., 158
West, 10, 16, 17, 38, 42, 78, 80, 81, 129
Western Reserve, 149–50
Whig Party, 9, 18, 20, 36, 131, 133
white supremacy, 2, 4, 6, 17, 18, 24, 39, 41, 56, 57, 59, 69, 73, 77, 84, 85, 88, 107, 109, 110, 112, 116, 117, 123, 124, 125, 128, 129, 143, 147, 148, 154, 155, 156, 158, 164, 165
Whittier, John Greenleaf, 169
Wigfall, Louis, 108
Wilmot, David, 37, 79, 83
Wilmot Proviso, 37, 79, 80, 82, 133
Woman's National Loyal League, 173, 174
Woman's Suffrage Association of America, 176
women: ideas of their role, 44–45, 47–48; status of, 3
women's suffrage, 43
Wool, John, 96
Worth, Jonathan, 152
Wright, Paulina, 169

"Young America," 77

RECENT BOOKS IN THE SERIES
A Nation Divided: Studies in the Civil War Era

The Weaker Sex in War: Gender and Nationalism in Civil War Virginia
Kristen Brill

Young America: The Transformation of Nationalism before the Civil War
Mark Power Smith

Black Suffrage: Lincoln's Last Goal
Paul D. Escott

The Cacophony of Politics: Northern Democrats and the American Civil War
J. Matthew Gallman

*My Work among the Freedmen: The Civil War and
Reconstruction Letters of Harriet M. Buss*
Edited by Jonathan W. White and Lydia J. Davis

Colossal Ambitions: Confederate Planning for a Post–Civil War World
Adrian Brettle

*Newest Born of Nations: European Nationalist
Movements and the Making of the Confederacy*
Ann L. Tucker

The Worst Passions of Human Nature: White Supremacy in the Civil War North
Paul D. Escott

*Preserving the White Man's Republic: Jacksonian Democracy,
Race, and the Transformation of American Conservatism*
Joshua A. Lynn

*American Abolitionism: Its Direct Political Impact
from Colonial Times into Reconstruction*
Stanley Harrold

*A Strife of Tongues: The Compromise of 1850 and the
Ideological Foundations of the American Civil War*
Stephen E. Maizlish

*The First Republican Army: The Army of Virginia
and the Radicalization of the Civil War*
John H. Matsui

War upon Our Border: Two Ohio Valley Communities Navigate the Civil War
Stephen I. Rockenbach

Gold and Freedom: The Political Economy of Reconstruction
Nicolas Barreyre, translated by Arthur Goldhammer

Daydreams and Nightmares: A Virginia Family Faces Secession and War
Brent Tarter

Intimate Reconstructions: Children in Postemancipation Virginia
Catherine A. Jones

Lincoln's Dilemma: Blair, Sumner, and the Republican Struggle over Racism and Equality in the Civil War Era
Paul D. Escott

Slavery and War in the Americas: Race, Citizenship, and State Building in the United States and Brazil, 1861–1870
Vitor Izecksohn

Marching Masters: Slavery, Race, and the Confederate Army during the Civil War
Colin Edward Woodward

Confederate Visions: Nationalism, Symbolism, and the Imagined South in the Civil War
Ian Binnington

Frederick Douglass: A Life in Documents
L. Diane Barnes, editor

Reconstructing the Campus: Higher Education and the American Civil War
Michael David Cohen

Worth a Dozen Men: Women and Nursing in the Civil War South
Libra R. Hilde

Civil War Talks: Further Reminiscences of George S. Bernard and His Fellow Veterans
Hampton Newsome, John Horn, and John G. Selby, editors

The Enemy Within: Fears of Corruption in the Civil War North
Michael Thomas Smith

The Big House after Slavery: Virginia Plantation Families and Their Postbellum Experiment
Amy Feely Morsman

Take Care of the Living: Reconstructing Confederate Veteran Families in Virginia
Jeffrey W. McClurken

Civil War Petersburg: Confederate City in the Crucible of War
A. Wilson Greene